Undoing the Silence

Undoing the Silence

Six Tools for Social Change Writing

LOUISE DUNLAP

New Village Press • Oakland, California

Published by
New Village Press
PO Box 3049
Oakland, CA 94609
510 420-1361
press@newvillage.net
Order online: www.newvillagepress.net

New Village Press is a public benefit, not-for-profit publishing venture of Architects/Designers/Planners for Social Responsibility. www.adpsr.org

Second printing 2009 in the United States of America.

In support of the Greenpress Initiative, New Village Press is committed to the preservation of Endangered Forests globally and advancing best practices within the book and paper industries. The printing papers used in this book are acid-free and have been certified with the Forest Stewardship Council.

Book design by Leigh McLellan.

Cover and chapter heads illustrations were derived from "We Bostonians" Quilt Two, a community-based artwork produced through the Faith Quilts Project founded by Clara Wainwright.

Quilt photo by Richard Howard.

Back cover author photo by Marissa Carlisle.

ISBN 978-0-9766054-9-2

Library of Congress Cataloging-in-Publication Data

Dunlap, Louise, 1938-
    Undoing the silence : six tools for social change writing / Louise Dunlap.
        p. cm.
    Includes index.
    ISBN 978-0-9766054-9-2 (pbk. : alk. paper)
    1. Authorship--Social aspects. 2. Authorship--Political aspects. I. Title.
PN145.D86 2007
808'.0663--dc22   2007032039

Contents

Acknowledgments

As a Buddhist saying goes, I offer gratitude to parents, teachers, friends, and numerous beings. My parents, David and Elizabeth Dunlap raised me to love language and know its power in the world. Teachers in many fields helped me refine my understanding, including Charles Muscatine, Ann Berthoff, Peter Elbow, Mel King, Thich Nhat Hanh, Jun Yasuda, Donald Moyer, Angela Farmer and Victor VanKooten. So did many who co-taught and collaborated over the years—Marlene Griffiths, Susan Andrien, Doug Sherman, John Lesko, Karen Christensen, Ben Harrison, José Alicea, Amy Schectman, Lyne Bernard, Karen Hurt, Gary Delgado and Ann Markusen. And friends too—so many friends who helped at every stage—Bill Shortell, Betty Burkes, Cathy Hoffman, Gill Hart, Loretta Williams, Meck Groot, Bobby Marie, Shamim Meer, Alissa Fleet, Marissa Carlisle, Dan Turner, Joan Schwartz. And friends in many writing groups—Clare Cooper Marcus, Jane Midgley, Mary Leno, Betty Holt, Susan Moir, Christle Rawlins-Jackson, Minga Claggett-Borne, Soul Brown, Wendy Call, Jorgette Theophilis, Donna Bivens, Curdina Hill, Joan Ecklein and many more.

The "numerous beings" reside in the many communities that energize and sustain me—the Cambridge Peace Commission, the Boston Old Path Sangha, the Eviction Free Zone, the Park View Coop, the National Writers Union. They include legendary editors Pat Farren and Patricia Watson of the American Friends Service Committee's Peacework; Susan Moon and Maia Duerr of the Buddhist Peace Fellowship's Turning Wheel; and Lynne Elizabeth, Karen Stewart and Eric Broder of New Village Press. Most of all, I am grateful to the generations of students and clients whose triumphs over silencing ground this book—some named here, many not. And two very special beings: my youngest sister Susan Dunlap, whose untimely death deepened my work, and Skip Schiel, social justice photographer par excellence, who has collaborated with me on so many projects for social justice.

Foreword

Louise Dunlap's *Undoing the Silence* accomplishes what other books on writing do not: it links our writing to our beliefs, our activism, our voice. Dunlap begins one of her early chapters by observing, "most people will do just about anything but sit down to write, even though all of us have powerful voices somewhere inside." Citing her own experience in the Free Speech Movement, she reflects, "in that atmosphere of heightened awareness, we found strength to say what was hard, even painful—to think and articulate in ways that would stand up to scrutiny. Every person became eloquent. This was democracy."

All of the examples in this book not only show us new ways to unearth the power of our own experience, they connect the writing struggles of peace activists in California, labor organizers in South Africa, and community organizers in Boston with the changes these people are trying to make in the world. So, although the book is very much about the personal writing struggles of activists from many social justice organizations, Louise gives us a context, a reason, for them to duel with the silencing ghosts of their pasts.

The tools Dunlap offers include *freewriting* techniques, strategies for reaching our intended audience, an innovative exercise for feedback, and tactics for rethinking, editing and rewriting our free flowing drafts—all effective tools to improve our writing. But for me, the exploration of the writing process is even more valuable. Louise has opened up a whole new arena by giving me a way to think about my own writing process. As a researcher and occasional journalist, I write all the time. My goals are to produce analytical pieces on deadline that are relatively easy to follow. Sometimes the writing flows and sometimes it doesn't. It is sometimes magic, sometimes painful, often both. But Louise's book has shown me that I have never given the process much thought.

In the beginning of the book, Dunlap cites a South African activist who observes that, "We do not yet feel free to write what we think—and that means we aren't even thinking it fully." *Undoing the Silence* helps us delve into our psyches to explore our true feelings about a subject, freeing us enough to think fully and then write what we think. It also teaches us how to analyze our own writing process so that we can recognize the power of our own voice.

Gary Delgado
President Emeritus
Applied Research Center
Oakland, California

CHAPTER ONE

We Are the Second Superpower

Mainstream Americans are reluctant to speak out in writing, even when it can make a real difference. How can we shift that reluctance and turn writing into action? This chapter suggests six tools to undo the silence by setting aside self-judgment, releasing fear and tapping our common heritage as powerful thinkers.

On one side of the country, earth-conscious activists in suburban Silicon Valley are pushing themselves to write letters to the news media. The terrifying reality of global warming is not getting honest attention; government and fellow citizens seem to be ignoring a crisis that will soon be overwhelming. Rather than sit back isolated and helpless, this group wants to mobilize public attention with letters and articles. To get themselves moving, they have organized a writing workshop.

Three thousand miles away, inner-city tenants are also organizing a writing workshop. Many are about to lose their homes as government money for affordable housing pours into a murderous war that makes terrorism a greater threat than ever. They have marched in Washington and demonstrated at landlords' homes, but now one organizer believes they need to make their case in writing. These tenants face an official silence. They hardly ever see their story in the media. Invisibility and their vulnerability to eviction force the public silence inward. Few are confident with the written word. But like environmental activists—and others facing the enormous crises of our times—their truth is deeply felt, prophetic and urgent. Putting their voices in print, sharing their vision, can help change a disastrous course of events.

Can ordinary people make a difference? There are times when we feel it happening. As the United States prepared for war in Iraq, huge demonstrations in major U.S. cities and also around the world prompted a *New York Times* journalist to declare that there were now two superpowers: the U.S. government and world public opinion. Voice by voice, ordinary people can make themselves into a superpower. When we are willing to speak out and to write, this kind of miracle is entirely possible.

I travel from coast to coast to work with both tenants and environmentalists. Our world needs their voices now, and I have tools that can help. I'm not surprised to learn that both groups are already very vocal. They talk to neighbors. They call elected officials. But their spoken words haven't made enough difference—both groups feel their most vital insights remain unheard. Both want their stories in the news. But speaking out in writing brings up fears and old habits that deepen the silence. Even outspoken people can feel a lack of confidence and know-how when they try to put their passions into the written word.

I'm not surprised that both suburban professionals and inner city people feel the same pressures. This silence touches everyone, and it is not the peaceful, voluntary, nourishing silence of reflection. This silence threatens survival, and it is deeply embedded in our culture. The workshops begin to shift the silence. In both groups there is support in being together. People start to write letters, celebrate achievements and get some of their writing into print. *This* is what democracy looks like.

When I learned the word "democracy" as a child, gatherings like these workshops were what I pictured—ordinary people getting together to speak their truth, maybe disagreeing, but putting their voices out there and bit by bit changing the dominant dialogue. This kind of effort is part of our history. Small, locally based citizen groups kicked off the independence movement. In colonial America, when most communication came by boat or by foot, local "committees of correspondence" met to write letters and reports to send from city to city, sharing ideas about oppressive conditions and building the will to transform them.

Today, citizens concerned with our daunting problems have hundreds of outlets for written opinion—blogs and web-based alternatives, press releases, policy memos, articles and written testimony. All of us can write proposals and community newspaper columns and pamphlets, and email petitions and letters to editors or decision-makers. And many of these written efforts have documented effectiveness. A recent study found that 96 percent of congressional staff say personally written letters have "some" or "a lot of" influence on our representatives' decisions. More and more ordinary people are taking the risk to write their truth. Writing isn't easy for most people but, with the right tools, all of us have what it takes to be part of this new movement for change.

Shifting pressures

There have always been strong pressures to remain silent. Most of us have felt a fear of being seen as different. And author Frances Moore Lappé reminds us that fears about standing out from the crowd may have a genetic basis. For early humans, rejection by the tribe meant starvation, predators and death. Lappé suggests we may be genetically hard-wired to go along with the mainstream. That instinct once protected us, she argues. But evolutionary times have changed. With our "tribe" heading for environmental chaos and permanent war, the only hope for planetary survival may mean breaking with the fearfulness we carry in our DNA and taking the risk to voice dissent and new vision.

Each time we don't act on an urge to write, we add another layer to our habits of silence.

Yet today's climate intensifies the fear and the risk—with color-coded warnings, new laws like the USA PATRIOT Act and legal retaliation against dissidents. Free speech seems a distant fantasy. But looking back to times before silencing became so obvious, I see that people I've known have never felt easy with writing—not environmentalists, not inner-city tenants and not even policy researchers in the academic world. Because a few seem to rise to the occasion and make their words felt, we imagine that writing should come easily. But most of us don't write much. We don't have time. We can't get started. We don't think we have the tools. We don't want to rock the boat—or at least not right now. Sometimes we're nervous about political repercussions or job security. Sometimes our resistance is deep and touches old pain. Usually we think we're the only one who feels uneasy about writing. Most of us have no idea how important our ideas are or how powerful we can be when we speak up. But each time we don't act on an urge to write, we add another layer to our habits of silence, burying more deeply our power of voice, and losing touch with the active expression that nourishes our sense of hope and grounds democracy.

I know about these habits because I too have a story of silencing. I grew up during World War II and the Cold War years, another period when fears about national security were rampant. Ideas that weren't part of the mainstream were called unpatriotic—a lot like today. And we had our own version of the USA PATRIOT Act—a congressional committee on "Un-American Activities" designed to suppress alternative views in the name of security. There was so little grassroots dissent that we were known as "the silent generation." I was no exception, growing up with many privileges—not wealthy, but middle class and white, the oldest child in my family, with a mother who studied ancient languages and a lawyer father who made his living with words. Doing well in school, my deep roots in the status quo kept me from speaking my own thoughts and blocked my ability to write on certain subjects.

My family reinforced subtle pressures. There were lots of do's and don'ts about what we could and couldn't put into words. A very early memory is my mother shushing me for asking in my loud child's voice why Ina had such dark skin. Ina was an African American woman who did our ironing every week. Later I realized that, for different reasons, there is silencing around the issue of race in Black families too. A former southerner, my mother had a reputation for challenging racial hate-language, but even she thought it wasn't polite to discuss color and race in daily life. Mentioning color might hurt someone's feelings or cause problems, she insisted. Income level, social status, political views and sex were also on her "no-no" list.

Now I see that, no matter how well meant, politeness is a kind of organized silence. Not discussing race helps keep racism in place and is part of the invisible system that maintains injustice in our society. What you can't name is hard to think about, so I, and many others in my generation, grew up polite but silent and ignorant on a lot of important subjects. We didn't build skills for discussing the hard issues. But I was lucky. A more open era and a unique transformative experience began to undo the silence for me.

The Free Speech Movement

I was a shy 26-year-old when a spin-off from the civil rights movement plunged my university into what history calls the Berkeley Free Speech Movement. In 1964, we called it the FSM. During a short two months, students challenged campus restrictions on free speech that now seem unbelievably harsh, even by today's standards. Our struggle began with authorities restricting where students could distribute literature and recruit for causes. It escalated into failed negotiations, a massive sit-in with 800 student arrests and a campus-wide boycott.

For thousands of us, this was our first experience with social action and the need to take sides on something serious. I can still feel the excitement—standing elbow to elbow in a crowd that filled our whole plaza and listening to ordinary students like myself speak from the top of a police car. The faces around me wrestled with new and challenging issues. Why was one of the most outspoken of us imprisoned in this car? The freedom to speak out—and act—when things weren't right was essential to what we'd been taught about democracy. Yet this basic principle conflicted with campus and state governance, invisible to us until then. Nothing was simple; each day's developments brought new contradictions and energy. Who made more sense: classic American writers like Henry David Thoreau who urged us to speak from conscience even if it meant civil disobedience, or our parents who thought we'd been duped by "outside agitators"?

In this challenging atmosphere, there simply was no silent majority. Conversations, speak-outs at daily rallies and writing assignments stretched all of us to think through and articulate our deepest beliefs—to convince each other, our professors, our parents. We learned to make arguments, to blend the heart and the head. Every day at noon, students spoke at public rallies. Newsletters, position papers and leaflets, even poems flowed onto campus every morning from secret mimeograph machines, the old-fashioned, hand-cranked kind that left the paper damp with yeasty-smelling purple ink. There was no email then, so we scrawled notes on leaflets and sent them to friends at other colleges so they could learn what the media did not report and share our exhilaration.

Our world was in flux during those special days and weeks, and there was a heady feeling that the ideas we voiced would have the power to change repressive policies not only in our university but also in state and local government. Our words—written, spoken and shouted—did change the Berkeley campus as we watched. And already we could see that other people's words—and the actions of millions of Americans—were shifting entrenched segregation policies in the South, challenging the war in Vietnam and reframing deep-seated attitudes toward women and the environment. We learned what it feels like when the people become a superpower. A lot of citizen effort poured into letters to decision-makers and the press, while people took to the streets with signs and pamphlets. After all those silences of the 1950s, we were seeing that the word could make change in the world.

The word changed us too. My first time teaching during the FSM, I noticed the same general malaise and discomfort with writing that I would come to expect in classes over the next forty years. But in this group, I also noticed that when they wrote about the turmoil around them and the justice issues that touched their daily lives, every person seemed to become a powerful, confident writer. I remember reading through 25 papers on how Thoreau's ideas on civil disobedience applied to our campus and marveling at each paper's special brilliance. It wasn't polemics or the shallow "political correctness" of today. At that time, with our new awareness, we found strength to say what was hard, even painful, and to think and articulate in ways that would

> *There was a heady feeling that the ideas we voiced would have the power to change repressive policies.*

stand up to scrutiny. Every person became eloquent. This was real democracy. The heightened passion of this historic moment, our sense of quandary and discovery of truth, brought out layers of intelligence and creativity normally locked away inside us. In giving voice, we realized how we had been silenced, how many thoughts we had not felt entitled to talk about, how much in us had seemed out of tune with the norm, unacceptable to express.

Hidden silencing

Until that magical FSM year, I was a "good student." I'd been praised for my writing and had won a scholarship and a teaching assistantship. If anyone had asked me how I felt about myself as a writer and thinker, I would have said, "Just fine." But the "good student" label was misleading. In fact, writing came very hard and painfully for me. Lots of my papers were late. And, to be honest, I saw myself as powerless in the world of ideas. There seemed no way my thinking, my writing, anything coming from me, could ever have influence in the world. Out of touch with my creativity and strength, I remember the first time I ever spoke up in a big FSM meeting. I said something very brief—about keeping our leaflets for an archive—but I felt a surge of energy as I saw the hundreds of people in the room hearing and supporting what I said. Something in this moment affirmed my voice, my will to express and act, that years of good grades had not.

"The power of speech is what marks us off from the stones and the stars."

I was not the only one to feel the miracle of speech in action. One of our most beloved leaders was Mario Savio, a tall young man with bushy hair that was rare in the early '60s. He was an inspiring speaker who had a way of collaborating with his audience that I admired and learned from. He seemed to raise the questions we all had on our minds and then answer them, as if in our own words. More than any of us, he took free speech seriously. "The power of speech," he reflected later, "is what marks us off from the stones and the stars." Mario died of an untimely heart attack in the 1990s, and it was only at his memorial service that I learned that this most articulate speaker had once been silenced by stammering. The FSM had marked Mario's turning point. Years later he told an interviewer, "In addition to its political meaning, and its moral and philosophical meaning, the Free Speech Movement was a pun: (It was) my free speech movement, the free movement of my speech. So I was deeply, viscerally involved."

An ally for silenced writers

For me the free speech experience confirmed a vocation to work with writers who had experienced silencing. My own struggle helped me to listen with empathy, to understand why their voices were blocked, and, more important, what they were trying to say. A few years later, I taught in an urban university in the northeast, in a culture very different from Berkeley's. But I remember how a young working-class student evaluated one of my earliest classes. "She is able to understand our innermost thoughts," he wrote, "even when we are unable to put them in words." Strange as that must have sounded to my supervisor, it went to the heart of what I knew I must learn to do and eventually to teach. Words cannot change minds unless we understand what is already going on in those minds. I would come to realize that listening and gaining a feel for audience is as important to social transformation as the outspoken words of student leaders atop police cars. Free speech is a first step, but real communication matches speech with listening and understanding. That is when thinking shifts and change happens.

Over time, I moved into some unusual settings to teach writing. I needed to go where the silences were deepest because I realized that my work aimed not just at teaching but also at healing—both individual voices and our ailing collective voice. So I went into VISTA programs where young people without a formal education were developing leadership skills. I taught in bilingual community programs where activists from other language backgrounds were organizing immigrants. I even went to South Africa after the fall of apartheid, where community organizers, labor leaders and health workers who had been denied resources under the old regime were pooling their skills to set up a new kind of country. I found silences everywhere, in places you might not expect them: privileged graduate programs at Massachusetts Institute of Technology (MIT) and University of California Berkeley, well-financed nonprofit organizations, and leadership circles for the women's, labor, anti-racism and peace movements.

It's a thrill to see another person come into the power of voice. There was Greta, my neighbor and a single mom who joined with others after the dreadful high school shooting spree called the Columbine Massacre and organized the Million Mom March in Washington DC on Mothers Day, 2000. Greta told me she was holding back because of all the writing and speaking involved, so we sat down to talk it out. "Who's going to listen to me?" she worried. Yet every time she spoke, Greta made us feel her concern for her son's generation if the tide of street weapons could not be stemmed. "Write the way you speak," we encouraged her. And two months later, Greta had written everything from stirring newsletter articles and press releases to registration forms for the buses to Washington. More important, she had become a confident, dynamic speaker and writer who continues to take leadership on issues she cares about.

At MIT I discovered Melvin King's program for community scholars, a program that specialized in developing confidence and leadership through voice. Each year students came to Mel from all over the country. They were Apache, Anishinabe, Cambodian, Dominican, African-American. They were filmmakers, dancers, preachers, computer-whizzes, geographers and poets (like Mel himself, who coined the expression "Rainbow Coalition," later popularized by 1980s presidential candidate Jesse Jackson). I sat around the table with them each year as Mel talked about the African American anthem. "The song says 'Lift every voice,'" he would tell us, "and it means *every* voice. We need *every* voice if we are going to be about transformation." As the writing coach for Mel's program, I was privileged to watch powerful voices emerge from histories that often included severe silencing. You'll read many of their stories later in this book.

Everywhere I found that speaking out vocally and taking action with the written word were closely related. Maybe one skill is stronger than another to begin with, but when you work on writing, the silence starts to unravel on other levels. A tenant named Mark confirmed this for me four years after a workshop where he had written (and published) his first letter to the editor. "That's where it all started," he said in a group evaluation meeting. "Before I wrote that letter, I had no confidence in myself." (Mark was a working father of four so this was a big thing for him to acknowledge.) "After that I just learned how to do things: I went onto the steering committee, I started speaking at City Council, and now I'm on the Board where I live. I feel like a leader because I know I can say what I mean."

Tools to undo silencing

My early teaching strategies grew into six simple but profound tools. These tools have helped hundreds, maybe thousands, of silenced writers, many of whom didn't even realize they were stuck. These are not the same tools you learned in school, where writing is usually taught through models of good and bad imposed by someone in authority, like a teacher, supervisor or editor who supposedly knows the right way to say what you think. In fact, the authoritarian approach is a major factor in our silencing. The more we rely on how the experts tell us to do it, the more deeply we bury our own voices. Traditional schooling offers what African

American feminist writer Audre Lorde referred to when she warned that, "you cannot use the master's tools to dismantle the master's house." These "master's tools" are the rules and regulations of "good writing": *Watch your commas, be sure you understand yourself fully before you write, and don't rock the boat. Be polite.* Tools like these could not free enslaved people and they cannot help you free your voice. The tools, themselves, are silencers. As Einstein put it, "No problem can be solved from the same level of consciousness that created it." If we want to transform a problem as major as our silencing—or as overwhelming as the poverty, war and violence in our world—we need new and different tools.

Unlike "the master's tools," the ones in this book work because you are in charge. Based on ways writers have helped each other for generations, they grow out of a nurturing, empowering vision of society rather than one controlled by masters or experts. The tools help you get in touch with two essential things: your passion and clarity on what you have to say, and your readers' way of thinking, so you can frame ideas they can hear. When you discover both, you become the expert on how to write. Used over time, the tools help shift self-judgment, release fear and tap our innate power as communicators. Here is a brief preview of the six tools.

> **If we want to transform a problem as major as our silencing, we need new and different tools.**

The FREEWRITING Tool   This first tool is a way of writing quickly and freely without judging yourself. It expands your comfort zone, helping you connect with the depth of what you have to say and your own natural way with words. With practice, you'll use this tool to write spontaneously, as if you were talking to yourself on paper. And no one will read it unless you ask them to. Freewriting helps with a whole range of silencing problems, like "grammar fear" and fluency when English isn't your first language or you've always felt better speaking than writing. Mainly it gives encouragement, making writing doable for everyone—even pleasurable. Ideally you freewrite nearly everyday, like a runner trains for a road race. And once you get the hang of it, this workout is easy and has many health benefits because it also releases feelings of stress from other parts of your life.

The PROCESS Tool   This tool helps you time the various activities that go into a writing project, so you can be free of destructive self-judgment at the beginning and save your ability to judge and evaluate until after you've written a draft. The tool is flexible because each situation is different. Once you get used to the five core activities that are part of this tool, you can trust yourself to finish even challenging pieces of writing without agony. With this tool, your inner "judges" stay quiet until later, so your writing—and your ideas—can come in stages, even if they're messy and confusing. When you aren't criticizing yourself it's much easier to write a first draft. And this process saves time because you won't procrastinate or wait to get everything "right" because you know you'll be able to revise later.

The THINKING Tool   One reason people get stuck is they don't have good ways to organize what they want to say. This tool offers a wide range of options for thinking ideas through and presenting them more effectively. Some, like hierarchies and grids, come from people in positions of authority. Others, like stories and diagrams, come from artists and indigenous people all over the world. Together they liberate the powerful thinking that is our common birthright.

> *"We are only useful where we understand how we are understood."*

The AUDIENCE Tool   Misperceptions about readers can be a great silencer, especially when we picture them as judges or try to ignore them. This tool helps us look accurately at the people we're writing for, figure out what they think and believe, and shape a message that can change their attitudes. It includes strategies for introductions and re-organizing ideas to get readers involved. As Buddhist teacher and author Hilda Ryumon Gutiérrez Baldoquîn said recently, "We are only useful where we understand how we are understood." This tool helps us understand how readers will receive our words.

The FEEDBACK Tool   This tool takes us even more deeply into readers' minds to learn how our words affect them and how to improve our work. Traditionally, feedback is criticism and evaluation (very much "the master's tool"). But with this tool a small group of ordinary writers respond to each other without activating the judges. Totally without evaluation, the tool reveals so much about readers' reactions that it can strengthen writing and build a nurturing community at the same time. Even though it's been everyone's favorite tool over the many years I've used it, this kind of feedback isn't easy to learn. It can be hard to give up our tendency to judge our own and others' writing. If there's no group to work with, you can adapt this tool to elicit non-judging feedback from one person.

The WORD-POWER Tool   Rushing to edit or correct your writing while you write can put you at risk from your internal judges because grammar rules can silence us. Even so, it's important to know how structuring sentences, choosing words, and cutting out what isn't essential can make ideas more powerful and more accessible to readers. Used at the end of your writing process, this tool helps make your language accurate and convincing.

How to use this book

After taking a deeper look at why the silence happens, this book offers a separate chapter on each of the tools. In these chapters, you'll find guidelines, examples, stories of people using the tools, and exercises to help you learn by doing. Use the book in whatever way works best for you. You can skip through to the tool you need at the moment or read the chapters one by one to get the big picture in all its fullness. I hope you'll use the book with a few people from your work, school, neighborhood or activist community—sharing ideas and writing as you go. That's how the people you'll read about in the book have used the tools. Changing longstanding and unconscious habits of silencing is a major undertaking, and the book is set up to help you do this over time either by yourself or with a supportive community. Even if you're not taking the full-book approach, I recommend you start using the first tool, FREEWRITING, right away and keep your freewriting and any exercises you do in a journal or notebook as you go.

The book is set up to give you information and assistance when and where you need it. For instance, if you're writing to get funding or convince voters, understanding your audience is crucial, so go to Chapter Six, "The AUDIENCE Tool." Each chapter is set up to help you locate what you need most. The first few pages explain how the chapter works and which parts will be most essential. The rest offers greater depth for a longer read. You may be able to get what you need just from the charts, examples, or bullet points or from the appendix at the end of the book. Part of gaining power and confidence is that you choose how much to read and when. I hope you will find every word useful, but you are the best judge.

CHAPTER TWO

Understanding the Silence

What keeps us from writing to make a difference?

Grassroots educator Paulo Freire saw "silencing" as part of our culture. This chapter explores what keeps us from writing and shows people undoing their silence and using the written word to play more powerful roles in a more democratic society.

For decades I have listened carefully to people's stories about why it's so difficult to put challenging thoughts into writing. Just mentioning my work with silenced writers brings up yet another story—not only in classrooms but also in cafés, boardrooms, church basements and even my own living room. The stories come from people at all levels of education, including some who are accomplished writers. Everyone's experience is different, but the overlap from story to story shows that the pressure to remain silent in the face of injustice is not just a personal issue but has deep roots in our social and political culture.

Struggling with the silence

Clara's story caught my attention at a leadership training for nonprofit staff. Her workplace focused on bilingual women's education in English and Spanish and Clara was good at both. This woman loved her job and her co-workers—until one day they asked her to handle all the writing for the organization. Suddenly Clara was under pressure as she wrote not only newsletters and grants but also countless routine letters to an enormous variety of people. It was hard enough writing to people in different professional roles—funders and board members. But Clara's readers also came from a range of cultures where she felt like an outsider. She knew she could irritate someone from Honduras or Mexico with the same expressions she used naturally as a Cuban American. And when she had to write for the white grant-makers who held so much power over her organization, a voice inside kept saying how clumsy each sentence sounded—not the English but her way of expressing herself. So Clara wasted hours rewriting or mailed out first drafts she felt were embarrassing. In an environment designed to support women, Clara's own confidence was plummeting. Like Clara, many of us feel intimidated when people we write for have control over our jobs or our future. I had seen this dynamic so often in universities when students wrote for teachers, especially when gender, race and class privilege deepened the power differences.

My work often connected me with people who had wrestled with silencing all their lives. I met Timothy at an alternative college for working adults. Long ago, inner city teachers had torn apart his vocabulary and quashed his youthful poetry, leaving Timothy in fear of misusing the simplest words. In this one chance at higher education, he was determined to regain his confidence with words and find a job helping today's African American children get the good schooling he had missed. Another case was Jim, a photographer and risk-taking peace activist since the Vietnam War. Raised Irish Catholic and a former priest, Jim had been ridiculed in parochial school for spelling, grammar and ideas that didn't follow the norm. Though a wonderful speaker, Jim felt terrible about his writing but struggled to write the stories of Latin American farmers affected by U.S. development policies. While we were working together, he began to write and publish op-ed columns. Jim's experience with liberation theology would help me understand the roots of silencing.

Once in a while people told me they weren't affected by silencing, but usually—when we looked deeply—it was there. Jane was a good example. She came from a family that wrote and spoke out. She'd been known as a "good writer" for many years and was great at speaking up for justice in any forum. But there was a book Jane wanted to write that could help everyday people get more active in shaping national priorities. She even dreamed of reaching academics and economists with this book. But here Jane's dream made things difficult: like Clara, she found her more powerful readers intimidating, and it was hard to get started. Whenever she sat down, silence stretched out before her, the kind 1970s author Tillie Olsen called "hidden and foreground silence"—waiting so long before you write that no one ever sees your writing. Olsen had focused on women, but also saw the pattern in men, afflicted by the "age-old silencers of humanity, class and/or color." Once Jane began to meet with other silenced writers, she saw that she, herself, was also affected, and that there are ways out. In Chapter Six you can read more of Jane's story and the tools she used to finish her book—which is now in print and contributing to social change. The six tools helped Jane, Clara, Timothy and Jim, but an understanding of how silencing happens was also important.

A "culture of silence"

Silencing isn't just personal, though it can feel that way. When so many are affected, there's something going on across the board. The best explanation comes from the great Brazilian educator, Paulo Freire, who wrote about silencing, voice and the word in a classic called *The Pedagogy of the Oppressed*. His literacy work with peasants and factory workers (in the 1960s, when powerful grassroots voices were emerging around the globe) revealed the often-subtle pressures that keep people quiet in order to maintain oppression and block full human expression. His work shows how people in what he called the "culture of silence" take on the thinking of their oppressors and fear to speak their own truth. It explains why university students repeat their professors' ideas even when they have new and better ones of their own. It explains why activists find it hard to write about things not already covered in the media and why people who think differently can't make themselves heard. It explains why all

GOOD SILENCES

Freire always reminded us of complexity, even in language. The word "silence" stretches way beyond oppression. It also describes something we seek and treasure. It's in silence that we gather our thoughts, center our energy, feel the love and understanding we need for taking action. Quakers, Buddhist meditators and many others use silence to connect with forces larger than ourselves. Freire also valued the reflective possibilities of silence. In 1985, I heard him speak about what he called the "tensions between silence and voice." Silence, which we often see as empty, can represent great activity. "I can spend one hour silent but totally alive. I can speak a lot in silence," he told a crowd at Harvard University. Freire warned teachers not to "emphasize our own voice so much that we impose silence on students" but to "feel out how to get voice from the other side...how to, little by little, get students' voices into speech while we [the teachers], little by little, go into silence." When we truly choose it, silence is a powerful ally to speech.

"fear to speak their own truth."

of us have so much trouble saying things powerfully in writing—to the point that sometimes we don't say them at all.

Later I would work with my own neighbors as they wrote to defend federal housing subsidies. Alas, not one of them felt comfortable acknowledging publicly that they received these subsidies. Part of this was a vulnerability to reprisals that I could understand, but something more subtle was going on. Where I saw these tenants as intelligent, hard-working people shut out of a shrinking economy through no fault of their own, they had internalized negative imagery from the culture and our press—the message that "tenants don't deserve handouts." Freire spoke very directly to their situation when he wrote that oppressed people often "*house* the oppressor" inside themselves. In his view, the oppressor lived inside these tenants in the form of negative self-images. As their writing coach, I was challenged. Without speaking directly from their own experience with subsidies, they would lose the chance to tell the personal stories that could make their arguments powerful. That is silencing.

But silence isn't limited to people denied their rights. Freire insisted that highly privileged people, too, could be victims of silencing—though they'd find it even more difficult to acknowledge. Polite, educated, privileged citizens could be filled with the thinking of the oppressor and could actually fear freedom. I knew from my Free Speech days that I was a good example, and I knew from the stories my students shared that there were others like me.

The knot of silencing

Freire's and Olsen's ideas about silencing and oppression gave me a framework to interpret what I kept hearing from those I worked with and what I felt in myself. I began to picture the silencing of our voices as a huge stifling knot, layered together with tangled strands from many aspects of our culture. In this knot, impulses we regard as deeply personal are interwoven and reinforced by the institutions around us such as schools and the media. In this mix, it is difficult to know the cause of silencing from the effect, but following the strands can help us loosen the knot.

Many of the strands have already surfaced in the stories so far, and they correspond with the forms of discrimination we know from social justice work—not just racism and sexism but all the ways people in our culture can be targeted as "less than." If you are treated as "less than" because of race, like Timothy, or class, like Jim, or language of origin, like Clara, you are tackling this form of discrimination whenever you want to speak out. And the challenge can intensify when the zones of discrimi-

> *Gay and lesbian voices have been so deeply silenced that, for many, the very term "silencing" evokes a gay person's dilemma—being "in the closet," unable to voice one's truth.*

nation overlap: Timothy faced more than one, and so did the tenants writing to defend their homes. Discrimination takes forms that affect everyone. Children are "less than," supposed to be "seen but not heard." And the youngest ones in a family—without the skills or vocabulary of the big ones—may be ridiculed for "baby talk." Old people, people with illnesses or disabilities, people with non-mainstream views, like socialists or Sikhs, can face similar treatment. People without higher education can be targeted. The list goes on and on. Every time people in a targeted group speak, they're up against an intimidating audience that may or may not listen, that may judge or reject what they have to say. And some will take that judgment inside themselves, so that they won't be able to help seeing themselves, at least some of the time, as "less than."

Being a woman is the most clear-cut target area for me. Even though I have what are seen as advantages like color, class background and higher education, I still feel silenced at times as a woman. I notice at public meetings who it is with the confidence to step up to the microphone. People of my gender hold back, and I sometimes do too. Over decades women and men have worked for more consciousness of this dynamic, but I haven't seen a dramatic change. From feeling devalued myself, I've been able to guess what it's like to be in the shoes of others who are not supported by our culture. Speaking up about being gay or lesbian, for instance, has been taboo in most circles I've moved in—even many progressive ones. Gay and lesbian voices have been so deeply silenced that, for many, the very term "silencing" evokes a gay person's dilemma—being "in the closet," unable to voice one's truth.

With all the forms of discrimination, silencing works in two related ways. There is subtle (and sometimes overt) censorship: in staff meetings, for instance, people may not listen to the ideas of a woman until a male colleague voices them later. As North Americans responded to the 9/11 attacks, The Center for New Words, a feminist organization, reported that women had authored only 8 percent of the op-ed columns shaping public opinion in major newspapers and were only 15 percent of those consulted as experts on major TV stations. In such a climate there is also self-censorship. *Since no one is going to listen to me, why should I even try to raise my voice?* With two faces to the silencing, there are two ways to counter it: demand accountability for the shocking discrepancy and work among women themselves to create more confidence and empowerment about speaking out.

Where does it all start? As babies, most of us feel free to scream about our needs even though we don't have words yet. But adults quickly shut us up, so by the time we learn language we've lost our original power of voice. Then, as we grow up, being treated as "less than" reinforces powerlessness. But we react in unique ways: not every big sister speaks out and some little sisters develop strong voices for self-defense. The pressures and counter pressures that mark our early lives intensify in the institutions that surround us afterwards.

Pressures from institutions

Family dynamics can intensify the pressures. Sisters, brothers or spouses who are "the writers in the family" often figure in the stories I hear about why other family members think they can't write. And more than once I've heard of parents who "yelled and screamed about mistakes in writing," especially when they were not confident writers themselves. I think they desperately wanted their children to succeed, but couldn't help passing on the same fears and habits they'd learned as children. This way silence can span generations.

Schools and churches also set limits on what children can and can't say. I loved hearing about Jim's childhood, the former priest mentioned earlier, who had so much trouble as an adult writing about liberation, peace and justice. Jim always rocks the boat with his thinking, and, as a child, I'm sure his views troubled the Catholic nuns who were his teachers. Visionary children look like troublemakers in a world that is trying to teach "obedience," and the rest of us learn lessons about silence and compliance from watching how they're treated. Peer groups could support children's authentic voices, but in my childhood they had the opposite effect—none of us wanted to express anything that might make us stand out as different.

Public media play a crucial role holding silence in place by shaping societal thinking that will not rock the boat.

As adults, some of us find new institutions that validate and support us in expressing our vision of justice. The Free Speech Movement and other groups in the 1960s helped my generation. But even alternative institutions can reinforce politeness and comfort zones. It may be easier to talk about food or the weather than vital issues of survival on the planet. Perhaps we don't want the fear and challenge of a truthful discussion of global warming or nuclear weapons. But meanwhile our ability to speak truth together gets buried more and more deeply in habits of group silence.

Public media play a crucial role holding silence in place by shaping societal thinking that will not rock the boat. Our press sets tacit limits on what is acceptable to talk about by headlining sensational topics like murders and wealthy people's issues and keeping quiet about Salvadoran farmers impoverished by our trade policy or events like the 2007 U. S. Social Forum, which brought 15,000 people together to say "Another World is Possible." The low-income tenants mentioned earlier had never seen media coverage that explained how they were barred from the kinds of jobs that could buy them a condo. Nothing they had read or heard on TV showed their struggles in a positive light, validated their lives or prepared mainstream readers to understand them. So their truth was very hard to voice, much less get into print. Excellent analyses of media, government and corporate complicity now exist in a remarkable range of alternative media, but you have to hunt for them. Mainstream media still exert a firm hold on public thinking. What fills the public airwaves affects us even when we're conscious of alternatives.

APARTHEID-STYLE SILENCING

When I visited South Africa after the fall of apartheid, I found that even courageous activists who had brought down the regime continued to feel traces of institutional silencing. One workshop brought women together across class, race and language differences. There were tensions, but these women recognized something very deep in common. All had felt silenced under apartheid and that feeling had stayed with them, even though the regime itself was gone. The younger African women still struggled with "the language problem": their work had to be in English, a colonial language they'd once been forced to learn by rote. Women of South Asian descent also experienced English as the colonizer's language. Amazingly, the white women, who'd grown up with more privilege under apartheid, also felt judged and silenced when they wrote. They felt pressured to conform to rigid standards in the most authoritarian of societies and surrounded by a culture they said did not "valorize" their sense of injustice. This group helped me see how institutional silencing can last for generations and real change can take a long time.

Think about the workplace. So many of us get our paychecks from organizations that are part of the problem—like one woman who worked with the elderly. I met her when she was struggling to write an expose of illegal restraints in nursing homes. Employed as an "advocate" by the industry she was supposed to monitor, she had witnessed old people tied up against their will, an injustice that touched deep personal chords for her. But words just wouldn't come; she had spoken to her supervisor about the problem to no avail. It was clear that breaking the official silence would mean losing her job.

The need to make a living can silence us in less dramatic ways. We must make choices about how to spend our time and energy, choices about whether to establish our own security before taking risks, choices to support our colleagues even when they're not always right. Less than consciously we take on the subtle values of the organizations we work for, and most of them include not voicing original critique, not rocking the boat.

My workplace, for many years, was higher education. From the outside, colleges and universities may look balanced and fair, open to ideas and hostile to censorship, but inside I found serious limits to what could be thought and said. Listening for the sources of silence, I heard stories of Latino students given poor grades for criticizing "manifest destiny," of graduate students shifting their research away from controversial "women's issues." In one school, students told me they avoided mentioning social class in their research, and sometimes race. How could they develop powerful thinking on these subjects if they had to protect themselves by not using the words? I myself heard one influential faculty mentor label other scholars as "fuzzy-headed Marxists," seeking to silence a way of thinking respected around the world at that time.

Silencing and fear

The fear at the root of silencing came clear to me during a thesis seminar in the 1980s, which had drawn outstanding students from all over the world. One man from a Middle Eastern country was describing his research on land ownership and his difficulty expressing ideas straightforwardly. (His professors kept telling him to state his meaning more directly.) Exchanging glances with other classmates from his troubled region, he chose his words carefully for the rest of us, "I don't think you can appreciate what it's like where we come from. There are so many political crosscurrents. It isn't safe to say these things, so we find ways to hide them, to self-censor. We know a few like-minded people will understand what we're really saying." I wasn't surprised by his revelation. A student from Central America had told me he feared death squads if he published his research results.

What surprised me was the reaction of the North American students. Looking around the room, I saw that all of them were nodding their heads. "It happens here too!" they affirmed, deadly serious. In their own ways, these promising young adults from New York, Chicago, Kansas and the Boston suburbs felt their most important ideas were unsafe to express in a university setting. Was this just their perception or was there a reality behind it? Either way their voices were silenced. The discussion offered a sobering view of the main challenge I would always face as a writing teacher for highly educated people—their genuine difficulty in coming out and saying what they knew, especially if it did not mirror what others were saying, their reluctance to affirm their main ideas in simple, direct, accessible words. Rather than being eager to say something new and original, they were, in their way, terrified of sounding different.

Thinking through something new creates its own fearfulness. There is loneliness, an uncertainty, a real stretch to find words for what hasn't been said before. You're in unfamiliar territory, where fear is natural. Writing can easily bring you to this frontier and we'll look, later in the book, at how to pass through this fearfulness. Meanwhile it helps to separate the fears that come with new thinking from anxiety about who will read. When we feel entitled to express ourselves, words come more easily.

The culture of judgment

Thinking through something new creates its own fearfulness, a real stretch to find words for what hasn't been said before.

The glue that keeps the knot of silencing in place is what I have come to see as a culture of judgment—an authoritarian attitude that permeates family, church, schooling and public decision-making. Linguist George Lakoff helps explain this authoritarian attitude. His work shows how two very different kinds of thinking clash in our society and shape our lives and national politics. The more authoritarian view sees government as a family run by a powerful "strict father" who knows "right" answers in a dangerous world. To teach traditional morality, this figure judges and punishes citizens (the "children" in the family). Fear is a given, and obedience is a key value. But Lakoff also describes a more progressive way of thinking where government is like a family that works through discussion and negotiation—with the goal of helping everyone towards full development. In this view, nurturance and empathy are key values and dissent is important in making good decisions. Not surprisingly, the two ways of thinking often exist side-by-side in a given person, family or institution, which explains why many of us struggle to free ourselves from leftover aspects of authoritarian thinking, even though overall we're more progressive.

Lakoff's ideas have special relevance to free speech, silencing and the culture of judgment. Whatever our political values and beliefs about child-raising, all but a few of us learned to write by the "strict father" method. Judgment was key. Someone in authority (a teacher or a parent) knew the "right" way to say something and evaluated or corrected our spelling, our sentences and our thoughts until we got it "right." To succeed as learners and stand on our own in this system, we learned to internalize the judges, to embed judgmental voices inside ourselves to do the work of the expert. We had to adopt the voice of outside authority as our own—in Freire's terms, to "house the voice of the oppressor." Most schooling, no matter how progressive, works by teaching self-judgment—how to judge yourself "right" or "wrong"—especially as our schools return to more test-based teaching. Even in fields like humanities and social sciences that emphasize negotiation and human potential, expectations about writing are often the last remnants of the authoritarian mindset.

Think about how you learned to write. At every stage you probably received evaluation and judgment rather than reactions to what you said in the writing. Note that even positive evaluations, "good" or "excellent," are still judgments, not a response to your ideas. And any judgment reinforces the authoritarian approach and the culture of judgment. Peter Elbow, an influential teacher who has worked for decades to change this dynamic, recalls that parents greet our first spoken words with delight and praise—no matter how inaccurately we form the sounds. But for our first written words, they correct the misshapen letters, in effect judging us and sending us a different message about our competence and worth. After this we have grammar school teachers with red pens and professors, editors, supervisors and friends who practice "constructive criticism"—all of them reinforcing the idea of judgment, rules and a "right way" to formulate our thoughts. But real communication depends much less on rules than on understanding who you are talking to. And this we cannot learn from rule-based training.

> *Real communication depends much less on rules than on understanding who you are talking to.*

Of course we have to use some judgment and critical thinking before a piece of writing is finished, but the timing is crucial. One of the master's main tools is the gut-level, criticizing kind of judgment that undermined our power and intelligence in school. Fear of negative judgment becomes our own inner judge, criticizes us even before we get words on paper, and stops the flow of words right there. Clara felt this writing letters for her organization and Jane felt it trying to start her book. Most of us are barely aware that we have internalized negative judgment.

The most important instruction we can give ourselves when we sit down to write is to be aware of self-judgment and set it aside. In the long run, evaluating what we've written will be a strength. But if we start by looking for mistakes, we'll scratch out half our words and be unable to move forward. But setting self-judgment aside, we can disengage from the culture of silence—from family, teachers, colleagues and even friends, who may reinforce our sense that what we're saying and how we are saying it are not good enough.

Undoing the silence

There is much more to understand about silence and the culture that maintains it, but this book is about moving forward. When things get really bad and people feel their most treasured values at risk, dramatic events like those in the 1960s can liberate tremendous will to break out of the silence, to take a stand on the vital issues of the day and to do it in a convincing and effective manner.

A year after the Free Speech Movement, the attack on civil rights activists in Selma, Alabama, sparked nationwide outrage and a flood of public sentiment that began to reverse official attitudes. Political scientist Taeku Lee recently studied simple letters to the president from average citizens during that time, showing how the enormous shift in our national priorities really started with grassroots voices. The silent generation experienced a transformation. Ordinary people felt compelled to defend the democratic values of equality and fair play and did so eloquently, both in their letters to decision-makers and on the streets. The politicians followed their lead.

Since the 1960s, the culture of silence has set in again, leading Vermont's Bread and Puppet Theater to portray mainstream Americans as "sleepers"—huge puppet faces and bodies deep in slumber while atrocities are committed in their name at home and abroad. What if all those sleepers awake? What if we learn to use our potential as the world's second superpower? As this book emerges, we are seeing increased silencing— harsher regulation of free speech in a fear-driven climate—and also more vocal dissent. The cataclysmic rise of environmental destruction, poverty, racism and war are moving many citizens to take the risk of voice. A report by a Quaker organization shows that already more people are writing letters to their congressional representatives. In her book *Democracy's Edge*, Frances Moore Lappé looks at hundreds of ways citizens are giving voice and taking action below the radar of media silencing. And there are many small and larger ways all of us can add our voices to the democratic dialogue, now and for the long haul.

Writing for social transformation

North American schools rarely showcase the kinds of writing that can make things happen. To many adults, "writing" means either dull school assignments or poetry and novels written by artists only. But when my neighbor Greta plunged into public involvement with the Million Mom March in the year 2000, just about everything happened in writing. Some of it was creative and inspirational, like personal testimony for hearings and articles for newsletters; some was routine, like proposals and registration forms. All of this writing was essential to democracy. Every piece of it helped Greta undo her silence and become a community leader.

HIGHLIGHTING THE "GUEST OPINION COLUMN"

Among all the ways for writing to make a difference, one with untapped potential is a short, 600-700 word article that appears in small local newspapers, sometimes called the "guest opinion column." These columns are usually more personal and community-focused than the op-ed columns by major public figures that appear in big city papers. Most small papers can't afford many staff writers, so they welcome community input. And controversy sells papers—so they also welcome dissenting views. Over the years, I have been in several groups that shared responsibility for weekly or monthly guest columns. My all-time favorite column was one written for over ten years by my friend Betty Burkes on Cape Cod in Massachusetts. Betty struggled with all the faces of silencing discussed in this chapter—and used her friends for feedback and support.

Betty lived in one of the most beautiful areas of Cape Cod, where visitors marvel at the serenity of dunes, salt marshes, winding roads and the elegance of colonial homes associated with early democracy. But Betty and her young daughter were not part of this history: they were African American. One day twenty years ago Betty told me about her child's terrifying experience returning from school along these same secluded roads.

As one of only two or three children of color in her school, Betty's daughter was followed home and taunted with hostile, racist language. Betty and her daughter were up against the old terror their ancestors had faced during slavery and afterwards. Throughout our history and as recently as 1998, dark nights on country roads have been fatal to people of African descent in America. Betty felt the terror would not end until deep-seated attitudes could be brought up and changed. She knew there was no way she could keep quiet and hope for the best. A favorite writer, Audre Lorde, had warned about keeping quiet, "My silences had not protected me; your silence will not protect you."

So Betty decided to try something far outside her comfort zone. She began to write bi-weekly columns in the local Cape Cod paper to make the issues more visible. Her first column promised to give readers "greater access to stories of people of color—their fears, their anger, their hopes, their celebrations, their lives." Twice a month for over ten years, Betty wrote stories: about the local Wampanoag people keeping their culture alive on the Cape, about Black sailors on old-time whaling ships, about Jamaican seasonal workers, about a ten year old Cape Verdean boy abused by teachers, about a racist incident on Fourth of July—and also about celebrations like Kwanzaa. Always she wove in her own, deeply-felt, family history, combining research and interviews with the voice of her heart.

Writing these columns wasn't easy for Betty. She would put them off to the last minute, then agonize over how to express painful issues she knew only a few would easily accept. It's hard to find words for something too challenging for others to hear, but she found support in friends and neighbors who would read drafts of her columns. Betty's writing had impact; in fact it became the lightning rod for the paper, the thing readers would call or write in about. Some white readers wrote to thank her for speaking out, but many expressed hatred and anger. That couldn't have made it easy, but Betty persisted, laying her heart out on the page twice a month for over ten years and shifting the level of discussion about race in one white community where the issue had remained invisible. (You can read one of Betty's columns in the appendix.)

The written word drives social change for the long haul. Every time I walk past the coffee grinder in my grocery store, I think of a writing project that made a huge difference in the world. Back in the 1980s, Rink Dickinson got teased in grad school for a vision of economics others didn't share. He was upset that our system didn't provide a fair living to southern hemisphere farmers, who grew most of our food. In those days, there was no such thing as "fair trade"—the term hadn't come into use. But Rink didn't let this silence him. He teamed up with two friends to write a business plan based on what he saw as a fairer system, at least on a small scale. He proposed a venture called Equal Exchange.

Rink did draft after draft of a five-page proposal. He was writing for people who didn't know economic jargon, so he had to make technical ideas accessible and exciting. In the end, his argument was strong enough to draw a few investors to a small coffee-importing business with no middlemen. The fair value of the coffee would go directly to cooperative farmers in Central America and East Africa. As the new business got off the ground, I proudly drank Cafe Nica (from embargoed Nicaragua) and Cafe Libre, "the anti-apartheid coffee" (after Tanzania's stand against apartheid).

Twenty years later Equal Exchange coffee, tea and chocolate can be found all over the United States. Now worker-owned, the company advertises widely and educates at the same time, through written materials and overseas tours to show customers the politics of coffee first hand. Equal Exchange went on to co-found a thriving "fair trade" federation with alternatives to the so-called "free trade" of huge companies and government treaties. And this movement has become a sizable fair trade sector giving hope to embattled farmers in the Global South. Today's consumers know Equal Exchange products and accept the concept of business that Rink put into words in those few pages of writing twenty years ago.

Writing is rarely done completely alone, as we're expected to do in school. Most of Greta's and Rink's writing was done with others—sharing ideas and feedback. Even when you're writing something very personal, other peoples' feedback and support strengthen your voice. So the writing you'll hear about in this book comes not just from lone writers but also from collaboration in community organizations, small citizen groups and local government offices that are working for a better world.

IDEAS FOR WRITING THAT CAN MAKE A DIFFERENCE

Writing on your own:

- Letters to the editor and decision-makers in media, government or business
- Op-ed and other columns and articles for small or larger newspapers and magazines
- Blogs, websites and discussion lists; print or e-magazines and newsletters

Writing with others:

- Group-written letters, articles and reports
- Press releases and other media campaign materials
- Letters of inquiry and funding proposals
- Position papers for your organization, decision-makers, or regulatory bodies
- Publicity materials, flyers, brochures, manuals or guides
- Speaking materials—public testimony for hearings, scripts for political phone calls

Writing that makes a difference doesn't have to change the whole economic system. The shortest flyer or phone banking script, the hastiest letter or email—all play a role. As activist-historian Howard Zinn told a crowd recently, only half humorously, email is "one of our main forms of dissent these days." Lobbying groups tell us every communication with politicians, CEOs and others with the power to make change is helpful. But more than this, every time we put a vision of change into words, we are beginning to act on that vision, to undo what holds us back and create positive movement forward. "To speak a true word," Freire said, "is to transform the world." And anyone who's taken part in social movements knows what he means.

CHAPTER THREE

The FREEWRITING Tool

Letting go of self-judgment

Most people will do just about anything but sit down to write, even though all of us have powerful voices somewhere inside. This tool helps end harmful self-criticism, reach buried insight, and create pages of energetic writing. Stories and exercises make getting started easy.

> *Most people will do just about anything but sit down to write, even though all of us have powerful voices somewhere inside.*

When I went to South Africa a year after the fall of apartheid, I wanted to see how people were recovering from a regime that had silenced citizens by outright terror tactics like arrest and assassination. The first South Africans I met there were community organizers helping grassroots groups gain a voice in the new system. Yet even these leaders struggled with silencing. I remember the sun of a winter morning pouring into a spacious training room filled with eager faces. Everyone in that room came from ethnic and language groups that had resisted apartheid; all had spoken out and many had been imprisoned or in exile. Now they needed to write reports to influence the new government that they had brought into being. But writing reports was different from shouting slogans in the streets. Now they had to work in a language and style of thinking associated with the old regime and rooted in their painful history of colonialism. The new South Africa recognizes eleven official languages, yet English—the mother tongue of less than ten percent of the population—is the main language of decision-making. Everyone in this room was struggling with it.

I always start by asking what problems people want to resolve as we work together. In this group, the brainstorm began with language itself. Items like "proper grammar," "correct use of jargon" and "how to structure a policy report" went up on the flip chart. Eventually people began to mention things like "confidence" and the fact that their supervisors—also former anti-apartheid activists but mostly white and highly educated under the old regime—didn't appreciate their way of thinking. Then they grew quiet and I waited, unwilling to cut off the brainstorming.

At that point a man named Brian Moholo spoke up. Brian had been a union leader during the apartheid years and was the person who had invited me there for the training. "All of these things are important," Brian said, "but our biggest problem here is *freedom*. We do not yet feel free to write what we think, and that means we aren't even thinking it fully. I am hoping this workshop will help us learn to feel more free." I knew from the sigh that moved through the room that Brian spoke the deepest wish of everyone present.

In the rest of the English-speaking world, many think of ourselves as free, but Brian hit on something pretty universal. Over and over I find Americans who don't feel entitled to write what they really think or even to have thoughts that might rock the boat. Surprisingly, even people who are successful as writers feel this way. Many of us have learned to get our writing done, whether we're speaking in our full power or not. I can't tell you how many people who seem too successful to be struggling with writing have thanked me for the tool in this chapter. Until they tried it, they didn't realize they were missing out on something.

With Brian's word "freedom" on the flip chart and echoing in our heads that morning in South Africa, it was the perfect moment to introduce the freewriting tool. And, after they tried it, this roomful of anti-apartheid leaders began to buzz with conversation and laughter that felt like applause. It was thrilling to offer a tool that went to the heart of the problem.

Over and over I find Americans who don't feel entitled to write what they really think or even to have thoughts that might rock the boat.

What is freewriting?

Freewriting is an exercise to undo your own personal silencing, a tool that enriches your life in general, not just a writing project. Over time, it can address profound issues like freedom, but its immediate purpose is to strengthen yourself as a writer and thinker, both overall and for the task at hand. Especially if it's hard to find words for your thoughts, or if it's easier to speak than write, freewriting is something to build into your life for at least a few minutes every day. Try it in a notebook while waiting for the bus or on the keyboard whenever you sit down at your desk. This tool needs to become a regular practice, like stretching for runners or playing scales for pianists. It's a way to get yourself comfortable with writing and at the same time find your true and most powerful voice. It can also help you think more powerfully and form words more fluently. It is especially important if you've been neglecting your intuition, if you struggle to combine creative and analytical thinking, or if English isn't your first language. The exercise is to write for a limited time period, without stopping or judging yourself and without planning to show it to anyone.

The goal is to get yourself writing without evaluating what you write. Five minutes works as a start, but the exercise feels so good that most people want to increase to ten or anywhere up to 45 minutes or even more. Freewriting is not new. It has been taught in many U.S. classrooms since the 1960s, but it comes so naturally that earlier writers must have used freewriting without giving it that name.

Remember that freewriting is private. It is for you only, not for readers. In the time you give to freewriting, you are exploring your own relationship with language, thinking, and yourself at a deep level. On paper, freewriting may look rough, experimental and personal, completely different from the finished writing you'd show to readers. No one is looking over your shoulder when you do it, and you never need to share your freewriting with others unless you really want to.

How to use this chapter

Freewriting is one of those things—like music, yoga or a sport—that you can deepen and develop over a lifetime, but just starting out helps people enormously. Afterwards there are many ways to intensify the practice. This chapter is arranged in three parts so you can choose either the quick or the more thorough approach.

- Part one gives you a brief overview plus the basics of the tool.
- Part two helps you develop deeper awareness of your freewriting.
- Part three helps you use the freewriting tool in your writing life.

However you use the chapter, I suggest you do a lot of freewriting as you go along. You will feel the real benefit if you use this tool a few minutes each day, or at least four or five times a week. Sometimes you'll simply write about whatever's on your mind that day. Other times, following the suggestions in this chapter will bring new energy. While some people like to freewrite very casually on paper to throw away, I suggest that, while learning, you start a notebook or loose-leaf binder so you can save it all in one place. A file in your computer also works. Occasionally the exercises ask you to look back over what you've freewritten, not to evaluate or judge it but for greater awareness of yourself as a writer.

Getting comfortable with freewriting

This first part of the chapter gives the bare bones "rules" of freewriting to get you started. Simple as the tool is, it can be very difficult for some people, so stick with it until you start to feel at least a little free. Then you can decide whether to go beyond these first steps with the second part of the chapter.

How to do it

Sit down with paper and pen or the computer—whichever feels better for you. Then write without stopping for a given time period. You are talking to yourself in writing and keeping your mind as free as possible. Each person finds his or her most natural way to do this, but ironically, most of us need rules to release ourselves from all the critical voices inside.

FREEWRITING "RULES"

- Time yourself for five or ten minutes and write without stopping
- Don't try to mentally control what you write, no outlines or plans
- Don't cross out or change anything
- Don't worry about grammar or spelling
- Let your mind go wherever it wants
- Honor your own "craziness"

- **Time yourself for five or ten minutes and write without stopping** for the whole time. Keep writing even if your foot itches or the telephone rings. Above all, don't pause to think about what you're writing, even about your next point. Stopping, even for a microsecond, opens the doors for the judges inside you to get critical.

- **Don't try to mentally control what you write, no outlines or plans.** Don't try to be logical or "good." Let the words and ideas come out intuitively from within, even if you find yourself shifting your direction, going in circles. There is no "off the subject" in freewriting.

- **Don't cross out or change anything.** If you don't like your words, note your feeling, put your dislike aside and go on writing.

- **Don't worry about grammar or spelling** and give yourself permission to shift into another language if you feel like it. This includes actual languages like Spanish, Cambodian or Ebonics as well as the many wonderful informal "languages" you may use with friends on the street, in the shop or at family gatherings. Forget all you've been taught about proper English. (Yes, this is just the opposite of what the South Africans and most others expect will help them learn better writing!)

- **Let your mind go wherever it wants,** even if you started out writing about something specific. Stay free in your head. Be open to changing your thought and let whatever is deep within come out on paper.

- **Honor your own "craziness."** If wild, scary, risky, or dangerous thoughts come up, try to stay with them, even things you'd censor immediately if you knew someone would read them. Taking risks may be exactly what you need to get in touch with your true power and freedom.

> *If wild, scary, risky, or dangerous thoughts come up, try to stay with them.*

Relax and let the freewriting stimulate your mind with whatever comes up. Freewriting is never an assignment. Give yourself permission to jump all over the place regardless of logic. It's amazing where our hands and intuition will take us if we just free them up.

If words do not come, keep your hand moving anyway. Write spiraling lines, write nonsense words, or continue to write the word you got stuck on until your mind clicks back into action and more words come. You can write, *My hand is tired, my hand is tired;* you can leave blanks, make up new words, whatever keeps your hand moving and your mind free of the judges.

Exercise

Try it now!   If you are learning this tool just from reading this book, please stop reading right now and try five minutes of freewriting. Just reading about it is too controlled, too passive and too mental. You may think you know what I am talking about, but until you do it, you won't know it in your bones.

One way to start is to write for five minutes beginning with the question "When is writing easy? When is writing hard for you?" Or substitute an emotionally loaded question of your own. Write whatever comes from your mind at this moment, and keep writing without pausing even if you find you've gone far beyond your original starting point. Invite yourself to try it now.

Reflecting on your first freewriting

The South African organizers were so delighted with their first freewriting that, when we finished, they spontaneously turned to their neighbors to talk. It helps to hear others' experiences, so I usually ask for reactions. Here are some I've heard over and over:

> *I didn't believe I would be able to write for as long as five minutes! I had no idea I could write so much in that time.*
>
> *I actually found myself thinking in English when I usually struggle to translate from my first language. (Or I found myself easily writing in my own language and skipping back and forth into English.)*
>
> *I never believed I could feel this comfortable writing.*
>
> *I found myself writing things I didn't realize I knew. I really made some discoveries.*

If you felt just a trace of any of these feelings, your first freewriting was a big success, and you have more discoveries ahead.

The "gong," the "supervisor" and the internal judges

For many people, the first freewriting doesn't feel very free because the exercise can bring us up against the root mechanisms of silencing. Here are other reactions:

> *I keep thinking about what others might say about my writing. I can't feel free.*
>
> *I don't think I will ever be able to feel free when I write. My supervisor in Japan used to walk around the office on a special platform behind where we sat. He would look over our shoulders and catch mistakes as soon as anyone made them. I spent ten years in that office, and I can't get my supervisor out of my head.*
>
> *I keep hearing the gong. My third grade teacher used to make us stand in front of the class and read our writing out loud until she heard a mistake. Then she would ring a gong and we would have to sit down. I carry deep shame about my writing.*

Most of us expect our writing to be criticized, so we protect ourselves by not writing what we really mean. This is how silencing works: we develop our own internal judge. The blocks to freedom are right inside us! So learning freewriting really *is* learning freedom—and it isn't easy. At first, just be aware of when you are not free. From there you can move on to look at the big picture. It has taken a long time to develop the thinking that prevents freedom. You've been creating those internal judges for your whole lifetime and you can add in the years that shaped your parents' and teachers' attitudes and even the centuries that shaped our culture as a whole. It is going to take more than a few sessions of freewriting to liberate your voice. And even then, most of us experience freedom off and on, hardly ever a solid, confident state. I speak from painful experience when I say that continuing to practice freewriting keeps us making progress.

Could we be resisting freedom?

With lifetimes of being unfree behind us, we have a habitual "comfort" with the status quo, so we find ways of resisting freedom without knowing it. For instance, our minds and bodies may refuse to work together, making freewriting physically painful:

> *My wrist hurts.*
>
> *My thoughts move too fast for my hands to keep up.*
>
> *My thoughts keep jumping around or I have too many thoughts at once and can't decide which to follow. This chaos is mentally painful.*

At first it seems impossible to coordinate the hands and the mind, but gradually, with practice, this changes. When I notice that my wrist hurts or my mind is racing ahead, I can slow down, try to take the hurry out of the practice. Eventually the hand and the mind learn to cooperate. Thinking slows down just a little and the hands speed up. A certain harmony develops. The mind gradually gets comfortable with the exercise and eventually with the whole writing process.

And if your mind is jumping around, let your freewriting jump around too. Write choppy sentences. Write non-sentences. Trust the chaos and write whatever comes up. If you give it a chance, your deep mind can help you find connections between ideas when your surface mind sees only disorder. Freewriting is a good place to get comfortable with the chaos that can lead to powerful thinking.

Freewriting is a good place to get comfortable with the chaos that can lead to powerful thinking.

The "boring" judgment

Even though the freewriting goal is to be free of judgment, for most of us, it's hard to let go of judging ourselves:

> *What I wrote looks childish and boring when I read it over. How can this put me in touch with powerful ideas?*
>
> *Nothing special seems to be happening. What's all the hype?*

Where do you think this reaction is coming from? Who is judging? If you were to share your freewriting—and remember I said not to do this unless you really *want* to—you might find it appeals to others. What you fear is "boring" probably isn't.

And freewriting is a practice, not a test of "good" writing, so it's often boring and rambling by literary standards. The person who coined the term "freewriting" says he usually throws his away. Another famous freewriter says she has filled countless notebooks with boring writing. We can't get attached to quality here. We're doing this to keep our writing muscles alive, to nurture ourselves for the long run. Boring may mean that we feel bored while writing, simply because we're not yet free enough to get in touch with our deepest thoughts. Going deeper comes as we get more free.

Any of these responses are valid reactions to freewriting. Locating the supervisor or gong somewhere in ourselves is part of the ongoing struggle to free our minds. When we're aware of internal criticism, it quiets down and our real voices emerge.

Exercise

Naming the judges   As you were growing up and developing your way of writing, what interfered with your natural freedom? Who were the judges? Parents or particular teachers? Did you pre-judge your own work to protect yourself? Most of us were penalized in school for crossing out or changing words in our papers. We had to stop and think carefully before writing each word. Our parents may have had strong reactions to what they saw as "mistakes."

Staying as much as possible in the spirit of freewriting, list five or more experiences that may have helped create "judges" in your mind. Don't censor! Then freewrite about one or two experiences you feel most strongly about. What actually happened and how did you feel? If possible, try to relive the scene as you write about it.

Energizing freewriting with questions

We want this power to be easily accessible, not just an occasional miracle we can't repeat.

At times there's something almost magical about freewriting with no agenda at all. New thoughts burst forth energetically. At other times, lethargy sets in and we worry about whether we've done something wrong and lost the magic. Don't be fooled by the judges in another of their disguises. There's nothing wrong with "low energy." Ups and downs are very natural. On the other hand, the more freewriting you do, the more you experience its power to liberate words and ideas—your creative energy. We want this power to be easily accessible, not just an occasional miracle we can't repeat.

Starting with questions as prompts can trigger the energy of freewriting:

- *Can you remember the first time you saw the ocean (or mountains, or people from another country)?*
- *What was the first experience of being in nature that you can remember from childhood?*
- *Can you remember a time when music (or painting, sculpture, poetry, dance) was transformative for you?*
- *What smell (or sound, taste, etc.) can you recall from your childhood? From yesterday? From this morning? What sensations are you noticing now, as you write?*
- *What would your mother (father, grandmother, great-grandfather, etc.) have thought about the issue you're writing about?*
- *What got you interested in improving your world?*
- *Can you recall a time when you felt fear (or anger, sadness, joy) while struggling for your rights?*

Understanding why questions trigger energy for writing can help you come up with your own. The best ones take you into specific experiences, inviting you to recall real people, places and objects. They often touch on deep, magic-like dreams, ancestors, birth or death—things we rarely talk about. Most of us want to write about important ideas, but we mask them in our daily lives. Powerful questions have a surprise element, lifting you out of the ordinary so you can't hide behind what's "proper." A good question is emotionally loaded for you. It will touch on what Paulo Freire called your "generative themes," issues that motivate you so deeply you can break away from the judges inside.

A word of warning: questions that are really assignments can throw you right back into the hands of the "judges." Remember the classic school assignment question, "What did you do on your summer vacation?" This one can zap your energy. Not only is a teacher asking it, it's also too vague and broad to be stimulating—no surprise, no generative themes. If you ask the question to yourself in a more specific, sensory way, you might find good freewriting energy: *What tasted (smelled, sounded) best last summer? Were there any times I was afraid? What was my most profound experience of community?*

When freewriting without a question works for me, it is usually because I have a question already in my mind that I am barely aware of. Some call this an "itch" or a "felt difficulty." Being aware of the itches—the themes that have energy for us at particular moments—is crucial to writing powerfully. There's always a question that will spark your creativity.

Exercise   **Finding questions that work for you**   If you have been doing freewriting for a while, examine five or six freewritings that have a lot of energy. Notice whether you had an unstated question on your mind and identify other factors that stimulated you— a word you'd never heard before, an unusual place to write, a particular time of day, a dream the night before. Now list ten things that have the power to energize your free-writing, and freewrite for 10 to 15 minutes about where your freewriting gets its energy. Building on what you discover, end by listing five to ten questions for future freewriting.

When speaking is easier than writing

Socially active people often do better speaking than writing. A particular friend comes to mind. Harley had started out in the machinist's union, cutting metal with a lathe and speaking effectively in crowded union halls and tense negotiations with management. When I met this man, he was working in research, helping to build a labor-friendly point of view among policymakers. Even though he was writing a lot and had finished his first book, Harley found writing painfully different from speaking.

Harley told me how energized he used to feel among the political tensions of a typical organizer's life. Speaking before an audience, he could sense their reactions and this stimulated his thinking. Without those faces before him, he could write words on a page, but they seemed lifeless. To find words for his best thinking, he needed to feel his lis-teners' reactions. The way he told it, speaking and writing came from two different thought processes on "two different conveyor belts." His best thinking came on the speaking belt, and he couldn't seem to get at it through writing. Nor could he fool himself by speaking into a tape recorder because his key stimulus—the audience—was missing.

I thought immediately of freewriting, and Harley decided to try using this tool as if he were speaking. As he wrote, he imagined a tense, crowded room, the sound of his voice in the microphone, the pauses, the crowd's reactions, their applause, disagreement or support—everything he knew would energize his voice and his thinking. After trying this different kind of "production process" for a while, Harley gained the awareness that helped him switch from speaking to writing. A few years later, he told me he'd become comfortable with writing as a way to express his best thinking.

Exercise   **Switching conveyor belts**   Try doing your next freewriting as if you were speak-ing. Mouth the words, say them out loud if necessary. Imagine the faces of listeners and respond to their reactions as intuitively as you can. You can't stop and think— you just have to keep talking or in this case freewriting. Notice the rhythms of your "voice" and allow them to come through in the writing. When you're finished, reread to see what came out, but don't judge yourself. Keep repeating this exercise until you start to feel the processes of speaking and writing begin to merge. (To heighten awareness of the two processes, read Peter Elbow's work on speaking and writing listed in the resources section.)

Letter writing as freewriting

> *I began to feel in touch with the creativity I had always believed was in everyone but had rarely felt in myself.*

People often tell me they are fluent as letter writers but can't translate that fluency into other writing. I can understand—I often feel freer writing to close friends than writing for myself. When international students at MIT asked if they could do their freewriting assignments as letters to loved ones half a world away, I realized this might help everyone. Years before email, one of these students wrote every week to his wife in China. He wrote page after page on the computer in English (which she also knew), telling her how he felt when the moon came up and he knew that, many hours later, the same moon would be visible to her in the skies of their home city. Even though he was writing for a reader whose first language was Chinese, he said it was the first time he'd felt comfortable expressing himself in English. He knew there was someone on the other end who cared about him and his thoughts, someone who would not judge him.

Does it work with email? Of course, if you are truly freewriting. Although email is often informal and casually composed, it's rarely as lengthy or personal as you get with freewriting. Sensory detail is rare. Most people write an email message to communicate quickly rather than to express what is in their hearts or to discover deep truths.

As you read about this tool, it may look deceptively easy. What could be simpler than writing without stopping to think, control or judge? I have to admit that when I first read about freewriting, it looked so obvious that I didn't even try it. I continued to believe that pausing and thinking about each word was the way to improve my writing. I continued to find writing painful and to leave many projects unfinished. Once in a while, late at night, some magic would take over. As I wrote page after page without stopping, I would begin to feel a voice, an energy propelling my words that came from somewhere deep inside. When I finally tried intentional freewriting, I realized it could give me access to this energy on a regular basis. I began to feel in touch with the creativity I had always believed was in everyone but had rarely felt in myself. I began to see how my own writing blocks and perfectionism came from the oppressor inside that Paulo Freire had described. This simple tool has revolutionary potential to undo the silence in all of us.

Freewriting may not produce miracles the first few times, but keep on doing it. For many of us it has become part of ongoing work to become freer human beings throughout our lifetime.

Tapping deeper insights with freewriting

When you begin to feel more relaxed and can keep writing in spite of inner judges, you can discover ways to get in touch with more profound levels of creativity. The balance works differently for each of us, so notice when a technique works toward your freedom and when it has the opposite effect. If you find yourself tightening up and trying to produce "good writing" or judging your freewriting "good" or "bad" in any way, back off from that technique for a time. By simply noticing self-judgment, you're beginning to break its hold.

There are eight techniques in this section. Some come from the authors listed at the end of this chapter who pioneered the concept of freewriting, but others come from ordinary freewriters like you. Some also resemble the THINKING techniques in Chapter Five.

1) Your freewriting environment To deepen freewriting, try arranging a writing space for yourself that helps you feel especially comfortable and creative. People's space choices vary tremendously: some like solitude at home or in a quiet corner of a library; others prefer the bustle of life in train stations or cafés. One friend has been writing for twenty years at small coffee shop tables. She concentrates best surrounded by other people (and she loves to nibble on muffins and scones). She rotates between six or eight cafes in her hometown. Other people establish special spaces at home for freewriting—somewhere with light, a cozy chair and an ineffable feeling of good energy. One friend feels most creative and safe curled up on the floor. Another has a writing space near an altar with photographs of inspiring people, a candle and flowers. Many do their freewriting in what they consider a meditation space, because for them freewriting, like meditation, encourages deep awareness. Some who are trying to fit a regular freewriting practice into busy lives use it as an early morning meditation.

2) Sensing and "simul-sensing" When freewriting feels most energetic, people often tell me they're engaged in details of taste, smell, hearing, touching and seeing—very specific details about what they perceive and feel. A natural way to bring this detail into your freewriting is to open your mind to whatever is going on in your environment while you write. If you're in a cafe and you hear a machine grinding ice or a nearby

If you're freewriting about a crowd of people that affected you deeply, invite your five senses to help you recall what touched off the feeling.

conversation, let these details weave into what you write. They aren't distractions to be screened out, but part of the mix flowing through your mind at that moment. If you're sitting by your window at home in the winter, stay open to snowflakes or drops of rain on the glass, cold feet, or perhaps a hunger pang if it's time for a meal. Let these things come out on the page. One friend freewrites every morning and always brings the weather into it, no matter what else is on his mind.

Once details start to come naturally, you can also awaken your sense-memory for what happened in the past. For instance, if you're freewriting about a crowd of people that affected you deeply, invite your five senses to help you recall what touched off the feeling. What did the people look like? What colors and styles of clothing were they wearing? What did their voices sound like? What was in their faces? What about the smell of tortillas on the little charcoal grills of the street vendors?

Watch out for the judges here. We don't want to confuse this technique with the writing instructions many of us received in school. If you hear the voice of a teacher asking for as many details as possible or more adjectives like "sky blue," "fragrant," or "billowy," try to return to the actual experience as you lived it.

People vary in their sensory awareness. Some notice tastes but not visual detail. Some remember touch but not smells. Some have vivid recall of the special nature of sounds they have heard. Others just hear them as "loud." Expanding our awareness helps all of us to awaken the sensory paths to language.

Exercise

Questions for sensing   If you notice that your mind doesn't recall sensory detail easily, then start freewriting with questions about the five senses. What smells do I remember from childhood? What could you see from the door of the house I grew up in? What are the subtle sounds that surround me now as I write? What are the touch sensations I experience on taking the bus to work? What does it taste like eating breakfast on the run? The goal is to extend your freedom into unfamiliar sense-territory.

Exercise

"Simul-sensing"   In the 1960s and 70s my students especially loved the invitation to get all five senses going at once. To try this, go to an unusual place to write—a library in a new neighborhood, an urban doctor's office, a park bench in spring, a concert. Being in an unfamiliar place helps with the surprise element. Spend a few moments noticing what you experience in this place, consciously exploring it with your hearing, taste, smell, seeing, and touch. Then stop thinking and freewrite about the experience while you are in the middle of it, including any thoughts, associations or feelings that pass through your consciousness while you are writing.

3) Metaphor Don't let this word make you uncomfortable. Metaphors are simple, intuitive ways of expressing thoughts about one thing with details from a completely different thing. "The *whirlwind* of my mind." "The *deep pool* of your mind." Like sense detail, metaphors come spontaneously when we're feeling free and in touch with intuition. Because metaphors are so important to thinking and feedback, there's more on them in the chapters dealing with those tools. For now, simply growing more aware of metaphors can energize your freewriting.

In South Africa I worked with a unique group of women committed to changing the apartheid policies on gender and developing powerful voices. Freewriting was essential. One stormy evening after the workshop, one of the women took me to walk along the bay surrounding Robben Island, where an infamous prison had held freedom fighter (later, Nobel laureate) Nelson Mandela for nearly thirty years. Huge waves crashed against a sea wall in the early darkness of a winter storm. The next day, after freewriting about our walk, she asked to share a metaphor that had come up for her. She could have written just "big wave" or "powerful wave," but what come out on the page was "lion-sea wave." The group was excited by the metaphor. It reminded us of the fierce African lion, of Mandela, and of this writer herself as a passionate activist who had been arrested by the apartheid government in her twenties when things were most dangerous. It spoke of the power of the Atlantic storm and the challenge that had drawn us to the workshop. Did the writer "think" about any of this during her freewriting? No. The words just came to her from deep inside. And when she shared them, they touched the whole group with their energy and power.

Metaphors don't have to be a big deal. We actually use them all the time. A job can be "a prison," strong feelings in a meeting can be an "explosion." And metaphors lie behind many of our action verbs when we say, "people *roared* approval" (another lion?) or "an idea *crept* into your mind" (a mouse?). In each case, our mind intuitively links two unlike things and helps us see the similarities.

To avoid self-judgment, we can't get analytical about freewriting metaphors, but we can be aware of them and encourage their energy. When you notice one as you write, tell yourself, *Oh. That's interesting. Look what I just said.* The deeper awareness may lead you in exciting directions.

> *Metaphors don't have to be a big deal.*

Exercise

Finding your own metaphors Reread several freewrites with a highlighter pen marking any metaphors you find. Look for the simple ones built into the verbs you're using ("roaring," "creeping") and dramatic ones like "lion-sea wave." Ask yourself about any connections between the highlights and the energy you felt while writing. If you feel inspired, try a freewrite about a particular metaphor you used. Remember we're not trying to come up with "good" metaphors but seeking to deepen awareness.

4) Diving deeper   When I had been faithfully practicing freewriting for many years and gradually opening up to its potential, another writer taught me how to take a giant step further in this direction, to dive deeper, avoid the internal judges, and find fuller, more powerful thoughts than those floating on the surface. Natalie Goldberg, author of *Writing Down the Bones*, urges us to pay full attention to feelings as we write. Notice when you are trying to avoid something painful because that's when we use vague words and shy away from our innermost thoughts. Goldberg encourages us to note when this happens without scolding ourselves. Instead we can shift gears and "dive right in" to an idea that seems scary or dangerous. The idea we're trying to avoid, she says, "probably has lots of energy."

In Goldberg's workshops, people go so deeply into themselves that they may cry or laugh or feel furiously angry while writing. It sometimes happens in my workshops too. When strong feelings come up—or when you realize you are blocking them—this is the time to feel brave and adventurous and plunge even deeper. Continue writing through the feeling, even if you are sobbing, gasping or pounding the table. You are onto something. If you can let yourself go, you may reach what Goldberg calls "wild mind writing," when your over-disciplined brain puts its training aside and trusts its raw power.

Exercise

Shifting the block   For me, diving deeper has only been possible as I become aware of when I'm "weaseling" around powerful ideas. (My students came up with this metaphor.) To gain awareness, read through a freewrite you have just finished. Use a highlighter pen to identify places where you came close to scary thoughts, then weaseled around them. What happened at those moments? Is there any pattern in them? Next time you freewrite, see if you can find the courage to go straight in.

5) Painful or negative material   Going deep can bring up painful feelings we usually see as "negative." Yet anger, fear and sadness have a lot of energy, and writers have traditionally sought access to this energy as a source of powerful writing. But our culture encourages us to cover up hard emotional realities with "nice" or "positive" thoughts—a sign of silencing. Many who have grown up repressing painful thoughts make tremendous progress with their lives as well as their writing through free-writing. Expressing and discharging negative feelings in the safe privacy of freewriting can get them off our backs and release a power we may feel as increased vitality in all dimensions of our lives.

But at times feelings that seem negative are so raw and confusing they endanger our well-being. I'm thinking of an African American friend, Amatul, who is now a successful performing artist and outspoken leader in my community. Ten years back, using freewriting to express anger about racism and sexism, she came to our group with questions about whether to continue. Her freewriting was generating painful feelings that seemed endless, sucking her into a whirlpool of negativity. Freewriting deepened her depression rather than clearing or liberating her energy. The prospects were terrifying. Would it be better to put the lid back on?

Where freewriting feels too painful, the tool needs to be used with great care, and not in isolation. Fortunately, Amatul was part of a compassionate community that had come together for a year to work on projects to benefit their communities. As soon as she shared her painful feelings, peers encouraged her to carry on. With their support she was able to keep freewriting and, later, to take on significant work for change in the areas which had been most painful to her.

When your own balance is at risk, you need to talk, not just write. You need a friend, a counselor, or a writing support group—a community for sharing your feelings (and maybe your freewriting). Find people who can listen with deep attention without trying to rescue you or give soothing advice, people who respect you for risking deep feeling. Their listening can bring out your strength. Along with the whirlpool of negative, depressed, or hopeless feelings, there is bound to be some genuine hope and encouragement, maybe deeply buried. Active listening, not advice, can help you find it.

Each of us is different, but when my emotions grow too raw, it's often because I am pushing myself too hard. Social change issues seem to grow more challenging every year. Sometimes it makes sense for me to step back temporarily from the distress and cultivate peace in my heart before returning to the painful dilemmas of our times.

6) Affirmations Another technique for those times when personal confusion and negativity seem overwhelming comes from Julia Cameron's *The Artist's Way*, a book that connects us with our creative energy. Affirmations are simple sentences affirming your own strength and creative purpose. You choose one and write it over and over (ten times!) to see what it brings up for you. Some examples:

I am full of creative energy.

I am putting aside my hang-ups with writing and giving my full attention to this project.

I am dedicating my energy to ending racism (or whatever you feel strongly about).

To do this in the spirit of freewriting, include everything that comes to mind while you're writing the sentence. When I do affirmations, my mind resists with counter-thoughts—*This is absurd. Creative?! I don't feel any energy at all!* Cameron calls these "blurts," the voice of our internal censor trying desperately to keep us from getting free. The most powerful part of the exercise comes from writing out the blurts and any thoughts or memories that come with them. I find myself writing between affirmations about what has held me back from my strength and what I can do to change. Sometimes what I discover between the lines leads me to adapt the words of the affirmation, and by the time I've copied it ten times, it has grown into something very different.

AFFIRMATIONS

Here are some that work in my groups. Cameron's are marked with an asterisk (*); the others my students and I invented. Always feel free to change any words in an affirmation to fit your own beliefs. Just be sure to keep the meaning positive.

1. I dedicate my work to my own healing and that of my community.

2. As I create and listen, I will be led. *

3. My creativity heals myself and others. *

4. Through the use of a few simple tools, my creativity will flourish. *

5. As I write, I set my good intentions.

6. My creativity always leads me to truth and love. *

7. I am willing to use my creative talents. *

8. I am willing to be of service through my creativity. *

9. I know there is strong creative energy in me.

10. I am willing to speak out.

11. What I have to say is important to many people.

12. I am willing to risk completing this project.

Affirmations emphasize what you *will* do and your positive feelings about your intentions. They are exactly the opposite of that old childhood punishment where you had to copy "I will not talk during class" one hundred times. Punishment strengthens the internal censor, while affirmations strengthen our inner sources of creativity and goodness. The spirit of affirmation is a powerful ally in freewriting.

Exercise

Affirming your energy and purpose   Even if you are a practical, no-nonsense person, please try this exercise. I have to admit that affirmations sounded like a sugar-coated pill until I gave them a try. They are much more. Choose or adapt one of the sentences in this section—whichever one speaks loudest to you at this moment. Then begin to copy it in the spirit of freewriting and stay open to any negative "blurts" or positive insights that come up as you write. Explore all of it in your freewriting, then return, when you feel ready, to the affirmation you began with, repeating this process over and over, moving back and forth between affirmation and "blurt." Feel free to change and adapt the affirmation as you go. End when you have written out the affirmation at least ten times.

7) Clustering   One complaint practical people have about freewriting is that it is often so rambling, circular and indirect. It seems to take forever to get to clear thinking. Clustering is a wonderful, common sense tool to organize spontaneous thinking without killing the imaginative quality of freewriting. It was popularized by Gabriele Rico in a fascinating book on right- and left-brain thinking, *Writing the Natural Way*. In clustering we express our ideas in diagram form before freewriting, circling the words and connecting them out from the center.

> *In clustering we express our ideas in diagram form before freewriting.*

Here's how to cluster: draw a circle in the middle of a large piece of paper. Then write a word or phrase in that circle to get you started. This word gives a preliminary name to the issue you want to talk about. Choose something that is "loaded" for you: "love," "anger," "fear," and "sadness" are emotionally loaded for almost everyone. Words like "community," "red-lining," "cooperatives" and "equality" can be loaded if you feel passionately, one way or the other, about them. Even technical terms like "Community Reinvestment Act" or "chlorine compounds" work for some people, but only when the technical meaning connects with deep personal themes. Start clustering with words you feel strongly about.

Next spend several minutes writing out free-associations with your word in cluster form. Add one idea at a time, circling each new word and connecting it with either the last one or an earlier word. You are creating a web diagram of connections, with lines like spokes on a wheel. Every

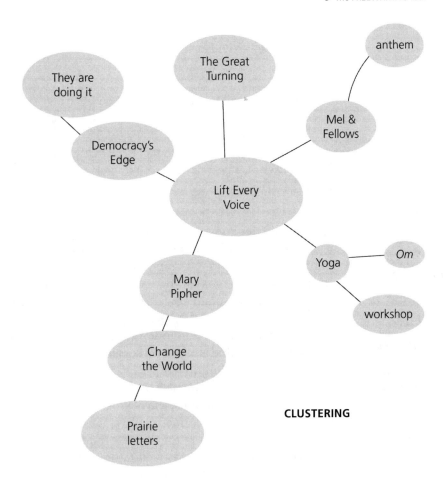

CLUSTERING

set of associations roots back to the central starting point either directly or indirectly. Move quickly and spontaneously, as in freewriting, without stopping, thinking too hard, or trying to be logical. As you continue filling your page with connected words, you will suddenly experience what Rico calls a "web shift." This is the moment when your mind tells you, very naturally, "Now it's time to write."

At this point, put aside your diagram without trying to remember it and begin to freewrite, following whatever flow of ideas comes to you at that moment. The diagram is there, but don't try to follow it as you write. In fact, you may end up writing about something completely different. But drawing the diagram helps you arrange your thoughts and warm up to the subject at hand. It helps your unconscious mind to organize in a unique way. Sometimes what you find yourself writing after clustering is astonishingly vivid and deep.

Exercise

Clustering   The next time you freewrite, try clustering with a loaded word or expression. If you don't have a good one in mind, search through recent freewriting for a starter word to explore further. Draw the circles expanding your diagram quickly and spontaneously, until the urge to start writing hits you. Then freewrite for ten or fifteen minutes. Does this work for you? If so, begin to keep a list of words you think will work for future clustering.

8) Signs of "freedom"   You can tell if freewriting is working by how you feel while you're doing it. You'll start to develop what Buddhists call "mindfulness"—an awareness of just how free or un-free the act of writing is for you, moment by moment. Are you still trying to control what you write to sound "good" or are the words pouring out, as if on their own? Do you genuinely feel free to go anywhere with your thoughts or are you trying to stay on topic? Is there a feeling of ease or are there tensions in your mind and body? (Remember, don't analyze or judge, but seek this awareness intuitively.) It's hard to put in words what freedom feels like, but you will gradually come to recognize it.

Is there a feeling of ease or are there tensions in your mind and body?

If you're like most of us, the feelings of freedom will ebb and flow with your mood and the situation. Despite years of practice, I still don't feel free when freewriting for the first time with new people. I'm too preoccupied with my role as facilitator, so I usually write only about that and feel very inhibited. Days or weeks later with the same group, I may unwind and discover wild and amazing ideas during freewriting. On a daily basis at home, my freedom also varies; I've come to accept ups and downs in freewriting as natural.

The South African women who liked the lion-sea metaphor loved the feelings of freedom so much that they created a list they called "signs of freedom," what they found in their freewriting that felt most free.

- Partial sentences. One- and two-word sentences.
- Repetition of words and ideas.
- Energetic informal words—slang, words from another language, private words you use with intimate friends.
- Nonsense words, made-up words.
- More feelings than analysis.
- Memories that don't usually come to the surface.

- Sensory language and detail.
- Playful rhythms—sometimes repetitious, sometimes jazz–like.
- Playing with the sounds of words (including rhyme or alliteration).
- Shifting voices (angry to sad; professional to personal).
- Linking things that are usually separate (battery problems in an old car with depressed feelings). Sometimes metaphors.

They noticed that some of these signs are also marks of excellence in literary writers' work:

- Sentences that sound like real people speaking
- Metaphor or sensory detail
- Repetition and rhythm

Freewriting can help you find the kind of style that makes a great writer, but that's not the goal, and it can be a big distraction. As soon as you think about greatness, the judges can come right back into the picture and before you know it, you're evaluating yourself again. The goal of freewriting is to get free of self-judgment and more openly explore words and ideas. Don't look for signs of freedom unless this helps you feel more free, not less. It's a difficult balance—to seek creativity and power in your writing but not push or judge yourself.

I've had to struggle with that balance too. Recently I was feeling vaguely dissatisfied with my freewriting. Wishing it were "better," I kept remembering a highpoint some years back when each freewriting session seemed magical, full of deep, heart-wrenching insights. Words I had never used would come to me just when I needed them and powerful insights flowed freely. I thought I had finally connected with a universal creative force, energizing my voice and my thinking. This time had seemed like a writer's heaven, and I wanted things to stay exactly as they were. But that's not how real freedom works.

When I realized I was pushing myself to get back to that highpoint, and losing my freedom by pushing, I decided to reread my freewriting during that period. To my surprise, I found the special energy came from major life struggles, not just from the freewriting tool, and I knew I did not want to repeat the pain of those times. My mother had just died and my father was on his way. I had just lost a job. Global politics and global warming were at cataclysmic turning points, and I was about to lose my home of twenty years. Each of these crises stirred me deeply with vivid dreams and perceptions of the people and events around me.

Probably this was one of the most intense periods of my life, and I was meeting the challenges actively and reflectively with the help of freewriting. No wonder every word I wrote felt charged with energy and meaning. Writing highs like this are exhilarating, but the true gift of freewriting is not to maintain a high but to keep ourselves writing through whatever is happening right now in our lives. Instead of pushing or comparing or judging, we have to follow the practice wholeheartedly to see what it brings.

| Exercise | **Finding your own ways to deepen freewriting**   After working through this part of the chapter, try freewriting about your freewriting practice itself. When is it most energetic and alive? What events in your life energize freewriting for you? What are the four or five ways you might bring more energy and depth to your freewriting practice at this point? Most important, how can you nurture your freedom and your awareness of that freedom? |

Using freewriting

Even though the point of freewriting is to stay free of judgment and the need to "produce" for an audience, there are times you will use this tool to work on a formal piece of writing. And there is a contradiction here. Every time you load practical expectations onto something that is supposed to be free of them, you risk the judges. But you can live with the contradiction if you've developed a strong freewriting practice. Here are seven ways to use freewriting while working on a writing project. Some are discussed more fully in the next chapter as part of the PROCESS tool.

- **Getting started / "Instant version"**   Before planning or strategizing for a letter, memo, or other piece of formal writing, freewrite an "instant version." So named by Peter Elbow, this is a quick, loose draft of what you think you want to say. Write without stopping or "thinking." Leave blank spaces or guess at information to prove your points. Trust your instincts and write whatever comes to mind without judging it. If material that is not part of the piece comes up, write that down too. Stay fast and free and use what you write as a brainstorm to identify what needs to be figured out.

- **Mad draft**   Very much like an "instant version" but usually comes after more planning. Write an entire draft quickly and freely. In a mad draft, stay as free as possible—even if there is a plan—by not feeling bound to that plan if new material comes to mind. (Mad drafts are a key step in the next chapter.)

- **Daily warm-up for long term projects**   As you work day after day on longer projects, use freewriting to warm up when you sit down at your desk. Rather than plunging directly into the work of the day, spend ten or fifteen minutes freewriting about whatever mixture of ideas is on the top of your mind. After this you'll feel freer to enter into the discipline of your work. You'll also use time for writing that might have gone to procrastination.

- **Freewriting during research**   Too many people separate research (reading and taking brief notes) from actual writing, allowing their best creative thinking to drop between the cracks. Freewriting as you go along by writing out your insights on readings, interviews, or other research will be much more valuable than brief notes when you write up your results. (Of course you need the notes too!)

- **Before or after meetings**   The same thing goes for writing down insights after listening to people speak in a meeting (very helpful if you're taking minutes) or as you think through your own strategy for presenting testimony in the unpredictable atmosphere of a hearing. I also use freewriting to prepare myself for important interviews.

- **When you get stuck**   Freewriting can be mental or emotional therapy in the midst of the writing process. If you realize you're stuck, stop and freewrite to gain awareness of what's holding you up and how to move forward. Put your draft aside and talk to yourself about your ideas and feelings at this moment. Freewriting can help you vent your frustrations in a constructive way or get at hidden feelings that are blocking you.

- **Focused freewriting**   When your project is particularly complex or challenging, such as a term paper or a report on a many-sided issue, try focused freewriting before planning or organizing. First pose questions to explore the subject, then freewrite with the questions as your focus. Focused freewriting is tricky because it's so easy to slip back into the "assignment" mode. Protect your freedom by staying open to unplanned ideas that crop up as you write. These could lead to your most important breakthrough.

- **Generating expressive detail**   The most powerful and convincing writing—no matter how technical—always has details that

Too many people separate research from actual writing, allowing their best creative thinking to drop between the cracks.

come from the heart. Whether it's the brief personal story that gets readers on your side in a letter to the editor or details about housing conditions that need changing, freewriting gives you access to genuine, heartfelt language that has the power to move others.

Sharing freewriting

The whole freedom of freewriting is that no one can make you share it. But good things can happen when you want to share and do. I realized this while co-teaching with José, a talented community organizer you'll read more about in the next chapter. After freewriting sessions, José would usually beg to read his, which was always lively and passionate. My favorite was a vivid memory of sunshine as he stood in a river helping his mother wash clothes during his Puerto Rican childhood. José's delight in sharing sparked others' enthusiasm, and soon there were four or five people wanting to read every time he did.

Keep the sharing free of critique or analysis. Even praise—like "Excellent!" "I really like that!"—is evaluation. People feel bad if some get it and they don't. Non-verbal acknowledgment seems to work. In their talking circles, the Lakota people respond to each speaker, with affirmations like "Ho!" and "Hmmm!" Brian Moholo's colleagues in South Africa always broke into spontaneous applause when someone read writing aloud. Deep, silent listening can also be satisfying. If readers look up at their listeners, they will often see emotion in the faces—maybe even tears.

Creative self-esteem gets a boost when you read your writing aloud. Until you've taken the plunge, it's hard to imagine anything so empowering. It's also great to hear other people read. Each voice sounds unique and inspirational. There is something lively and real about these words. An energy builds—synergy, really—and everyone gets ideas about what to try another time. Sharing builds group intimacy and solidarity. As a community organizer, José saw this at once. If you don't have a group, try sharing freewriting out loud with a friend who promises not to comment. And never pressure anyone to share freewriting. Respect each person's right to decide what risks to take and when, and make it comfortable for people to pass if they don't feel like taking a turn.

What freewriting can and can't do

When I first taught freewriting, I found some people resisting what they saw as a "touchy-feely" activity that would not be graded or produce tangible results. I didn't want to force freewriting, so I always made it optional. Fortunately enthusiastic people like José created the kind of friendly peer pressure that got everyone trying. Once the doubters gave it a chance, it always had benefits for them. Freewriting became the key to the toolkit. It almost always shows results and is the one tool that directly addresses our empowerment as writers, helping us raise self-esteem and break through the many blocks that keep us silent. Now, decades later, freewriting is the one tool I never leave out of a workshop.

I've seen freewriting turn many people around—not just Brian Moholo's comrades with their yearning for freedom after apartheid, but many others who had no idea they were unfree. As a regular practice, freewriting has helped people deepen insights, think more clearly and keep written records of their thoughts during long projects. It has sharpened use of

MORE RESOURCES ON FREEWRITING

How to tap intuition is an age-old dilemma. Art and design students, for instance, have told me their training includes "free-sketching"—moving the pencil around the page without stopping to think or plan—to release the spontaneous, intuitive spirit from the censoring, logical mind. The judges are always with us.

Freewriting, as we know it, was popularized in the 1960s by writing teachers like Peter Elbow and Ken Macrorie. But looking back over a hundred years shows writers like Charles Darwin, Gertrude Stein, the surrealist poets and Virginia Woolf were also freewriting. Even S.I. Hayakawa, who wrote the textbook on logical thinking that guided my education in the 1950s, (and later became known for his repressive educational philosophy) encouraged a similar practice. In 1962 he wrote in *College Composition and Communication* that college students "should be told that the lid is off, that they can write and spell and punctuate any damn way they please—but that they must write daily and copiously . . . rapidly and continuously for [fifteen to twenty minutes] without pausing, without taking thought, without revising, without taking pen from paper."

Since the late sixties, freewriting has become a fixture in American culture. Under various names, it is taught to help with everything from better writing and thinking to stress relief, personal therapy, spiritual insight, team-building and leadership development. And our bodies benefit too: a recent study found that people who freewrote every day about painful events in their lives healed major symptoms of asthma and arthritis. A control group—who freewrote every day, but about ordinary, not painful, events—also improved, though less dramatically. The popularity of freewriting reveals a pressing social need. Something in our relationship to external authority blocks our access to deep inward strengths of insight and expression.

> *The challenge of most writing projects is to combine our innate intuition and creativity with our logic and organizing ability.*

language and given writers a sense of greater power, creativity, and awareness of their thinking process. It has helped them relax, treat writing as something natural, and even find pleasure in the process. And many, many effective letters, articles, reports and book chapters have come out of freewriting.

But it's important to remember that freewriting is mainly a practice, an exercise, a way to stay in shape and not a substitute for the whole set of activities that makes up the writing process described in the next chapters. When you are writing about a new subject or one with many parts to integrate logically, when you are including researched material from many sources, or when you need to frame your message to reach a difficult audience, freewriting by itself can be frustrating and inadequate. You need a fuller range of tools. The challenge of most writing projects is to combine our innate intuition and creativity with our logic and organizing ability. Freewriting strengthens the first half of this mixture.

CHAPTER FOUR

The PROCESS Tool

Finding a flexible writing process you can trust

There's no single recipe for all writing situations, but you almost always save time by doing more than one draft, taking things step by step. Writing comes more easily when you know you'll be able to change it later. Stories and exercises in this chapter show five core mental activities to mix or match for each project.

In the 1990s I worked with the Community Fellows Program, a remarkable effort that brought activists from all over the United States to MIT to develop projects for improving their home communities. People came to this program with a dream—a cultural center for a small town along the Mississippi, a health program for the White River Apache, a youth leadership program in Seattle based in poetry and non-violence, a support system for young grandmothers in Boston's Roxbury. Many stories from the program are in this book. At the outset, most of these dreamers and doers had little experience with the practicalities of funding their dreams; they came for support with the research and rethinking that turns a vision into something grant-makers will fund. My job was to help with the part of this work that involved writing, and we began with two pages the very first week.

There was always chaos and agony over these first two pages. Even though there would be nine months to improve on the writing, I could understand. People everywhere stress out over the process of writing: they don't like looking at the blank page or painfully coughing up the words. This starting moment is when the silence is strongest. The judges inside are very active, especially when there's funding at stake. With their home communities waiting for the results, most of the Fellows hadn't done much writing beforehand and still had lots to think through on their projects. It was never easy to write those two pages.

But one person looked like she might breeze through. Marian told us she loved writing and was used to doing it on the job. She had already worked out the details of her project, and she had a promise of funding. A mid-western foundation was enthusiastic about her plan to design a spiritual component for youth training in the national organization where she worked. Along with funding, Marian had already secured the support of the Dalai Lama and other Nobel Peace Prize winners for a manual that would help youth leaders deal with the stress of front-line violence-prevention work through meditation, journal-writing, prayer, nature walks and yoga. Marian had a unique opportunity to get mainstream funding for something that would really make a difference to youth of color.

All the funders wanted from her was "a few words on paper," two pages maximum. It didn't sound like much, but Marian was seriously stalled. She came to the group in great distress to tell us she was sitting up late into each night at her computer, doing all kinds of other writing instead and feeling worse and worse about the two short pages. She was a sleepless wreck; all her issues were coming to the surface, and nothing was getting written. How was she supposed to get started and keep going on this project? Others in the group felt even more stuck.

Writing intensifies the pressures we face already. The self-judgment we struggle with in freewriting can be even harder on us when we sit down to a major writing project, especially when people we think are very powerful—like funders or Nobel laureates—are going to be reading our writing. But there is a tool that helps us move forward even while we're struggling to be freer inside. I know, because I used to get stuck on writing projects and still do sometimes. What helps now, besides freewriting, is knowing that writing takes time and comes in natural, balanced steps or stages. Like living your life one day at a time, you can't worry too much about the final product—good or bad—all you can do is keep writing. Take the freedom of freewriting into as many of the steps as you can and stay away from self-judgment. Once you have done one or two projects with the step-by-step approach, confidence slowly becomes a possibility. You *will* finish and the writing *will* be good. Once you know and trust your own process, you'll move right through challenging writing projects just like Marian and the other Community Fellows did once they began to use this tool.

What is a writing process?

However simple it may look on paper, writers work hard to get to that final product. Their process is invisible to readers, yet the mental activities they go through are accessible to all of us who want to write. You don't have to be part of a talented elite to use them effectively.

A writing process includes everything that goes into a piece of writing—the thinking and information-gathering, the conversations, the notes, the flashes of insight, the time we spend actually writing (and having new insights along the way), the feedback and the layers of changes we make before we're done. It includes everything from strategizing about how to reach an audience, to going deep into our own psyches to explore our true feelings about a subject. It includes amazing changes in our early thoughts that give us far greater power to change minds and hearts. Also, it includes last minute decisions about the language of a final draft. Anyone who sits down to write is blending a complex set of mental, emotional and interpersonal activities. But we have so little awareness of these activities that the process often breaks down under pressure. Awareness brings trust. The process gets easier as you learn to trust that it will work for you. This trust allows you to undo the silence.

> *The process gets easier as you learn to trust that it will work for you.*

Avoiding the "dangerous method"

During those painful late nights, Marian was more focused on turning out a product than on her writing process, but she had already gone through many of the mental steps to write her two pages. She had done the thinking and research. She'd had conversations with her audience to find out what they liked about her message. But when she started to put it on paper, Marian was using what writing teacher Peter Elbow calls "the dangerous method." Because she knew her subject so well, she expected to write the two pages perfectly in one sitting. For most writers, this one draft method—trying to get it right the first time—looks like an efficient way to make every moment count. But people who write this way do not save time. Getting it "right" means critiquing and editing as you go, as well as lots of inner torment, especially if you have important outcomes depending on your work or are struggling with your share of negative self-judgment. If you can get started at all, it takes hours to write just one paragraph this way, with no momentum to carry you forward.

Once in a while the dangerous method may work, but most of us wait, clean up our desks and procrastinate. When the time is up, we have to settle for something very far from perfect. Or we get so tormented, we just give up. These responses strengthen our original feeling that it is painful and frustrating to write. We dig ourselves deeper and deeper into our "dangerous" habits and our silence. We become more and more reluctant to undertake the responsibility of writing. We don't have a realistic process, so of course we can't trust the process.

It doesn't have to be this way. Peter Elbow, the teacher who popularized freewriting and coined the term "the dangerous method," urges writers to "divide the available time in half" and use the first half to get a rough draft on paper. The second half is for changing, perfecting and revising not just the words but the ideas. This two-stage method isn't fancy, but it is a process.

Like most of us, Marian had heard of rough drafts and revising, and like most of us, she felt she was too busy to try them. But when she did, the effects were magical. As soon as she told herself, "this is just a draft," Marian was able to write two pages. The pain had left the process: she got a good night's sleep, looked back at what she had written, changed a few things, got feedback from the group, made some more changes and—several drafts later—sent the two pages off to her funders, feeling very positive about this work. From then on, Marian had the bare bones of a writing process she could trust for all the writing she would do as her project evolved. Once you experience a good process, "the dangerous method" won't be so tempting.

MARIAN'S PROJECT

That year, Marian David wrote funding proposals, publicity materials and a draft of her training manual, "Sustaining the Soul That Serves"—promoting her vision of youth leadership. She'd been disturbed at the tough emotional situations young leaders faced in troubled communities across the nation as they dealt, on a daily basis, with emotional violence and deprivation without techniques for cultivating their own inner peace. Marian's materials became the center of a non-profit organization, where they're now available to anyone helping socially engaged youth with burnout. (The materials also work for adults!)

How to use this chapter

This chapter shows ways to divide and use your time while you write. Although the PROCESS tool is the second tool, it's also the key to the whole kit because all the other tools link with this one as part of the writing process.

I wish there were a simple step-by-step recipe for all writing, but no two situations are the same. A letter to your boss is different from a magazine article. Marian was ready to write, but her friends needed more preparation. All of us have different ways of working. Each project may have a different first step, but every writer uses certain core mental activities that you can mix and match to create your own recipes for writing. Here's what the chapter covers.

- What happens during a writing process
- Core activities that get you to a first draft
- Core activities that lead to a final draft
- How to vary and adapt the core activities to fit your unique writing situation

Why We Need a Process

Trusting herself to a multi-draft process worked for Marian in a practical way. Once she felt free to write something that wasn't perfect, the pressure was off, the inner judges quieted down and she could write. But there's another reason to avoid "the dangerous method." Taking the project in stages helps us make the most of our creative minds. We need to balance the dramatically different kinds of thinking we're capable of so they support, rather than fight, each other.

People sitting down to write often feel a conflict between the head and the heart. *Do I write from my passions or do I stick to logic?* My answer is: both. The best explanation comes from recent thinking about the left and right sides of the brain in human creativity.

> *We need to balance the dramatically different kinds of thinking we're capable of so they support, rather than fight, each other.*

Left- and right-brain thinking

The left side or lobe of the brain handles our analytical thinking—counting, adding, memorizing, learning grammar rules and categorizing. Here we analyze, separating ideas so we can understand their component parts and deciding whether our words are accurate. The right side of the brain handles visual thinking, emotions, metaphors and intuition. Here we synthesize, discovering relationships and coming up with new and powerful ideas. Freewriting gives us access to this often-neglected side of the brain.

People like Marian and her colleagues helped create this chart of left- and right-brain activities as mirror opposites.

LEFT AND RIGHT BRAIN STRENGTHS

Left Brain: "Critical"	Right Brain: "Creative"
Ability to think about the parts one at a time	*Ability to see the whole* in a flash
1+1=2 style logic	intuition, insight
careful, step-by-step work	spontaneity
linear thinking, one dimensional	visual or spatial thinking, multi-dimensional
memorizing	improvising, playing by ear
grammar, spelling, technical skills	flow, rhythm of sentences (or music)
structuring paragraphs & ideas	visual images, picturing your thought
numbers, facts, statistics, measurements	emotions, feelings, visions, dreams
evidence	metaphor, illustrative story
strategizing to convince an audience	trusting what you feel
tables like this one	drawings or stories
separating ideas/ANALYSIS	connecting ideas/SYNTHESIS

Inspired by Gabriele Lusser Rico, *Writing the Natural Way, Using Right-Brain Techniques to Release Your Expressive Powers*, J.P. Tarcher, Inc., Revised edition, 2000.

We need both sides of the brain to do our best thinking, and most forms of human creativity use them together.

We need both sides of the brain to do our best thinking, and most forms of human creativity use them together. A musician uses her left brain for the technical operation of her instrument and balances it with a right-brain feeling for the music. A Scrabble player uses his left brain to calculate letters and points, but his game becomes brilliant when he combines those numbers with right-brain insights—words that "just pop into mind." When I worked with former South African freedom fighters in the mid 1990's—who loved this way of understanding things—they added "fighting" to the list of activities that balance the two sides of the brain. They said that fighting has to strike a balance between calculated strategy (left brain) and intuitions about what is needed in the moment (right brain).

They chuckled when I said that writing works exactly the same way. Writing balances technical awareness about grammar, paragraph structure and sound arguments with sudden insights and feelings that just come. If you are stuck in the detail work, it's hard to see the big intuitive picture, and if you are stuck in feelings and passions, your writing may be chaotic and may not accomplish your goals. Why we get stuck is part of the silencing.

The freedom fighters were amazed to hear that the U.S. educational system prioritizes memorizing and the left brain without helping us develop insight and intuition. They knew this was true in their own apartheid system, which had sought to prevent them from doing their best thinking, but they imagined things were different in a truly democratic country. Alas, in most of the world, young people whose intelligence shines when they dance or perform poetry or respond intuitively on the sports field may never get credit for being smart if they aren't good at memorizing information. By the time we're adults, our natural balance of left and right brain strengths can become distorted. Most of us default to one side or the other.

Balancing the two kinds of effort in the writing process

It's not easy to balance. Most of us use our left-brain, critical mentality, prematurely. We begin to evaluate and criticize what we are writing before we have a chance to get it on paper. Typically, we interrupt ourselves with our own criticisms even on the first page, in the first sentence. This short-circuits our creativity and the many acts of intelligence that are part of writing. We lose out on wholeness of mind and voice, on our full power as writers. Our creative and critical voices clash instead of working together—a recipe for silence. Regular freewriting helps us gain balance in the long run, but how can we balance our efforts under pressure in a real-life writing project?

Taking a writing project in stages gives each side of the brain a chance to do its thing. We may vary the time frame (it doesn't have to be exactly fifty-fifty), but dividing allows the two kinds of mental activity to work in harmony. The first half of a good writing process emphasizes right-brain creativity and thinking ideas through from your own point of view as a writer. Hundreds of people I've worked with over the years—including Marian and just about everyone else mentioned in this book—have added their insights to my understanding of the writing process. We've looked at some research, compared it with our own experiences and given names to the activities we feel are essential. In the first part of the process, we've identified three core activities: generating ideas, organizing, and writing a "mad draft." Some critical, left-brain effort is involved, but mostly these three stages rely on the strengths of the right brain, giving

CORE ACTIVITIES IN A WRITING PROCESS

Generating Ideas
Get our ideas out on the table, via
discussion, exploring, brainstorming, listing, freewriting.
Mostly right brain

Organizing & Strategizing
Plan how to organize your ideas
logically for an audience.
Right and left brain

Revising
Rethinking, rewriting, editing.
The longest stage of the process.
Experienced writers go through
several cycles of rewriting.
Mostly left brain

Writing a Mad Draft
Get the whole draft written
quickly and freely. Freewrite.
Leave blanks to add more later.
Mostly right brain

Incubating
Let it rest. Open your mind
to new perspectives.
Mostly right brain

our thinking time to grow to full strength before we criticize, evaluate, or correct it. During this first period, we lean on the FREEWRITING and THINKING tools.

In the second part of the process we get back to more left-brained, reader-based concerns about final detail, connecting with an audience and correctness. This part has two activities—incubation, continuing the work of the right brain, and revision, where the left brain goes into gear for several rounds of rethinking, rewriting and editing. This is not a simple recipe that works for everyone at all times. Instead, most of the activities offer chances to blend left and right brain in different ways, varying with personality, state of mind and the kind of writing project. The last part of the chapter discusses some variations.

Dividing your writing process this way has three main benefits. First, it's easier to sit down and write when you know there are stages, so you can more or less eliminate procrastination. Second, you'll feel a sense of power. Dividing the time puts you in charge of your process and creates momentum. Third, and most important, giving time to both creative and critical energies gives your thinking time to mature. During a good writing process ideas will grow clearer and stronger.

| Exercise | **Naming your obstacles**   Before improving your writing process, take some time to give names to the things you think are holding you back. In many indigenous traditions, giving problems a name brings power over them. With paper and pen, crayons, or colored markers, ask yourself what stops you from starting and progressing and finishing a piece of writing. Draw your obstacles (no matter how rough and sketchy they look). Some may come from the world around you—like lack of time or bad vibes from bosses, teachers or "friends." Some may seem to be deeply rooted inside you, like worries about spelling or perfection. As much as possible, stay in the mindset of freewriting so the drawings come intuitively from deep inside, not from what you think you ought to show. When you have drawn your gallery of obstacles, give each one a name. Then freewrite about what it was like to name the obstacles. |

| Exercise | **Your left- and right-brain strengths**   When trying to overcome obstacles, it's important to know your strengths. All of us struggle to balance right and left brain in our daily lives. I've admired how a friend who's a community organizer balances left-brain detail work preparing for a meeting and then stays open to new right-brain insights while she's facilitating the meeting. Looking back at the chart of right- and left-brain strengths, where do you see yourself? Create your own chart with two columns for the strengths you have as a thinker, activist and communicator. Which are orderly, detail work (left brain) and which are intuitive (right brain)? After doing the |

61

chart, list some of your own forms of expression that balance right and left brain. Be sure to consider things like coordinating a busy household as well as sports, singing or drawing. After making your chart, freewrite on what you've figured out about your own use of right and left brain. How could you gain more balance?

Developing a Draft

The first half of your time aim for a loose (even messy) draft you can come back to later. It may work to sit down right away and write without any formal preparation. After all—and this is the beauty of dividing the time—you are going to have a chance to revise. However starting with a draft only works when what you want to say is already clear, perhaps because you've written many similar things or done an unusually thorough job preparing.

Most of the time we only think our ideas are clear. When we sit down to write and they don't come smoothly into words, it's time to work more on that clarity. Two core activities usually take place before the actual writing: generating ideas or bringing all the possibilities to the surface, then organizing and strategizing or finding a good way to get your message across to readers. After this you'll be ready to write a "mad draft"—a rough, messy version of what you want to say. Each core activity can take several forms.

First core activity: Generating ideas

While I was working on this book, I heard of a young woman with a huge writing challenge. A student from a Central American country that was stuck in poverty and the effects of war, she had agreed to speak at a major international gathering on childcare. I never actually met this woman, but I thought deeply about her dilemma because it was so central to this book. Important policy-makers would be at her talk, so it would be the perfect opportunity to speak out about the invisible situation for children in her country. But where would she begin? Out of all she knew and felt, what should she include?

Freewriting would have helped this woman realize how much she had to say and encouraged her thoughts to flow. But freewriting can't do it all, so it's important to get ideas out on the table by brainstorming—listing or sketching points on paper just to see all the possibilities. Most of us need to do this at the beginning of a writing process. Ask, *What are all the things I could possibly say?* and fill the page, or several pages, with words and phrases, jotting things down in the spirit of freewriting.

Don't stick with only the left brain and what you think you ought to say. Even if you're a person who likes neatness and order, allow some wild, crazy energy in your brainstorming, and your right brain will come up with unexpected possibilities. Generating ideas can border on chaos and, even though this can be a little scary *(Can I really deal with that?)*, chaos is a plus when it comes to creativity. Ancient stories from all the continents tell us the earth began in whirling, chaotic energy. Brainstorming stirs up the same kind of energy and coaxes ideas to the surface that are hidden even from ourselves. Don't censor anything at this point. You won't include it all in what you end up writing.

There are plenty of tricks for stirring more energetic and powerful levels of thought while getting started on the writing process. Some techniques are visual like drawing, diagramming or photography. Some are social and interactive like conversation, a lively meeting or a mental review of the readers you're writing for. Some involve researching your topic. Others help you gain better access to structures of thinking—for instance, mental diagrams, internal dialogue, and, of course, freewriting. More techniques to generate ideas come up in the next chapter on the THINKING tool.

It's especially important to put your brainstorming down in writing. How many times have you had new ideas—either in conversation or in your mind—without writing them down? They're so exciting at the time, it seems you will never forget. But the unwritten word fades very quickly. (Record-keeping is one of the main reasons we developed a writing system.) Our short-term memories hold things for 12 to 36 hours only. After that they begin to blur and become simplistic. A brilliant piece of reasoning becomes a dull buzzword. Detailed written (or recorded) notes are a must. One technique is to make note-taking a two-step process, as well. Write down a few key words in the heat of discussion or mental exploration, then go back to your notes as soon as possible to add what you remember. Write or freewrite in sentences and paragraphs to coax out your full memories. At the same time you will be deepening your ideas.

It's important to put your brainstorming down in writing. The unwritten word fades very quickly.

Exercise

Trying new ways of generating ideas   So much depends on how energetically you begin your writing process, yet most of us stick to the methods we've used before. The next time you write even a simple letter, try one or more techniques listed here, especially if they're new for you. (And remember, you can find more detail in the next chapter.) As you work, stay free from self-judgment to give yourself full access to right-brain creativity. Notice any ways the activity liberates your thinking or gives you extra energy for the project. If you feel a technique gives you less rather than more energy, put it aside for now.

- (Basic) List all ideas you have for the project and all relevant information, whether or not you think you'll actually include them.

- Brainstorm by answering the standard questions: What? Where? When? Who? How? Why?

- Ask yourself challenging questions (or get someone else to) and jot down the answers. What makes this subject so important? Why is _____ such a strong point?

- Pose questions from the point of view of someone who will not agree with what you want to say and try to answer them.

- Divide your paper into two columns and list facts in one, arguments in the other (or pros and cons, before and after, lessons and concerns, or whatever opposites make sense for your project).

- Freewrite two or more stories that illustrate what you want to say.

- Choose two photographs that express something important about your topic and brainstorm words you free-associate with the photos.

- Invent your own techniques or look ahead to the next chapter for more ideas.

After trying several techniques, use freewriting to reflect on which work best for you.

Second core activity: Organizing and strategizing

I picture the woman from Central America doing some of this brainstorming—talking to others and getting excited, listing points to include and quotes from people at home and freewriting a few stories to help bring her ideas to life for those who've never been to her country. She's found some statistics on the Internet, and she's beginning to feel like this whole project is doable. One day while she's waiting for the bus, she scribbles a few words on the back of an envelope. They have lots of energy and sound like an introduction. She figures she's finished generating ideas and she's ready to write. At her computer, she types in the sentence from the envelope. She's made a wonderful start, but nothing else "comes." What's wrong?

Right now she has pages of raw material, a promising introduction, and a rough, intuitive sense of where the writing is going. That's a lot, but there's one more mental activity needed before she can write with confidence—a conscious plan or strategy. Like everyone moving through the process of writing, she needs to organize.

Organizing might be as simple as writing 1, 2, and 3 on your notes to map out how you want the writing to flow. Sometimes the right brain synthesizes the chaos of brainstorming almost magically, and you know how to sequence your points without thinking too much about it. But when the magic isn't working, people get stalled for two reasons: first, the need to organize their thoughts *for themselves*—to clarify their message; second, the need to think through how to present the message *for readers*.

Organizing for yourself: what's your message?   There's a big difference between the facts you're conveying and the message behind the writing. A few years ago I worked with community organizers in an old industrial city with a culturally diverse population. They were fundraising for a big summer street festival, so we worked on letters asking local merchants for financial support. I noticed that the letters mainly gave information about the festival rather than showing why the merchants should support it. These organizers weren't the first to have trouble clarifying their message. For years I had worked with people in elite universities who approached writing projects as if their main job were to describe and provide information. Many were trained to include as much information as possible—neutral information, like in encyclopedias or high school research papers. This training is a big part of our silencing across the boards. People at all levels of education seem surprised to hear that factual information is not as important as our thinking about that information. Each piece of writing needs to have a message that shows the "why" not just the "what." In this case, the organizers were so absorbed in *what* they had planned for the festival that they weren't seeing the merchants' point of view. But the merchants would need to hear the *why* to be convinced to give money.

> **Factual information is not as important as our thinking about that information.**

MOVING FROM FACTS TO MESSAGE

Information: the "what"	Message: the "why"
The festival draws approximately 10,000 people to share the music and cultures of our city.	If you decide to sponsor the festival, approximately 10,000 people will learn about your company.
A large stage will be set up in our downtown park for round-the-clock performances of musical groups appealing to many ethnic groups.	You can support us and gain wide recognition for your products by financing the festival's main stage, which could then display your company banner.

Exercise   **Write a postcard**   When you want to be sure you know your message before trying to get it across to someone else, write it down in just one or two sentences on a postcard. It helps to imagine a friendly reader, someone you enjoy sharing your thinking with like a close friend, former teacher or mentor who really understands you. It also helps to write quickly without too much left-brain thought. Write a postcard like this:

"I'm writing a _____ (report, article, letter, etc.) to _____ (audience for your writing project) to tell them I think/find/want _____ because _____."

The last two blanks are the most important. The exercise is working if words flow and you find yourself saying something you hadn't quite said before. Articulating this message helps you see how to organize the longer piece you're trying to write.

Exercise   **Talking to the President**   There's an urban myth about one of President Kennedy's aides, who'd been asked to research and present recommendations in a half hour meeting. He came up with charts, diagrams, and information sheets and was going over his notes for the meeting when someone came to tell him that there was a time crunch, and he would have only ten minutes with the President, beginning shortly. In the next few moments, he had to revise his entire presentation to deliver in ten minutes. As he walked toward the meeting, going over his new strategy, the President's secretary rushed out to tell him that the ten minutes had been shortened to two and he would now have to argue for his recommendations while walking the President to a waiting automobile. Now he had just a few seconds to reshape his most important points into a few sentences that the President would be able to grasp on the run. Your task is to craft these few sentences for your own project. (These few sentences were the final product for the aide, but if we figure them out earlier in the process, it is much easier to strategize for a longer piece.)

Organizing for readers   The second hurdle in organizing ideas is figuring out how to divide up your points and sequence them for readers. In freewriting, thoughts come crowding in all at the same time. But readers need one thought at a time. So it's easier to write a draft if you think of your message in parts, taking readers one step at a time toward full understanding. If more writers knew this, reading their articles would be less of a chore. Many don't divide ideas into manageable chunks or put them into a readable sequence. When something is a pleasure to read, it's usually because the writer used basic organizing strategies such as:

- "This comes in two parts"—or three or five
- Story plus lesson

- Theory plus evidence
- False version followed by true version *(People think it's like X but it's really like Y.)*
- Familiar to unfamiliar *(Once you get point A, you're ready to understand point B.)*
- Easy to hard, safe to risky, local to global or any other pattern familiar to readers.

These simple patterns for organizing ideas are discussed in more detail in the AUDIENCE chapter. During early stages of your writing process, you can map the pattern for yourself with any of the following:

- **Numbering and arrows:** Number the chunks on your brainstorming notes and draw arrows to clarify connections for yourself; then use this diagram as a writing plan.

- **Headings or subtitles:** Use one or two word reminders for each step or chunk. I enter mine right into the computer to begin with, so I have a clear plan as I write.

- **Lead sentences:** Talk yourself through all the stages of your argument and write down the opening or lead sentences for each step you want readers to take. As you write your draft, these sentences will become the opening sentences of each paragraph, and you can add details to explain their meaning.

- **Rough outline:** Combine headings and sentences, list the points you want to make in the order you think best and write down sub-points under each one so you know where you want to go within each step. Don't get too fancy. People often feel stuck with the formal outlines they learned to make in high school, which may leave no room for thinking to evolve.

- **Diagram or "tree":** Sketch a diagram of your sequencing. Just be sure you have one you can follow step by step like the "tree" described in the next chapter. It's hard to write from diagrams that take you around in circles.

Research shows that writing itself stimulates more thinking—thus better writing.

Remember you're trying to make the thinking easier for readers than it was for you. If you put your points in the order you discovered them, you may plunge readers into the same confusion you experienced. And remember that as you write, and especially as you revise, you'll have new insights that improve your thinking, so you'll adapt and change. Research shows that writing itself stimulates more thinking—thus better writing. You probably remember a project that started out hard, but by the end became easy, maybe even fun. This was because you wrote yourself into understanding your meaning. What we're trying to do with the process tool is to reach this enlightened state sooner.

Pat Farren, beloved founding editor of *PeaceWork* magazine who believed in "empowerment journalism," once told me: "It doesn't have to be perfect to be wonderful!" Wanting perfection keeps many of us silent. Go ahead and write a draft even if you don't have it all figured out. The whole point of trusting the process is that we *will* figure everything out as we write. By the time we finish, our thinking *will* be clear.

Exercise

Talking readers through it   I often set up my sequence of points while taking a long walk and talking out loud to an imaginary audience. Taking "step by step" literally helps me remember that people can take in only one thought at a time. What thought follows from the starting point? What thought follows from that? (I watch their imaginary faces.) Am I taking readers where I want them to go? Am I taking time out to explain what they need to know? Am I giving them the help they need to follow my thinking? In talking out loud to them, I also gain confidence from the sound of my own voice.

Exercise

Making it easier for your reader than it was for you   Once you know your message, take a moment to review how you got there. Probably you had to struggle with a lot of confusion. How can you save your reader all that extra work? What path can you take readers on to make things easier for them? Hint: think of a specific reader, even someone who might not actually read the piece. One student pictured his thirteen year-old niece and organized his statistics paper so she would understand. There may be times when you want your reader to struggle—as part of a learning process—but a strategy like that takes even more careful planning.

Exercise

Contrasting strategies   The next time you write something so simple you could probably use "the dangerous method" without getting in trouble, take some extra time on the organizing step, just for practice. After generating a list of points to cover, map two strategies for getting them across to readers, making the two strategies as different as you can. If you're writing to request that your child be excused from school because your family is going on an educational trip, try putting the details about what he will learn and why you think this is important first, so you can end with your request. Also try putting the request first. Ask yourself which strategy feels more natural for you and which might work better for your reader? What is it like to have different options for organizing?

Third core activity: Writing a "mad draft"

> "It doesn't have to be perfect to be wonderful!" Wanting perfection keeps many of us silent.

Once you've created a "map" to write from, you're ready for the most energetic and freely creative part of the writing process. You are ready to sit down and write a draft—but it needs to be a "mad draft." This means you write out your whole piece as quickly and as painlessly as you can, leaving blanks for what's not clear to you yet. Handwrite, computer-write, whatever is most natural for you. You are trying for effortlessness, comfort and fluency. Your writing plan is a guide, but don't feel you have to stick to it if other ideas come up. Mad drafts are like freewriting. Don't worry about being logical or convincing your audience. Don't worry about spelling or grammar. Stay as free as you can so your intuition and intelligence will be there for you. You'll be a better critic of your work later, once your ideas are out on paper.

We have José to thank for the term "mad draft." The community organizer who liked to share freewriting, José was in his thirties when I met him, facing the intimidation of university life with a lot of fortitude. He told me about arriving at MIT, from the lively streets of his community—how he looked up at the imposing columns and wide stairway of the main entrance before first entering what we called the "infinite corridor." Surrounded by busy professionals from all over the world, José suddenly felt the huge differences between this place and where he was from. Later he began to feel the differences in training and culture between himself and students from Ivy League colleges. No one else in his class spent weekends in the National Guard earning income to support their kids. None taught salsa to neighborhood youth. Few seemed to have his fierce loyalties to class and community.

All of this reinforced silencing and made it difficult to write. José's preference for brief, concise expression—perfect for a community organizer—did not match his professors' desire for plenty of evidence for ideas. One of them shocked him by saying his writing was "like a blunt instrument." Although he knew more about English grammar than anyone else I met at MIT, José had to struggle with class and ethnic stereotyping every time he wrote. What helped the most was the idea of drafts—writing things loosely in the voice that came naturally to him, "blunt" or not—then changing them later. José was actually a skilled wordsmith. As a teaching assistant, he came up with the term "mad draft," and it stuck. Later, at Harvard for his doctorate, he used this tool to help other students defeat their silencing and took this practice into a successful career with non-profit organizations. José is now a dean of a college in his community and says he "writes on demand." He can turn out an effective report, memo, letter or article whenever it's needed.

Once you let go of the hope for a perfect draft to please all your critics, you'll invent your own ways to improve on drafting—as José did. Here are some hints to get you started with mad drafts:

- **Include more than you think you'll need.** Extra words, extra ideas and extra examples are fine in a mad draft. It's much easier to cut and combine them later than it is to return to the drawing board for new material. Cast your net wide at this early stage.

- **Include "iffy" facts.** The worst thing for a mad draft is worrying about accuracy. There's no way you can obtain all the facts you may think you need before you start the mad draft, so leave blank spaces and question marks when you aren't sure or make up things you can change later. Be sure to flag your "iffy" facts with asterisks or a code to catch your eye when you revise.

- **Take risks.** It is safe to say anything in a mad draft. When you write something important, silencing is always waiting to kick in. Do you feel uneasy mentioning key examples or names to the audience you're writing for? Could giving this information affect your professional reputation or win you some political enemies? A mad draft is not the time to worry about such things. You can cut or change later, but if you censor details now, you'll break your rhythm and inhibit your voice. And you may lose valuable ideas. It's hard to think clearly and watch your back at the same time. Taking risks in a mad draft really is safe, because no one but you needs to read this draft, and you will have time to revise.

- **Time your breaks.** If you're writing something short, push through and do it in one sitting. But crouching over your keyboard for longer than an hour, leads to stress-related injuries and burnout. For longer projects, take breaks on a regular basis, but plan them with awareness of your writing process. Your mind and your hands work well together when you're warmed up on a subject. Breaking at the end of a thought cools you down and makes it hard to start up again, so use your momentum from finishing one set of ideas to start writing the next. Then take your break.

- **Keep your brain in balance.** A friend says her right brain gets so active when she's writing mad drafts that she can't stand it for long without taking a break to file the papers on her desk. A classic left brain activity like filing gives her relief and a sense of balance. Learn to counter your own imbalances. If your right brain is overworked, maybe you can balance your checkbook, iron your shirts, or organize addresses or footnotes. If your left brain is exhausted, try gardening, stretching, or singing.

- **Above all, stay loose and tolerate the messiness!** A mad draft can be extremely chaotic. You may feel distressed because you know you're repeating yourself, using clumsy vocabulary, leaving out important material, or not creating good paragraphs or transitions. You may find yourself using street-talk grammar or a mix of English and another language. You may notice spelling and typing that are atrocious, or at best laughable. Don't let these things bother you. Keep reminding yourself you'll have time later to work on these problems. Don't let your inner judges put on the brakes. No one is going to evaluate. Keep on writing until you have the whole draft done.

For me what has made writing doable, and even a pleasure, is what happens after the madness. I know I have time to make changes and turn a wild messy thing into something I can feel confident about. I know I'll eventually be able to convey the message I want to put out. Because I've done it before, I know I can do it again—and that's what it means to trust the process. Finishing a mad draft—no matter how rough—is an accomplishment to feel good about and to celebrate.

Recently a whole roomful of people, who were addicted to "the dangerous method" of aiming for perfect first drafts, told me they felt extremely uncomfortable writing anything they knew was imperfect or unfinished. They said they preferred silence. If mad drafts hadn't been a course requirement, I think they would have refused to do them. But in the end, every single person realized that pushing through the initial discomfort helped them break the habit of perfectionism and trust their own natural thinking processes. Here's what Kelly, a masters student in the health field, had to say: "At first, I thought the mad draft idea was crazy! How could I just turn in my first thoughts, unpolished? But afterwards I realized it was probably one of the most useful writing tools I have ever used. To be able to just get it all out, not worrying about whether it was perfect, was liberating for me."

> *At first, I thought the mad draft idea was crazy! How could I just turn in my first thoughts, unpolished?*

Exercise

Writing a "very mad" draft. Some people need a special push to let go of perfectionism. Try writing a very mad draft, just to get the raw writing done. Give yourself ten minutes to write a letter that might normally take half an hour, and write "madly" with plenty of blank spaces, question marks, personal code words and spelling errors. Notice what feelings come up for you when you know you are making a "mistake" but don't stop to fix it. Afterwards do stop and celebrate completing the draft before you begin to edit or change it. If you don't feel freer, try the exercise again.

Revising

After a mad draft, it's time to get the writing in shape for others to read, with help from the careful, critical thinking of your left brain. This half of the process has two core activities: a short resting or incubation period to feed the right brain and a much longer, active left-brain revision stage.

Fourth core activity: Incubation

For the process to work best, you need to slow down and shift gears now. Drafting is intense—like driving your car all night on a long trip. If you begin to revise immediately, your thinking will not be at its best. Mental fatigue is one problem, but tunnel vision is another. If you look back over a mad draft immediately, you're still too close see what another reader would see, like spelling mistakes and gaps in thinking. The draft may look perfect or it may look terrible to you. In either case, your assessment is unreliable. You're still "mad," and not a good reader for your draft until your state of mind changes.

Everyone gains insight from putting the work down for a while. And this makes incubation very different from procrastination.

Amazingly, if you wait twenty-four hours, or overnight, the words no longer look familiar. Do something you love—walk or run, listen to music, do yoga, dance or meditate, have a reflective get-together with friends or a wild party. If there's less time, take a shower or get a good night's sleep.

More than just helping you unwind and find energy to continue, down time also opens the door to new insight because our minds keep working at a less conscious level. One scientist discovered the double helix through a dream after hours of difficult research. Einstein found the formula for his theory of relativity while sitting on a hillside watching clouds. Everyone gains insight from putting the work down for a while. And this makes incubation very different from procrastination—which happens before you begin.

When you come back to the draft, read it through quickly and see where you stand. This may be the time to show it to a friend (making sure she knows it is a "mad" draft and reads it supportively, not as a critic) or use the full FEEDBACK tool. Keep noting growth in your ideas. When you find yourself saying things in better ways, write them down. Now plan the time you have left for revision and editing.

Exercise   **Track your incubation process**   Make a point of "incubating" your next writing project. Take enough time out to erase the project from the worrying level of your mind. Let it sink down to a deeper level. Pay attention to what happens during your down time, by freewriting both before and after. As soon as you finish your mad draft, take ten minutes to write about what you see as the strengths, weaknesses, and meaning of the draft. When you've had a chance to unwind and gain perspective, give the draft a quick read and do another freewrite. Notice any differences in your perceptions.

Fifth core activity: Revising the mad draft—in three stages

Revising takes more time than any other core activity and is at least three activities rolled into one. Here the chaos and confusion of a mad draft turn into competent, influential writing. People often have a hard time changing what they struggled so hard to write the first time around, but I've watched many writers gain tremendous power through revising. One was Eugenio who, like Marian, was working on a proposal for his community.

Eugenio ran a youth program in a deeply impoverished neighborhood in the Southwest. His proposal envisioned a center where Latino and Native American youth could get the education they'd need for hard economic times. While working on his proposal, Eugenio had a pretty gutsy idea. He would write to a multi-national company with a computer factory on the edge of his neighborhood and ask them to donate a computer that he could use right away in his research, then turn over to the youth center once it got going. But who did he think he was, asking for a free computer? And how do you write a letter requesting such a big donation? The silencing effect was very strong. Eugenio tried every line he could think of but felt uncertain and apologetic writing his mad draft.

Sure enough, the first version of Eugenio's letter—like most mad drafts—grew so long he had to narrow the margins of the one page he'd planned. Even though he'd worked hard to sound good in this draft, Eugenio didn't really believe he was entitled to a free computer. So his letter didn't inspire confidence. To revise, he had to look closely at who would actually read the letter and why it was in the company's interests to donate. He had to turn his own struggles into a quick, convincing reading experience for the community outreach person at the factory, someone he had never met. In the process of revising, Eugenio realized that the company would actually gain community support by donating and that he was a very worthy recipient for one of their computers. After three more drafts, he came up with a half page version that explained everything and made his new point perfectly. (You can see his mad draft and finished letter in the appendix to this book.) Eugenio says revising this letter made him feel like a competent writer and gave him a writing process and a sense of entitlement he could use for the rest of his fundraising. Best of all, the company not only donated the computer but offered ongoing help to the youth center.

Eugenio's many hours revising his one-page letter are not unusual. A mad draft needs a lot of work. Some of us write too much and some of us write too little—or both. No matter how much preparation we do ahead of time, our first written version focuses more on our own struggles with the material than on what readers can hear. And we don't always say what we mean. Revising includes everything from re-examining our ideas and readers' needs to cutting out words. You are re-visioning everything about the draft, from its underlying thinking to the surface details of grammar, spelling and typing. But look at the deeper issues first. Otherwise, it's the same old "dangerous method," wasting time on grammar and spelling when big ideas need change. That's why revising includes three activities: rethinking, rewriting and editing.

> *That's why revising includes three activities: rethinking, rewriting and editing.*

Rethinking means looking at your writing with new eyes and from a reader's point of view. During first drafts we tend to put things in a way that makes sense to us emotionally but may not work for readers. Eugenio, for instance, was so worried about whether he was worthy of a computer that most of his mad draft spoke about himself and the prestigious university he was writing from. By the end of the letter he had mentioned the computer, but nothing about why the company would gain from donating. After his mad draft, he used the AUDIENCE tool to figure out exactly who he wanted to reach and what they might or might not respond to in his message. As soon as he realized he was writing to a community outreach officer—whose main job was to find local organizations for the company to support—he could see a better way to organize the letter. What did this person need to hear in order to understand and accept what he had to say? Eugenio also used the FEEDBACK tool to get closer to readers. His group saw right away that he wouldn't need to say anything at all about the big university if he printed the letter on official stationery. They also had questions about things he hadn't realized needed explaining.

Even without these tools, your message will shift or intensify after a mad draft, and you can now state it in a concise sentence or two. This is a good time to revisit the postcard exercise or try techniques from the THINKING chapter, especially the one called WIRMI. When your message changes even slightly during drafting, the whole thing needs adjusting so all parts can support the new, better message. The THINK-

ING chapter shows how to do an after-the-draft outline to see whether your message is consistent. What point does each paragraph and section actually make? Do you need each of these points? Do you need others that aren't there?

My father told a story about how messages shift in the process of writing. My dad was a lawyer and a very thoughtful writer, though I believe he suffered a lot over his writing and was inclined to "the dangerous method." Dad had great respect for a certain Justice Roger Traynor of the California State Supreme Court, with whom he had once shared a brief, person-to-person conversation. In that conversation, Justice Traynor mentioned how important it was that California state law requires Supreme Court judges to write out their opinions. Some states apparently let judges give the verdicts orally, without writing anything down. Justice Traynor told Dad that more than once he had considered all the facts of a case and decided on a guilty verdict before writing out his opinion. But as he wrote up the evidence, his thinking changed and he realized that the truer verdict was "not guilty." Fortunately, California law allowed him to rethink and revise.

Having time for rethinking is a real blessing because the act of writing makes all of us wiser. Putting things into words helps us know our material, our meaning and our audience. We understand it all much better now than we could while planning, organizing, or drafting. The more we plan time to make use of this new wisdom, the more we can trust the process.

Exercise

Too much or too little?   Rethinking shows some people they've put too much in a mad draft. Others find they've put too little, and still others—maybe most of us, including Eugenio—find a mixture. Once you've come up with a very realistic take on your reader and your message, here are some questions to help you see what to rethink and rewrite:

- Which thoughts speak to the message you want to get across?
- Which don't?
- Is there anything you can get rid of?
- Have you left anything out that a reader will need?
- Are you giving too much detail (which may confuse or bore the reader)?
- Do you have enough detail for someone unfamiliar with the situation to grasp it?
- Is every detail you include relevant to some part of your message?
- Can you take things out of the order you discovered them and put them into the order that makes things easy for readers?

Rewriting   means more than just changing a few things here and there. Be prepared for big changes to match your rethinking, like adding and cutting material or changing the order of points and even your meaning. The judge who changed his opinion while writing would have to go back and change most of what he wrote. But even radical rewriting to emphasize a completely different message is much easier than you'd think. Your mind is now at home with the material and can generate clear new paragraphs using the best words from the old ones. Introductions are a classic case because we tend to write them as a way of warming up to the material. While important to us personally in the writing process, they often don't match what we end up saying. I almost always change mine drastically during revision, when I'm clearer about what I want my reader to focus on. The AUDIENCE tool explores more about how to make an introduction reader-friendly.

As you move through what you wrote, ask yourself about each detail: Is this significant to my main message? Will this help or hinder readers? See if you can make your work "skimmable" by improving lead sentences and transitions and adding headings, bullets and white space. Readers need you to make ideas easy for them, packaged clearly. A warning: when you rewrite, you do need to think about readers, but you don't want negative self-censoring creeping back to haunt you. Writing teachers have plenty of stories of new writers who revised all the best words and phrases out of their writing because they couldn't appreciate their own power. Using the FEEDBACK tool with other people over time will help you see what is strong and distinctive about your work.

Computers make rewriting much easier than it used to be because it's so simple to add and delete, try out headings and move sentences around into a better flow. As you are making large structural changes, you will also be shortening your draft. Mad drafts usually have a lot of redundancy and repetition—a single paragraph may say the same thing four different ways. Right brain creativity works this way, but readers don't appreciate circular thinking. Here, you will also be improving on language and finding words or details for spaces you left blank.

My friend Ann, an economist and experienced opinion column writer, whose story is in the next chapter, calls rewriting "a great discipline." Because opinion columns have to be much shorter than most writers want—600 to 700 words—rethinking and rewriting are challenging. Ann recommends "starting with the 1200 words you think you want, then cutting it down. This means carving about 40 percent out of each sentence without losing what's important." Whether you are cutting at the sentence level or the idea level, rewriting makes your ideas more powerful and more readable.

Editing.   At last we come to the step that looms so large in most people's view of the writing process—improving on language, style, grammar and spelling. An entire chapter on editing and WORD-POWER covers this activity in detail. Word processing software can show you what needs work, but I suggest printing out your draft so you can see it on paper. If you have resisted the urge to tinker with words, you'll see why it's good to wait. Many of the sentences you would have spent time on are gone. You have not tormented yourself trying to remember grammar rules and censoring yourself at the height of your creativity. Now, at the end, you can afford to be critical about language; your left brain will serve you well. And since you now have a good sense of your audience, you can make decisions about grammar and language based on who the reader is. Pore over the paper carefully, combing your writing for trouble spots—like passive verbs, sentences you can't even read yourself, and confusing pronouns (like "it," "that," or "which") that friends or teachers may have said were problematic in previous writing.

What Einstein once said about scientific thinking also applies to writing, especially at this final stage: "Things should be as simple as possible—but not more so." The goal is language and ideas that are simple enough to be accessible yet are not simplistic. Research shows that most writers, even very experienced ones, can easily cut 20 to 30 percent from drafts without real loss of meaning. In fact, as Ann has found in her newspaper columns, cutting usually makes the meaning *more* clear.

A final step in refining language is to check for spelling errors and typos to avoid pushing the buttons of "gatekeepers," those readers who get distracted by what they see as mistakes and may shut the gate on your ideas. You can check spelling with your computer and double check it with a friend who has a good eye.

> *The goal is language and ideas that are simple enough to be accessible yet are not simplistic.*

Exercise

The Black Pen   My first two years at MIT, I wrote a regular newsletter column to help students, teachers and professionals with writing. One time I noticed that a column (on getting rid of unnecessary words!) ended up longer than usual, but I didn't think much about it. The following week I found the column sitting in my mailbox all scribbled up. A colleague had used a black pen to cross out exactly 30 percent of my words, with a challenge in crisp, firm handwriting: "Louise Dunlap: How do you like this?" No signature followed. To tell the truth, I didn't like it at all. As the new person in the department who was supposed to have expertise in writing, I felt it was a put-down. But I made this experience the focus of my next column, examining the suggested changes. In the end, I realized that more than half of The Black Pen's suggested cuts actually strengthened my writing. I got a lot of sympathy from other colleagues and students who knew who The Black Pen was because, they said, "he does the same thing to us." As an exercise, try being your own Black Pen, and ruthlessly cut your draft by one third. (Alternatively, try it on a friend's writing, with her permission, of course. Most people find this easier.) Which cuts add strength to the writing and which lose something important? Are there any patterns to learn from?

REVISING SCENARIOS

- **A one-page letter** You read it over with fresh eyes and see that your main point is buried among other points that will distract readers. Keeping your main point uppermost in mind, you quickly rewrite the whole letter, bringing the main idea out in the first paragraph and speaking more directly to your reader. You use some words and expressions from your mad draft, but mostly you rely on new, more effective language that now comes easily.

- **A two-page newsletter article** Most of it says what you want to say, but you think it needs a more engaging opening paragraph (what journalists call a "lead"), so you pull a high-energy story from the middle of the article and create a dramatic opening with it. You also cut about 20 percent of the language, partly to shorten the article for a 400-word limit but also to avoid repetition and keep things upbeat and energetic.

- **A twenty-page grant proposal** It's twice as long as the guidelines require, so you have to cut substance as well as words. Be sure that your main argument for funding stands out clearly at the beginning and throughout and that, in cutting, no important evidence for this argument is lost. Your approach involves cutting, pasting and matching the headings accurately with your content.

Building experience with the PROCESS tool is challenging:

- How do you know when you're ready to write a mad draft and when you're over-preparing, without leaving room for ideas to expand and grow?

- How do you balance the need to think things through with the need to keep your audience in mind? Is it better to be free and creative (and possibly off target) or to be practical and reader-based (and risk losing your insight)?

There's no one right way. Wrestling with these questions helps you grow as a writer. I suggest bending the rules, changing the order of activities and doing whatever helps you keep writing. The more challenges you move through, the more you will be able to trust your judgment and your writing process.

Adapting the Process to Your Situation

You can customize your writing process for different situations. Is your project short-term or long-term, about new or familiar material? Is it in a new or familiar format (letter, memo, proposal)? Do you feel comfortable with your readers or not, and are you writing in your own voice or for an organization, alone or with a group or committee?

Short-term or long-term writing projects?

So far we've been talking about medium length projects, articles or stories you could finish in a day or two. But sometimes you have only one or two hours to do a shorter project, maybe only a few minutes. Longer articles or proposals might take two weeks or two months. A book might take years. And you won't write steadily all that time. Most projects have to be sandwiched in with other work, including other writing.

For very short-term projects like routine letters or brief announcements, even if the subject is all too familiar, it's still important to do a mad draft, as opposed to a final, finished draft in one sitting. Jot down points you want to include. Then mad-draft for a few more minutes. Keep yourself writing, whether you like what you're saying or not. It's so tempting to revert to "the dangerous method." After drafting, break and move on to other work or, when feasible, let the project rest overnight. Give yourself time to rethink and revise before you consider this short piece finished. You may find a much better way to get your message across and catch glitches that might have made readers resistant.

Long-term projects, especially with unfamiliar material, obviously take more brainstorming and organizing. And you may have to write your mad draft in stages, some of them weeks apart. If you are working simultaneously on other projects, you may have to keep different sets of ideas in mind at the same time. Sometimes multiple projects complement each other, sometimes not. Be prepared to revise many more times than you expect. Well-known writer on politics and economics John Kenneth Galbraith once told me he always revised six or seven times; an urban myth about him ups it to fifteen! You can rewrite one chapter before drafting the next one. Or keep going with minimal revising. In writing this book, I bent my own rules by starting every morning looking over what I had written the previous day and making small changes—adding better details, clarifying what was fuzzy and removing obvious repetition. When I reached the end of yesterday's writing, I was warmed up for today's. Drafting over a long period of time has the advantage of built-in incubation. Your mind is always working on the project, whether you're aware of it or not.

Even a long-term writing project needs a tight, time-limited revision stage, when you get in gear and work through until it's done. Architecture students call this a "charette," a high pressure period for completing a design assignment. This siege of intense work, with all your feedback laid out before you, brings coherent critical thinking. Also, there will be a production stage, when you check for page formatting, graphics and final typographic errors. Allow extra time for this process. Just when you think you're finished, good editors or co-workers will come up with important suggestions.

Familiar or new subject matter?

You can cut corners writing about something you know well. If you've already written grant proposals for an organization, it will be easier to write a newsletter article about that organization. The AUDIENCE tool will help you organize and reshape the story for a new audience. You may be able to reuse whole paragraphs, but you'll need to change your voice: you're talking to everyday people now, not funders.

Even your finished product can be the starting point for another piece of writing.

On the other hand, if the subject is new to you, you'll follow the process more closely. Brainstorming and organizing merge with research, which most people don't realize is part of the writing process. Drafting is how you think things through, so expect lots of trial and error. Mad drafts can be extremely messy and revision extensive. Some people do their most powerful thinking at the very last minute, while deciding on clearer headings. I sometimes end a project with ideas so much better than I started with that I want to throw everything out and start over. Remember that even your finished product can be the starting point for another piece of writing. There is no last word on any subject.

Familiar, easy-to-write-for audiences or "tricky" audiences?

How well you know and trust your readers also affects your writing process. When you write for people who share your values, you save time on audience analysis and strategic planning. In a letter to close colleagues or an article for a national network you belong to, you won't have to worry about unfamiliar vocabulary or how to convince skeptics.

But social change writing can have complicated, "tricky" audiences—people who differ in social class, gender, age, training, or culture. Teachers are a classic tricky audience because of their grading power, and real world audiences are especially tricky when you're asking for money or resources. You might be writing for several tricky audiences at once. A short newspaper article correcting misperceptions about your organization goes to your coworkers (a familiar group), then to your boss (who may or may not be supportive), then to the newspaper editor (who's a "gatekeeper") and finally to a diverse reading community.

The AUDIENCE tool will help you frame your ideas for people different from yourself, and you can choose when to use it. Eugenio did a draft before he faced the full challenge of his audience. But you might want to analyze a complex, tricky audience first, along with brainstorming.

Exercise

Tracking your audience awareness   Next time you write, pay attention to how often and in what way you think about your audience. Do you think a lot or very little about readers? Who are they? Do you feel comfortable with them or do you worry how they will react? When your writing is finished, spend some time freewriting about your relationship to this group of readers. When you are fully warmed up to your freewriting, try speaking directly to them. Then shift voices and write as if you were the reader talking back. You can go much further with this with the AUDIENCE and FEEDBACK tools.

Familiar or new formats?

Letters to funders follow a different format from letters to the editor. Reports differ from articles. Once you have a basic process for writing, you can handle anything, but tackling a new format usually means prioritizing the AUDIENCE tool in your process.

Years ago I co-taught with a woman whose writing skills were legendary in the high-powered world of policy-making. Not long after graduate school, Amy Schectman had landed a job in an important state office headed by people who genuinely wanted to improve things. She was thrilled that her work would contribute. Because she had been considered a good writer in school, Amy's boss put her in charge of producing a "budget memo," the document sent every year to legislators to guide discussion on how the state should spend its money.

This was not only a very tricky, politicized audience but an unfamiliar format. Amy went directly to the files to look at past budget memos—exactly what you should do if you need to write in an unfamiliar format. In this case, the right approach didn't work. Amy's predecessors hadn't done a good job with budget memos. They'd written bureaucratic-sounding introductions followed by long lists of all the requests for funding they'd received. These memos were what the next chapter calls neutral writing: no message, no real thinking. Their intended readers in the state legislature would have a heyday fighting over who would get the money, with no guidance from those who had studied the budget needs. Amy and her boss had a different idea. They wanted their budget memo organized around a strong message identifying which projects made most sense with limited funding, and written so people across party lines could agree.

A few years later Amy had worked out an excellent format for these memos, one that was adaptable to other situations and similar to what is taught in business and professional writing. But her first memo—with no models to follow—was one of the hardest tasks of her life. Most of Amy's papers in school had used an approach that was the mirror opposite of the ideal budget memo. In those papers, she'd prided herself on weaving together as much complexity as possible. Her long introductions dropped contradictory hints to "draw readers in" to a rich mass of information. Only at the end of her papers (the longer the better) would she reveal her analysis of the problem she was exploring. The graduate school approach wouldn't work for readers in the state legislature. They weren't interested in complexity and didn't have time for it. They wanted to solve problems. Amy had to retrain herself to write in a way that would answer their questions quickly and help them agree. Memos for busy professionals reveal the message immediately—in the subject line, if possible—and give readers only the information they need to think through that message and come to a decision. It takes guts to write this way. You have to go out on a limb and say exactly what you mean. But Amy was good at this and at shifting her supporting information to an appendix to make the memo itself as brief as possible.

Hundreds of formats have arisen in the specialized worlds of government, research, grant-making, media work and business. Each expresses a special relationship between writers and readers. Each has a slightly different social purpose, which leads to different paragraphing, headings, organization and even a different voice. Like Amy, you will find the right approach if you give yourself plenty of time for the AUDIENCE tool and thinking through the expectations of the new format. Switching formats is challenging. Amy shifted from theoretical papers to something that would work in government settings; some people have to shift the other way when they go back to school after writing on the job. Learning to write effectively in more than one format deepens your ability to think strategically and gives you power in a wider range of situations.

> *Memos for busy professionals reveal the message immediately—in the subject line, if possible*

Exercise

Exploring a new writing format   Select a format you want to learn more about such as letter-to-the-editor, opinion column, report, or memo and study several examples of this one format as models. Ask yourself:

- What is the format? What are its "chunks," headings, etc?

- What can you learn about your audience by studying their preferred format? Are they in a hurry? Do they read for detail or just skim?

- Where does the audience expect to find the message or argument stated in this format? How do other parts help to support the argument? How does it feel to take the risk of speaking out boldly with your message? (Believe it or not, that's what most business and professional readers expect.)

- How can this special structure help you think through your own message? Is there a required section you could draft first to push your thinking along?

- Is the format really appropriate for your audience and purpose? Remember that Amy and her boss changed a format that was entrenched in old, disempowered ways of doing things. Changing an established format can be social action in itself.

"Sponsored writing" or your own voice?

Amy also faced the issue of voice. She wasn't just an individual writing to express her personal opinions on the job. The budget memos came out first under her boss's name and then, if approved, with the name of an even higher state official on the heading, as if he were the author. Amy's words became the voice of an entire branch of state government. ("Voice" is what we call the sense of values and attitudes that comes across in your words and writing style.) What Amy was doing is often called "sponsored writing," and it can be problematic.

Some complain about having to write in the dry voice of an organization or their supervisor. Tension between personal and sponsored voices can slow writing down, confuse thinking and even draw you into inaccessible jargon when you know better. So much in this book is about letting your own voice come forth. This means an important question is whether you have to silence that voice to write for your organization. I don't think you do, and Amy didn't either. With some ingenuity, she found a voice she was comfortable with.

To face this tension, your first resource is the flexible writing process. Use your most comfortable, natural voice to freewrite, generate ideas and mad draft. Switch to a sponsored voice only when you revise. Don't overestimate how formal the sponsored voice needs to be. Bureaucratic

> **You have more power than you realize to change an organization's voice and culture.**

expressions like "facilitate the development of" can probably be changed to "help." Second, you have more power than you realize to change an organization's voice and culture. Bureaucratic writing rarely serves the organization. With her boss, Amy created what she called an "upbeat" writing style, straightforward and accessible, that worked beautifully in the huge state bureaucracy. The WORD-POWER chapter can help you and co-workers make this empowering transformation.

Co-writing or writing alone?

In social change work, we hardly ever write alone. There's usually a group or team or supervisor to collaborate with. Activists and people from the corporate world who return to college tell me it's painful to shift from a setting that supports their writing to one that constantly tests them. But co-writing can pose its own problems, merging different people's writing processes. Some are stuck in "the dangerous method" and don't like to work on drafts. Some always make a formal outline; others never do. Some like to start with descriptions; others like to start with big, controversial ideas. Group writing tensions can culminate in final draft battles over relatively unimportant phrasing. Co-writing tensions teach us that there's no one right process or right way to say things.

In one group process, a supervisor may decide on the message and edit for voice at the end. Another group may work more democratically, with everyone taking responsibility for the ideas as well as the writing and editing. To head off disagreements, even when a supervisor is in charge, I suggest negotiating plans from the very beginning of the process. A graduate student once told me his group spent 46 hours arguing over language in a final edit of their client project. I'm guessing most of their disputes could have been resolved earlier by agreeing on a common process and exploring the AUDIENCE tool together to figure what voice would be effective with their readers. Then, dividing the work—with each person drafting a different section—group voice is more consistent. In one collaborative editing technique, a small subgroup listens carefully to all suggestions (and why the changes would help readers). Instead of everyone trying to agree on each change, the subgroup then synthesizes comments and comes up with a new draft. And using the FEEDBACK tool during drafting can help avoid the attack-and-defend mode that makes group editing such a nightmare.

Exercise

Jane's dilemma   Jane has worked in social change groups her entire adult life. She is a fine writer in her late forties, with a good sense of how to appeal to her audience. Nonetheless, she often feels tested to her limits fighting through an editorial process in a group. Tensions over things like passive verbs and buzzwords get her so upset she either wants to leave or take over and coerce people to do it her way. Recently Jane attended a conference where 200 people in an auditorium attempted to edit a mission statement drafted by the organizers. Late into the night, they stood in line at microphones, agitated and hostile, suggesting the same minor improvements. Like many others, Jane withdrew but kept thinking there might have been a way to change the experience into something more positive. What are you learning that might have eased the process of writing and editing the mission statement?

Some Final Words on the Process Tool

When I was in school in the 1950s, writing was taught by imitation. We studied examples of good writing, wrote assignments from these models and had them evaluated by teachers. We almost never rewrote after handing something in, and our work was often judged by how closely it measured up to an outline we submitted in advance. This meant we were very product-focused. Writing was like a factory assembly-line: we weren't encouraged to innovate or cultivate new ideas while we wrote, in fact we could lose points for doing so. In the 1980s, teachers raised in my generation developed a new approach: "Teach writing as process, not as product!" They began to research how people think as they write. Where do new ideas come from? What processes lead to creativity? What really *is* going on in that "black box" while we write?

In many ways this new focus on process was revolutionary and, for writers today, it has led to a kind of social change in itself. We do not need to practice factory-style writing or feel there is a "boss" standing over us. The new approach boosts awareness of how a writing process works, so we can take control, innovate and grow as thinkers and writers.

The PROCESS tool also has many practical uses. Besides helping us get started and keeping us moving, it helps us make the most of all our inner resources. To pace ourselves as writers, we need to understand our minds, just as long distance runners need to understand their bodies. Taking things one step at a time has taught me that even when a piece of writing doesn't come smoothly or looks foolish, sloppy or even "bad" to me at first, I know that later there will be a chance to improve it. No matter how messy my first draft, no matter how unfinished my thinking, I know that if I go through the core activities, one at a time, I will end up with a competent piece of writing.

CHAPTER FIVE

The THINKING Tool

Organizing ideas and framing your message

Learn how experienced writers organize ideas more powerfully with a set of techniques not taught in most schools. Stories, examples, and exercises boost your ability to think critically.

The first time I ventured outside the traditional classroom, a small, progressive graduate program asked me to give a workshop we called "Seven Ways to Organize Ideas." I was amazed that this title struck such a nerve. The room filled up with community activists heading back to school for a degree. Professors and staff piled in too. Everyone's eager looks spoke of a real hunger for the simple mental tools that can organize complex material into powerful thinking, and I did my best to offer an early version of what's in this chapter. The results astonished me. Most people, even those who'd gone to highly-privileged schools, had never heard of the techniques I considered so basic. "No one ever taught us these things!" they complained. Their resentment bordered on anger.

Later I came to realize that organizing ideas and framing a message was the most distressing part of the writing process for people in every setting I would work in. Even skilled researchers were often uneasy about taking a position on data they had collected. And the lack of good strategies for framing arguments was the most frequently voiced concern, not only of teachers but also of supervisors in the non-profit world. In truth, the mental processes behind critical thinking have not been taught to people in the mainstream, and that is a major pillar of our silencing.

Organizing ideas is thinking, and nothing about this process is simplistic or mechanical. Thinking is not a simple list of points nor a simple burst of creativity. Our minds are capable of a more profound activity that combines both the left- and right-brain energies described in the previous chapter. Throughout the process of writing, we are clarifying, analyzing and finding our message or argument. All of us can think powerfully and critically, but so much gets in the way, like negative reader dynamics, cultural differences and our own confusion. It is enormously helpful to become more aware of the basic mental processes that are part of our common heritage as thinkers. No aspect of writing is more challenging and less talked about.

How to use this chapter

Since that first workshop, my list of ways to organize ideas has doubled. This chapter starts by exploring what makes thinking powerful, then gives fourteen simple techniques to strengthen and clarify ideas and organization as you write. All of them are based in common sense. They're clustered to match the activities of the writing process. The chapter ends with a section on strengthening your message.

Generate and Deepen Ideas

1. Freewriting and clustering
2. Questions and conversation
3. Explaining code words
4. The funnel
5. Listing and grouping
6. Contradictions

Organize and Connect

7. The grid
8. The tree

Sharpen Your Argument

9. WIRMI (What I Really Mean Is)
10. After-the-draft outline
11. Gists and headings

Back to the Roots

12. Metaphor
13. Drawing and other art forms
14. Storytelling

For immediate assistance, look for the techniques that match your stage of the writing process, but remember that you can adapt any technique to any stage of your work. Together, all of them will give you confidence thinking through problems and presenting your position and will help you claim your power as a critical thinker.

What Makes Thinking Powerful?

Your own feelings are important, but real power comes from linking them up with information.

On one level, powerful ideas are whatever can influence or persuade others, and we explore persuasive thinking in the AUDIENCE chapter. This chapter covers the more private thinking that goes on inside your head: sifting through material, linking things together, coming up with ideas. In industrialized cultures like ours, this usually means what we call "critical thinking." This means more than simply listing information or reiterating the ideas of others (which I call "neutral thinking"); it means finding new ideas, analysis, and a position or argument. How do you sift through all the confusing ideas on a subject and come up with a persuasive argument, for instance, against preemptive war? Or privatizing water? Your own feelings are important, but real power comes from linking them up with information. You can't think critically by just listing points from an encyclopedia (as many of us were taught to do in grade school). In the world we want to influence, we have to articulate ideas, not just by giving facts or opinions or telling a story, but by doing it all together.

Freire, the peasant and the intellectuals

In his forty years of literacy work, Brazilian activist-educator Paulo Freire added a political dimension to the idea of critical thinking. He called it "criticity," which meant that the new ideas and the process of people thinking through those ideas can change social conditions, partly by empowering the thinkers and partly by creating new kinds of action. Both are important goals for writers who want to speak out in our times.

Although I was brought up to believe my own ability to think was innate and personal, I've learned that much of thinking is culturally determined. All over the world people have amazing and creative kinds of mental processes that differ from what we in the industrialized countries see as thinking. I heard Freire tell a wonderful story about intellectuals working with rural peasants in Brazil to solve problems in a remote village. The two groups thought in different ways, and each found the other's techniques frustrating. The intellectuals were sure their abstract ideas, separate categories and precise data were superior. As far as they were concerned, peasant thinking was story-like, childish and simplistic. But Freire noticed that the peasants thought very incisively, though in a more holistic way, through metaphors and stories. After a long meeting where the intellectuals narrowly analyzed a problem that the peasants knew first hand, one of the peasants got up to voice his frustration. "It's impossible for us to communicate," he said. "You are very interested in the salt. We're interested in the seasoning, and salt is only a part of the seasoning."

No one could say that the peasant had a "thinking problem." If anything, his thinking was more comprehensive and possibly more powerful than that of the intellectuals. But it was different. The thinking we use when we are trying to make a difference with our writing includes both his kind of metaphoric, story-oriented thinking and the detailed logical categories of a social scientist. It includes intuition and a right-brain sense of the whole as well as the left-brain ability to excel on the quick-answer, multiple-choice tests so common in today's schooling. Those of us who want to make our thinking as powerful as possible work to harmonize left and right brain and to cultivate ways of thinking not always emphasized in the dominant society.

Powerful thinking in industrialized society

The same thinking differences that frustrated the Brazilians cause trouble for us in the heart of the industrialized world, where we also have a wide range of thinking styles. Carol's story comes to mind. When I met her, Carol had a new, high-level job in a social service agency where her writing was supposed to argue for better resources and more enlightened policies. With a middle class background and a lot of higher education behind her, Carol was expected to shine in this work, but she was struggling. Colleagues said her writing was "length without strength"—all details and no analysis. We had to look hard for the reason: for years Carol had worked in an inner city clinic, writing daily case notes about her clients. There she had excelled in lengthy stories, including all details that might possibly turn out to be important. But the techniques that had worked for the case notes distressed her new supervisors. They needed something they could read and grasp quickly. They needed analysis not narrative, and they kept asking, "What's your point here?" Like many others, Carol felt an affinity for stories and couldn't seem to switch from stories to arguments.

Clarence also found analytical writing difficult, although his situation was slightly different. After finding his voice in the civil rights movement, Clarence had spent years working in Africa with an international organization. He was now back in the U.S. for more schooling. Although good at stories on the one hand and brief memos on the other, Clarence was stumped by assignments like a term paper asking him to compare and contrast five theories of development, the subject matter of an entire

PATTERNS OF THINKING

Years ago, scholars in a field called Contrastive Rhetoric diagrammed how writers from different cultures organize ideas. Without explaining everything or everyone in these cultures, the diagrams help people see how the way they organize and write may differ from what comes across most clearly in mainstream western culture. The four thinking styles show a lot about the purposes of communication in a culture. And cultures can have more than one pattern: Americans use the three on the right in poetry, fiction and music.

American & British	Hispanic, French, & Italian	Asian	Arabic & Semitic

Goes directly to the point. States the message directly and links sub-ideas explicitly. Everything is spelled out. What is most valued is a clear, direct message. Especially useful in communicating technical information and the command and control of an industrialized society.	Moves indirectly to the point, with many digressions and side issues. Writers go "off subject" on purpose. What is valued is richness of detail, whether or not it directly helps understand the message. Useful in communicating nuances of feeling and complexity of ideas. (The American way is seen as simplistic in this culture.)	Also moves indirectly to the point, by "circling" or revisiting each aspect of the idea without stating the message or the connecting ideas directly. Allows the reader to infer what the message is. Looks repetitious, confusing, and full of hidden meaning to westerners. (The American way is seen as blunt and rude.)	Sub points are made separately and not necessarily in the order westerners consider logical. The main message is not stated directly, and the connections between ideas are not stated but implied. What is valued is the challenge to readers to understand connections of ideas through shared assumptions with the writer. (The American way is seen as blunt and aggressive.)

Supposedly we share mental patterns for organizing ideas with our entire culture, but they can be mysterious, inaccessible or culturally biased.

course. He thought of describing each theory in a separate section of his paper and then trying to write a conclusion to pull it all together, but the whole plan seemed to lack power. He was also concerned that the theories (with names like "Modernization" and "Dependency") were so dry in comparison to what he knew first hand from Africa. Other students, especially those from more privileged backgrounds, didn't seem to have such problems with analytical assignments.

When people struggle to organize their ideas, they are usually trying to pull things out of story or narrative into some other form—out of the order in which things happened (chronological order) into logical order. Later this chapter will look at techniques to help Carol and Clarence. Shifting to a different organizing structure will actually deepen thinking, but over and over I have found people stumped and mystified by how to do this. Supposedly we share mental patterns for organizing ideas with our entire culture, but they can be mysterious, inaccessible or culturally biased.

Strengthening the thinking process

With all its emphasis on logic and analysis, our society does not give guidance on how to do the kind of organized thinking it rewards. Often teachers simply instruct students to "formulate your ideas" (assuming everyone already knows how) or "make an outline" (without exploring how an outline's logic works). They may teach students to write a "five-paragraph essay," fitting their thoughts into neat boxes, but not to make their thoughts powerful. Even now people in elite graduate schools and non-profit organizations are expected to pick up critical thinking by observing and imitating the "recipes" of other writing in their field. Not doing so can be a major barrier to advancement, a hard-to-discern glass ceiling, which is at the heart of silencing. Although we cannot afford to lose the ancient power of storytelling, people like Clarence, Carol and those in my earlier workshop are hungry for more awareness of the patterns of thinking that influence the worlds they want to move in.

Because we don't talk about it much, the thinking process is mysterious. Most people don't have a language for describing what goes on in their heads as they bring thoughts into words. The process seems magical, and we may imagine it is encoded in our DNA and beyond our power to change or strengthen. Yet in recent years teachers and researchers have studied the thinking process, especially the forms of critical analysis so valued in industrial culture. And not surprisingly, most people, whatever their background, already have many techniques for thinking and problem solving. Naming and growing more aware of our natural thinking strategies can strengthen them, which is one goal of this chapter. You'll notice that all the techniques blend the energies of left and right brain. Many rely on left-brain logic to divide and analyze material, but at the same time tap the right brain's intuitive power to synthesize.

Exercise   **Inventory your own techniques**   Before reading further, make a list of techniques you already use to refine and develop your thinking. Consider a time when you wrote something or solved a difficult mental or social problem (alone or with others). What are the things you did to help yourself think? Include everything from conversations to written brainstorming to drawings and diagrams. As you go through the rest of this chapter, build awareness of your own strategies. Most likely you already use a lot of those I will describe, and some I've left out. Your own tools are part of a diverse human heritage that we all share.

Generate and Deepen Ideas

The beginning of a writing project can be discouraging because there seems to be so much to say and too much to organize clearly. Or it might seem there is nothing to say; in some ways the two problems are related. Getting it all out on paper—the written brainstorming described in the PROCESS tool—helps move beyond this impasse. And as you brainstorm, the seven tools in this group can deepen and clarify your thinking.

As you explore them, remember the value of chaos. You may be aiming for a clear focused message, but powerful thinking—even the kind most valued in corporate America—often grows out of a wild, confusing mix of ideas. If you start by trying to tidy up your thoughts, they lose the chance to grow powerful. Be ready to get a little lost in the chaos and trust that the process will eventually bring clarity.

1. Freewriting and clustering   Freewriting is a primary tool for powerful thinking. Besides all the other benefits described in chapter three, freewriting helps you discover thinking your conscious mind has censored or is not aware of. While freewriting helps liberate right-brain thinking or "wild mind" writing, its companion technique, "clustering" (also covered in Chapter Three), can focus some of the confusion without losing the freedom. The spirit of freewriting—spontaneous, intuitive, sometimes rhythmic or visual, usually creative, and often surprising—is essential to the other tools in this first group. All of them have to be used with full freedom, where anything goes and there is no self-censorship. Remember you'll have time later to change anything messy that comes up.

2. Questions and conversation   Questions have a near-magical power to open up the energy of a subject. This means real live conversations are important during brainstorming. Start by telling someone what you think you want to say in a piece of writing, and see what questions they have. Listen carefully, respond in your own words, take notes on what you say or tape it, and let the conversation lead your thinking deeper. Conversations can reveal what your audience thinks, especially when your subject is controversial.

Thinking can take off when you brainstorm (or freewrite) answers to other people's questions, either from conversations or the formal questions in grant proposal guidelines or college applications. Instead of dreading these as challenges from authorities with too much power and different values from your own, or blanks to be filled in with the "right" answer, try approaching them in the freewriting spirit to inspire your thinking. If formal questions stifle your thinking, try ignoring them and write the proposal you want to have funded, just to get your thinking

USING CONVERSATION TO THINK THROUGH AN OP-ED COLUMN

An activist in her student days, my friend Ann Markusen is now an influential researcher with extensive knowledge of the military-industrial complex and a deep commitment to moving our country away from militarism. Realizing that no amount of research will change U.S. weapons policy without grassroots effort, Ann reaches out to the public through op-ed (opinion) columns in major newspapers. Since the end of the Cold War, she has published dozens of them on controversies like the military budget, the mergers of major weapons companies, arms sales abroad and the privatization of our military. Her op-ed columns challenge conventional wisdom and seek to present hopeful alternatives. (You can see one in Appendix B). Here is how Ann describes the conversations she uses to shape her thinking for these columns.

> To write an op-ed column that will really change minds, you have to ask yourself how people are going to hear it. A good exercise is to go talk to five average people about your idea. The person who cuts my hair is always one of them, because talking is what you do while you're sitting there. It's expected. You ask the person "What do you really think about this new atomic submarine or U.S. weapons sales?" or whatever it is you're writing about. Then you listen carefully to what they say, so you can repeat their argument. You have to really try to understand them. Then when you're planning your op-ed column, you can figure out what argument you could make that would help this person see things differently.

flowing. You can revisit it after working through the AUDIENCE chapter and look more realistically at the needs of your audience and the grant maker's guidelines. And you can always lean on the Who? What? When? Where? questions, which form the hidden structure of most newspaper stories, to draw out what you already know about a subject, even for a report or research project.

Questions are such important tools that they come up in almost every chapter of this book, so if you need a better handle on how to use them, look back at the FREEWRITING and PROCESS tools and forward to the AUDIENCE and FEEDBACK tools. However you use questions in this first stage of writing, brainstorm and freewrite answers to them and they will help you open the closed doors in your mind.

3. Explaining code words All of us have the tendency to think in code, to load special meaning into abstract words—like "success," "freedom" or "community"—without fully thinking it through. One person told me her professor had traced a hundred different meanings for "community." Some of us rely on code words like "interesting." If you think a particular neighborhood is "interesting," you may mean new immigrants from Haiti, Brazil, Cambodia and Cape Verde are mixing with older Italian and Irish immigrants. But for some readers the word "interesting" might mean a new shopping mall nearby. Words like "interesting" sound powerful as we write them (because our minds fill in the picture), but readers will often experience an emptiness, a loss of energy, about an idea they cannot see or feel. The real power comes when we carry "interesting" to a level of detail others can share. We need to show in detail what the code word means.

Details help readers, but exploring code also helps the writer, as university and community writing teacher Linda Flower, who named this technique, points out. It's amazing how often you haven't really thought about what was "interesting," "successful" or "great" until you try to show it with details. Doing so activates an important thinking strength—our ability to link abstract ideas with concrete detail. Teachers often call on us to do this when they ask for "evidence to support a point," but when we can get ahead of the game and explain code on our own during brainstorming, our thinking takes a leap forward. Over and over people tell me that explaining code is their most empowering tool for thinking issues through more fully.

The process works with words like "sustainable" and "community." We may believe these are fashionable buzzwords in powerful funding agencies and thus OK to use but their meanings vary tremendously.

Clarifying what you mean strengthens your case no matter who you are talking to. Politically loaded words like "racism" and "oppression" are especially tricky code words with direct and painful meaning for many writers that some readers may not share. Years ago a student wrote that the city's neglect of a once-beautiful urban park resulted from racism. Other students of color (who lived near the park) knew exactly what he meant, but for white readers, including their teacher, the meaning was not there. At first this student didn't want to explain what was obvious to him, but when he did, he created a powerful analysis that influenced readers, including that teacher. He began to develop a reputation as an incisive thinker.

Other code words are more technical—"red lining," "transfer tax" and "expiring use" have clear meanings for those who work on affordable housing (also a code word with several different meanings). But even other housing activists or people in government may react to these words with a blank stare. Your explanation educates them and you gain the ability to explain complexities. Technical code words can wield negative power to mystify or confuse. Remember how it feels to puzzle over big words in letters from the Internal Revenue Service or welfare system? Code words can be used to keep others powerless. We don't want to use language in a way that is part of the problem.

> *Code words can be used to keep others powerless. We don't want to use language in a way that is part of the problem.*

Exercise

Highlighting your code words   Awareness is the first step. After a rough draft or a freewriting brainstorm, highlight the code words. Don't be hard on yourself if you find a lot of them—mad drafts contain mountains of code, which you expect to explain in revisions. Think of code words as opportunities to expand your thinking rather than as mistakes. Now deepen your thinking by freewriting again about the words you highlighted; new language and ideas will come from exploring code.

Exercise

Deepening your awareness of code words   Look over several examples of your writing and make a list of code words you tend to use. Choose one of them as the central word for a clustering and freewriting exercise. Consider posting your list in your writing space and adding to it as you note more of the code words you tend to use. Or get together with friends and share short pieces of writing you suspect may have code in them. Read the pieces aloud one at a time and discuss them. Rather than critiquing (pointing out flaws—which may unintentionally strengthen silencing and self-judgment), have friends highlight the code words as opportunities. What words or phrases made readers want to know more? A third possibility would be to exchange papers and ask each person to circle what is code to them and write out their guess at explanations.

4. The funnel   Moving beyond single code words, whole ideas can be in code and thus too abstract for readers to get excited about. But there's a technique for linking abstract code ideas to the reasoning and concrete detail that give them meaning. I've been calling it the "funnel" because, when you diagram it, the broad abstract ideas are at the top and the specifics—tight and forceful—are at the bottom. It's a classic pattern, found in real, live conversations and in good op-ed arguments and research reports. And it always works.

If I said, *In this political climate, we could lose the Section 8 housing program,* a lot of people wouldn't get it because they don't know what political climate I mean or what Section 8 is and how it's funded. The only people who will know what I mean are people who are already struggling to keep their Section 8 subsidies. Details are energizing. I could add a concrete detail and say, *My friend Maria could lose her home.* But this wouldn't be enough; I need a logical sequence of ideas—from abstract to concrete—to get readers on the same page. A funnel starts with the most abstract statement and each statement that follows gets a little less abstract.

In this political climate, we could lose the Section 8 housing program.

If Congress keeps cutting social programs to pay for war, there won't be money for rent subsidies that keep working Americans in their homes when rents go up.

Already administrators are saying the program doesn't work: the law has been weakened and landlords are demanding higher rents. People who work full time and support a family can't afford local rents without government subsidy.

My friend Maria and her son will lose their home if this program ends.

In some ways each statement in the funnel makes the same point. What's special is each one has a different level of abstraction and the different levels form a line of connection between abstract and concrete, between the top and bottom of the funnel. That's what gives your thinking power. Picture two people talking through the Section 8 funnel with one person saying the sentences and the other person responding each time with *Really?* or *How come?* Real-life conversations often come out as perfect funnels, just naturally.

How can the funnel be helpful? It builds awareness of abstract and concrete, which are the two building blocks in a logical argument. You may find that your habit is to express yourself just at the abstract level, or just with details at the concrete level. Or you may find that one of the middle levels is more in your comfort zone. The funnel gives you a sense of the whole pattern and how to move through it. (You've probably figured out that you can move either down or up the funnel, depending on your starting point. I could have started this one by saying, *I'm worried that Maria may lose her housing,* and then worked up to Section 8.) Knowing the funnel can also help you put your thinking into smoothly flowing paragraphs, which often follow this same form.

Exercise

Your own funnels   Choose a sentence that appeals to you and fill in the blanks (or substitute your own full sentences). The sentence now becomes the top of your funnel. Fill in the top, bottom or middle of the funnel in any order; trying to come up with something at three or four levels. Do a first version in the spirit of freewriting and only then allow yourself to evaluate whether it really is a logical "abstraction funnel," or do a freewriting on your chosen sentence first, then create the funnel starting with sentences drawn from the freewriting and adding what you need.

I come from a culture where ___(family, music, honesty)___ is very important.

To me, "community" means _____.

Of all the challenges for the 21st century, I am most concerned about _____.

5. Listing, grouping and double-listing   Making lists is usually a left-brain activity, but right-brain intuitions and energy also guide this very basic process. Say you need to write about why your organization should support universal health care. During brainstorming, you list the reasons. As you jot them down in a column on paper, you find that one thought leads to another, especially when your mind relaxes as in freewriting. A relaxed mind is open to suggestions. *Good for children* might suggest *good for the elderly, good for working parents.* You're on a roll! Right-brain intuition chimes in and you end up with a list that is longer and richer than you realized when you began.

Your lists can teach you something important about logical thinking. Sometimes the points are similar or well-matched: *children, the elderly, working parents* are types of people who will benefit. Other times, the things you list are so different you wonder how you got them all onto the same page. *Poverty, democratic rights, infant mortality, Canada, medical ethics, Britain, AIDS, now or never* don't have one overall word that can sum them up even though they're all relevant to universal health care.

Trying to make sense of lists brings us face to face with the idea of groupings or categories, a very basic element of thinking. When a list helps us see similar items (for instance the types of people who will benefit), everything in that list is part of a similar category. As we make sense of a list, we look for relationships within it by grouping things into categories. Listing creates what information technology calls a database, and grouping or categorizing helps us find the logic that organizes this database.

Rough list	List with categories
Poverty	Urgent problems:
Democratic rights	Poverty
Infant mortality	Infant mortality
Canada	AIDS
Medical ethics	Now or never
Britain	Arguments in favor of universal health care:
AIDS	Democratic rights
Now or never	Medical ethics
	Success in other countries:
	Canada
	Britain

One way of enriching listing is to make two lists at once, for instance a list of problems from a child's point of view opposite a list of problems from an adult point of view. These two lists will usually give you differing takes on your material and the tension between the two may suggest a new line of thinking. Variations include listing ideas in one column and your reflections on these ideas in the other, or problems in one column and examples of them in the other. (This helps demystify code words at the same time.) Some call this kind of double-listing "dialogic" because the process is like a dialogue or conversation between one list and the other. The list of youth perceptions helps stimulate your thinking about the list of adult perceptions and the other way around. At some point, simply the process of listing may suggest how to balance the two points of view.

6. Exploring contradictions and synthesizing What happens if brainstorming turns up contradictions? You're listing points about a high-rise development that will disfigure a wild hillside you've always found serene and comforting. The project will threaten rare butterflies and native plants, and bring traffic, commercialism and toxic fumes right to the edge of a Native American burial site. You want to blast the developer. But there's something else. A newspaper article says this developer negotiated with Native and environmental groups and gave up the right to develop the sacred burial site. He calls this a "labor of love." What about that? Is this bad guy possibly a good guy?

Discovering a point that is just the opposite of what you want to say feels like big trouble, and your instinct may be to shut your eyes and pretend it doesn't exist. You don't want to weaken the argument or give any points to adversaries. But experienced writers see contradictions as a valuable opportunity to go deeper. If you ignore contradictions to keep your thinking unified, you'll write something that doesn't ring true to yourself and may get you in trouble with readers. And you'll miss a chance for deeper understanding.

Here's what I suggest to work with the contradiction:

- Explore it honestly through brainstorming and freewriting. List "pros and cons" or imagine a person on each side and list their feelings. Freewrite in the voice of someone really different from yourself—in this case the developer or someone who loves shopping malls. Enormous power can come from taking on the voice of an antagonist or social opposite. What does that very different person think or feel?

- Then state the contradiction clearly. Try several versions.

  The developer says he's building these towers out of love. But he's cutting into the earth ignoring plants and animals, and putting barbed wire around sacred sites.

  The developer and the press say this development is going to be one of the most lucrative of the century so far. The developer also says this is "a labor of love" because he negotiated with Native Americans and environmentalists.

- Now try to write one sentence that explains what makes it possible for both statements to be true. If you can, it will be a valuable piece of critical thinking, a "synthesizing" statement that pulls the opposites together into something profound. For instance:

  The developer used negotiation to put himself in a good light ("a labor of love"), but this makes his plan all the more offensive to people who think big profits don't go with love of the land and respect for sacred sites.

  The developer may believe he is acting out of love, but how can this be when his project puts high-rise towers on a beautiful natural hillside and brings big-box commerce and toxic fumes right to the edge of a sacred burial site?

Exploring contradictions can take you deeper into the truth of the situation and strengthen your point. Social justice groups often think they don't have the luxury to explore complications like this one. Or if they do take the time, they explore in divisive ways, with one group arguing against another and a whole movement splitting into factions over differences that could have been a source of strength. We need to go beyond simplistic, unanimous thinking to come up with ideas that are effective enough to bring real change.

Exercise

Exploring contradictions   You cannot know how this technique works until you try exploring some contradiction that has power for you. First make a list of several contradictions that concern you. A bottled water plant threatens your water supply but also provides employment. You believe in free speech but you don't like it when friends are hurt by hate speech. Then give yourself fifteen minutes to explore one contradiction on your list. After listing, debating and/or freewriting in your own and others' voices, state the contradiction clearly and ask yourself, "How can I pull all this together?" End the exercise by writing out one or more synthesizing statements, no matter how imperfect they seem to you at the moment. If no synthesis comes to mind, try freewriting for ten to fifteen minutes with no special agenda to see what thoughts lie buried.

Organize and Connect

If brainstorming is working well, you may come up with more material than you think you can use. But trusting the process means you *will* be able to focus, link, and connect the key ideas, which is the essence of powerful thinking. Look for two things when you organize brainstormed material: (1) ideas that are connected and (2) one message that stands out. Written communication is different from many thoughtful conversations. Instead of exploring many different ideas at once, a convincing piece of writing has one unifying idea, a synthesis; it can't have a "mixed message."

In other cultures, like that of the Brazilian peasants in Freire's story, synthesizing and connecting may come more naturally. In industrialized culture, we are usually working with ideas that are technical and unfamiliar, even to us, so they're hard to connect. Our so-called experts, too, often need to do a better job with connective thinking. Freire's intellectuals might have improved their narrow and simplistic analysis by using the two tools that follow.

7. The grid: A grid or matrix helps with a lot of confusing material in something like an article, report or grant proposal. It shows connections visually and helps you discover similarities, contrasts and completely new ideas. Building on the listing and questioning techniques in part two, it can extend the creativity of brainstorming. On a huge piece of paper (or a table in your computer) you list topics down the left side and questions across the top. Draw lines between them and you'll have a series of boxes to fill in with ideas and details. Grids are an especially good way to take your message out of story form into a more analytical form. Remember the two people struggling to organize their thinking at

CLARENCE'S GRID

Theories of development	Main ideas/ assumptions	Causal forces/ role of the state	Implications for develop-ment	Application to case X	Major critiques
Modernization					
Dependency					
World systems					
Mode of production					

the beginning of this chapter? A grid would have helped Carol pull the useful details out of the year's events for an annual report. It actually saved the day for Clarence.

At first Clarence thought of organizing his paper around the five theories mentioned in his assignment, with a section at the end to compare and contrast all five. Fortunately he decided to use this "recipe" to create a grid, not as a direct writing plan. It took a huge sheet of newsprint with the five theories listed down the side and, across the top, the questions the course had focused on including some he added himself. The list of questions grew as he worked, so he kept adding new columns.

Filling in the grid was at first like a review of the entire course (savvy students often review for exams this way). Mostly, Clarence worked theory by theory, filling in the boxes horizontally. From time to time, when ideas in one box suggested ideas for other boxes, he would skip around. As he moved from simple questions about each theory into the problems of applying the theories—especially given his own experience in Africa—new and powerful ideas began to come. He saw that there were two or three key messages about the theories to focus the paper and he was able to synthesize them into one unifying idea. After clarifying all this for himself and looking at other options, Clarence decided to go back to the obvious recipe for structuring the paper—five subsections based on the five theories. However, each section did more than describe the theory (as he'd originally planned). Each section began with how its theory compared (or contrasted) to the previous one and showed his point of view on the theory. Now, comparison was built right into the structure of the paper. Instead of a lengthy encyclopedia full of neutral information, he had done a powerful and well-informed critique of the five theories, supported by experience on the ground and his reading.

> *Now, comparison was built right into the structure of the paper.*

Grids helped with my first writing assignment in the planning field—a co-written article for people interested in environmental impact assessment (a way of checking in advance how a new highway or other project will affect the environment). The article focused on supposedly objective technical decisions that are actually shaped by the values of engineers and other professionals. I made several grids while working on the article, but the one I'm showing here focuses on a small part of the whole subject: how public participation in an impact assessment reflected values that decision-makers were not aware of. The chaotic material I started with came from a 30-page case story about relocating a major highway underground. In my grid, there were four hidden value choices down the left side of the page with two questions across the top.

While filling in material from the story, I was able to locate a unifying idea—a point that appeared in all the boxes and became the main idea for that section of the article. At the same time, key examples from the case study fell easily into the boxes of the grid. When it was time to write, they were easy to include in sub sections of the paper. In fact each box more or less became a sub section. Before the grid, the details had been locked into the chronological order of the case study. They looked like a fixed part of the story rather than evidence. Once the bits of information were loosened from the story, I could see them differently, move them around, and use them to make my case.

Issue	How Was It Handled?	Did It Affect Outcomes?
Did the team see public participation as really necessary or as a pro forma obligation?		
Did the team actively solicit public involvement?		
Did they see the importance of educating the public to increase the quality of participation?		
Did they expect the public to merely identify problems or were they also open to the public providing solutions?		

Exercise

Using the grid to solve common problems You don't need to be a student or a researcher to use this technique. The grid works on everyday problems that present both simple and difficult choices. Say your organization has interviewed three wonderful candidates for a job, but they're all good in different ways, and no one can figure out which person to hire. (Or maybe you have to choose among three jobs for yourself.) Select a situation like this from your own experience and make a grid listing three or more choices down the left side of the page and several questions or criteria across the top. Recently a group I know figured out which of two consultants to hire using three questions: What are the candidate's other work experiences? What are her ideas about our situation? What are the costs? Be sure to leave space for other questions that may come up as you work, and fill in the grid until your solution to the overall problem is clear. It's important to try the grid on an actual choice—even a very humble one like where you want to go for lunch. Once you've seen how well the grid works to help you make organized choices, you'll find plenty of use for this tool.

Exercise

Other people's grids   Put yourself in Carol's shoes and design a grid that would have worked for her. What topics and what questions might her grid explore? Or create a grid for a writing project of your own and get some feedback on it from an interested friend.

8. The tree   We are so smart! Most human minds can handle more than one thought at a time, so brainstorming and the grid really stir things up. But multi-task thinking creates a lot of distress when you try to write from it. Even in freewriting, people experience difficulty following too many thoughts at the same time. And how often have you gotten stuck drafting a paragraph with four or five points competing to be next? Unlike music and visual art, ideas in sentence form can only follow one thought at a time. This also goes for speaking, because communication with words takes place in a time sequence. You say one thing at a time and your audience hears and understands you one thought at a time. (Poetry can be an exception.) So how do we get from good brainstorming to a sequence of ideas to express in writing? We need a focused message and a conscious series of connections to find the system of logic in our ideas.

The beautiful, organic shape of a tree can help us order our many thoughts into a sequence we can write about. A tree has one trunk, several main branches and many smaller branches—all the way out to twigs and leaves. And we need to find this same branch pattern in brainstormed material so we can think more systematically. Here's a very simple tree diagram—upside down for easy understanding.

I jotted down this diagram recently during public comment in a city council hearing. While I listened to fellow citizens speak in favor of a city resolution to oppose the Iraq war, many ideas whirled in my head. I wanted to validate what the others were saying about how bad the war was but I also wanted to add ideas I thought would convince city officials. I knew I would have only one minute to speak. When the main branches of this tree came to mind, I knew I would be able to pull my thoughts together.

A tree shows a logical system of connections, linking ideas in horizontal and vertical ways. In my tree, the two main branch ideas are

TREE DIAGRAM FOR A BRIEF PUBLIC STATEMENT

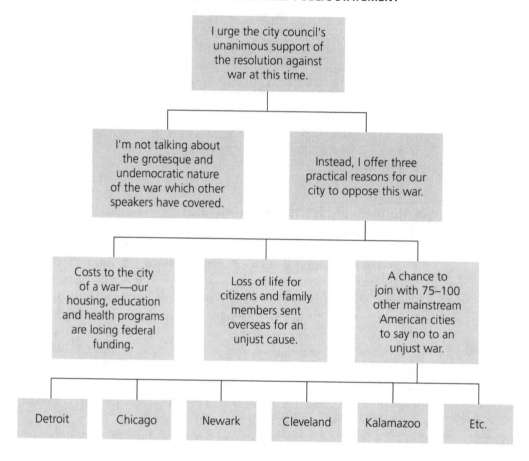

horizontally linked, from side to side of the tree diagram. So are the three smaller branch ideas (the *practical reasons*). Also the five cities connect horizontally. They are the twigs or leaves on one of the smaller branches. Whatever is connected horizontally has to be part of a set. I could add more branches, but they would have to match the set: I couldn't add a philosophical point about patriotism to the practical reasons. I couldn't add a country like Germany to the set of cities. That would have "mixed apples and oranges," and it wouldn't be logical.

Vertical relationships connect the abstract point at the top of the tree (*support*) down through each set of branches to the very concrete details of the tree (*the cities*). Each tier of branches gives us a less abstract version of the branch above it. So below the *three practical reasons* branch, we have the three actual reasons. Understanding how horizontal and vertical fit together in a tree gives us a way to organize even complex or confusing material.

You can see the tree structure in what I said when I spoke from the diagram:

> I urge unanimous support of this resolution. I'm not going to talk about the undemocratic and vicious nature of this war, which other speakers have covered. Instead, I offer three practical reasons for this city to oppose the war. First is the cost: cities like ours are paying for a war that is costing over two billion dollars—when our hard-earned housing, education and health programs are losing federal funding. Second is the loss of life for Cambridge citizens and family members sent overseas for an unjust cause. Third, Cambridge now has a chance to make a difference by joining with 75-100 other mainstream American cities to say "no" to an unjust war. If Detroit, Chicago, Newark, Cleveland and Kalamazoo have passed this resolution, Cambridge, with its history of standing for justice, should be among them.

I am proud that a lot of fellow citizens spoke out that day and that my city council passed this resolution unanimously.

How does the tree differ from other diagrams? Any diagram is a step forward, but I've seen many that made writers feel better without helping them write. Five circles and a box—connected by lines and arrows going up and down, back and forward—may feel helpful but it doesn't give you a writing plan. There are no horizontal or vertical relationships, so it's not a logical hierarchy. More important, there is no obvious pathway through this diagram, no way to take readers down the branches or across the tiers one thought at a time. If you can turn your diagram into a tree, you'll be thinking more clearly and much closer to a plan you can write from.

A classic outline is also a tree diagram—laid out on its side with subbranches, twigs and leaves under each main branch. People often ask why I recommend the tree over the outline. There are three reasons: first is all the negativity and misconception about the traditional outline. Most people had bad experiences struggling over outlines that did not match their thinking when it came time to write. And I see many so-called outlines that *look* good but the vertical and horizontal connections are not really there. Outlining has been taught in form only, stripped of the logic that makes it useful. For many, outlines have become part of the silencing. A tree makes it easier to see and use logic actively in your own way.

Second, it's much easier to change a tree—which is the whole point of a technique for strengthening ideas. An outline looks permanent once it's down on paper. Trees are more flexible and organic; you can

Outlining has been taught in form only, stripped of the logic that makes it useful.

107

move ideas around until they grow and evolve into their most powerful form. Third, moving the branches around means you can think about different sequences to cover first, second or third, making sure one idea leads to the next.

Exercise:

Tree versions   Take any brainstorm you have done (or start with another kind of visual diagram) and see if you can turn it into a tree. Decide what the "trunk" of the tree should be (main or unifying idea) and what the main branches are, then the sub-branches, twigs and leaves. You will probably find that your first version is too simple. Give yourself a few chances to restructure the tree, to add or remove branches, and to think about which branch you might like to describe first, second, third and so on. Be sure you include twigs and leaves (details, evidence). Notice whether working with the tree has given you any new insights about which thoughts belong at which levels of abstraction. Draw your new tree. Then try writing from it.

Sharpen Your Argument

Three linked tools help sharpen thoughts once they are on paper in a draft or mad draft. We clarify our message by stepping back from confusion and giving words to the thought that is there all along underneath. We have more thinking power than we realize!

9. WIRMI   These letters stand for "What I Really Mean Is." WIRMI is a simple, useful tool to use when we get lost in writing a paragraph, when thoughts are tangled up and seem to lead nowhere. Stop and ask yourself, *What do I really mean here?* Then write out your answer quickly in one or two spontaneous sentences. This technique—from Linda Flower whose book also covers code words and the tree—miraculously refocuses our thinking. Try it in the midst of writing, beforehand while organizing, or in the final editing stage when a paragraph seems unclear. Friends can also help you with WIRMI. Try telling someone what you are hoping to say (confusing as it may be to you). Then ask them to guess at your WIRMI. What do they think you are trying to say? One or the other of you will be able to verbalize the idea you are looking for. Write it down! Once you find it, you will usually put the WIRMI sentence into the writing, either leading off a paragraph or in some other important place.

10. After-the-draft outline   The WIRMI tool can also help you sharpen logic after you've written a draft, by outlining what's there and then improving on the outline. The whole point of writing without judging or censoring yourself is to get it out on paper without grief. But when you look back at a mad draft, it often wanders all over the place. Your thinking was evolving while you wrote, so mad drafts are full of repetition and need work on logic.

Here's how you do it: go through the draft, paragraph by paragraph, and write out a WIRMI (in sentence form) for each paragraph. Hint: the WIRMIs should be the ideas you want readers to catch while skimming. Write the WIRMIs neatly in the margins or on a yellow Post-it, or list them on a separate sheet. What idea comes across in each paragraph? If the WIRMIs say something different from what you meant to say, reword them to express your real idea (and change the paragraphs too). At this point you are looking at each paragraph as a unit of thought to see whether that thought is clear. But your mission is to look at all the thoughts together to see if they connect in a logical flow. So don't spend too much time tinkering with individual paragraphs.

Once you get all the WIRMIs written in the margins, check the whole list for its storyline. You should be able to get the meaning of the whole piece just from reading the WIRMIs. Check also for the systematic logic of a tree. Do the branches connect clearly? If your mad drafts are like many I've seen, the answer will often be no! But the WIRMI outline helps you spot where you repeated yourself, skipped something crucial, or connected ideas that don't really connect. Try rearranging the branches of the tree. Once you've made them visible, you can change them—and the paragraphs—to fit together more smoothly, getting rid of anything in the mad draft that isn't relevant. The outline you make now will be closer to your best thinking than any you made at the beginning of the process.

11. Gists or headings   Take your WIRMIs a step further and turn them into something even briefer and stronger: a two or three word gist or heading. These are the key phrases you see in bold type calling attention to sections of a report, article or longer letter. They're often memorable like headlines in the news. Here are three from the next chapter of this book: *Connecting with readers even when it's hard; Multiple audiences; Power differences.* Like good slogans or graffiti, they have a kind of emotional energy that activates the right brain and stirs readers. Also they accurately describe what follows, so readers get an overview just by reading the headings.

Thinking gets clearer when you work to improve headings. When I realize I can call a section *The second wave*, I see there may be a first wave and a third wave. Improving headings helps you rethink your subject and strengthen its logic. But beware. Many times wonderful, vivid headings show that the writer worked to sharpen her thought, but, alas, those new headings do not match the actual contents or the older, duller headings that still remain in the table of contents! Playing with headings profoundly changes the logic of your draft, so you need to retune everything else to match.

| Exercise | **Trying it**   WIRMI is so essential, you can practice it anytime and just about anywhere you write: a letter to relatives, a note to co workers, even (especially!) email. After drafting something, please try writing a basic WIRMI sentence about it, just for the amazing sensation of how this simple gimmick works. With a gentle push, our brains can usually stretch just that little bit further to clarify the thought that seemed so difficult to put in words. Try all three of the WIRMI techniques in this section as often as you can, so that you get good at this empowering mental practice. |

Back to the Roots

Most of the tools in this chapter help us think with the logic of the western world, of universities, governments and businesses. The tree and the grid help us process the confusing and massive amounts of information that mark public decision-making in our complex world. They help us talk to people clearly about this information, clarifying the relationships between facts and conceptual ideas. We can use these tools in letters to the media, lobbying elected officials, or funding solicitations to corporate foundations.

Yet even the most practical kinds of writing benefit from the intuitive techniques of right-brained thinking. The metaphors and stories that came so easily to the Brazilian peasant in Freire's story can energize dry reports, proposals or research papers. For real change to happen, we need to touch readers' hearts, so we cannot ignore the tools that give us direct access to feelings. These last three techniques offer an alternative kind of thinking so essential that without it, the others are not effective.

12. Metaphor   Metaphors came up briefly in Chapter Two as a way to energize freewriting. As thinking tools, metaphors can link two different things, such as a *job* and *prison,* to bring out similarities. The peasant in Freire's story used metaphor when he claimed the intellectuals were only interested in the "salt" while his community wanted "full seasoning." Obviously he wasn't talking about a stew but about the simplistic solutions the intellectuals were imposing on his community. Metaphor puts something real and concrete like salt in place of a more abstract thought and calls attention to characteristics we might not notice otherwise.

FORMS SIMILAR TO METAPHOR

Other word arrangements resemble metaphor. All of them work by comparing what you're talking about (a problem, a meeting) with something tangible that can be felt directly (a stew, a pie, salt).

1. **Analogy** is an outright comparison

   Let's compare this whole analysis with a richly flavored stew.

2. **Simile** is a metaphor that is pinned down with the words *as* or *like*

   As simple as pie. This meeting feels like a war zone.

3. **Folk sayings** often have metaphors in them

   Salt of the earth. Taste of success.

4. **Symbol** starts as metaphor but has an even wider range of meanings often varying from one cultural group to another. The *rainbow* is a good example, starting with the beautiful arc of colored lights in the sky after a rainstorm and taking on many other meanings. To mainstream Americans, it suggests a pot of gold, beauty, calm or promise of recovery after a storm; to former hippies, it's an annual community gathering in the woods; in the gay community, a rainbow flag means a gay-owned business; outside a town hall in South East London in 1991, it meant the Labor Party was in power; in Italy in 2003, it meant "no" to the Iraq War; for Native Americans of the Southwest the rainbow is a sacred symbol of peace and potential; to those involved in visionary political work, it's a coming together of people of many colors and ethnicities. The term Rainbow Coalition goes beyond metaphor to symbol when it activates all these meanings and more.

Through metaphor, the peasant was saying that the intellectuals' views shared certain qualities with salt. Both are strong, both are part of a mix of other tastes or factors, and both can dominate and spoil the mix if not kept in balance. (You may see other qualities—metaphors are very open and flexible this way.) The peasant used metaphor to explain the frustrations of the situation and to think it through for himself.

As expressions with at least two sets of meanings, metaphors are not just ways of communicating but also ways of thinking. To think in metaphor is to use comparison and also contrast, whether it's expressions like *belt-tightening, undermining,* or *rosy future* that once were fresh, live metaphors but are now ordinary language. If you find a metaphor like *rainbow* coming up, spend some time using it as a thinking tool. Ask yourself what *rainbow* means to you and then why you're using that metaphor or symbol. *(1) In what ways is our group like a rainbow? Do we represent new promise? Many colors? Something sacred? (2) In what ways are we* not *like a rainbow? Leaving out certain groups? Lacking harmony or democracy?* Exploring a metaphor is a right-brain way to analyze comparisons and contrasts—a different way in to some of what you may have found through techniques like double-listing or contradictions.

When I first wrote papers in graduate school, I was afraid they lacked original thought until a friend showed me how to organize with metaphors. For a paper analyzing a poem with a lot of small details in it, she suggested the metaphor of "tapestry." That meant I would use the idea of an "intricate weaving" to organize the paper. I mentioned the *tapestry of language* at the beginning, then used *weaving* words where I could throughout the paper—*colors, texture, thread.* The metaphor of *weaving* helped me see a lot in the poem that I would have missed otherwise, and my thinking became unique. Metaphors can strengthen other kinds of thinking and writing: a newsletter story about the different language and ethnic groups in your community with *rainbow* words like *promise, storm, colors, hues* and *working together,* or a press release for Martin Luther King's birthday that revolves around his stirring metaphor of *going to the mountain top* and uses words like *climbing, view* and *reaching for the sky.*

I have seen silenced writers discover metaphor and run with it. Please give this tool a chance, even if it isn't easy at first. We may not have a lot of comfort with an academic-sounding word like "metaphor." But all it means is the imaginative thinking of the eloquent peasant in Freire's story, a kind of thinking that is available to all of us.

> *I have seen silenced writers discover metaphor and run with it.*

Exercise

Awareness of metaphor   Spend a full day trying to remain aware of all the metaphors that pass through your experience. Jot them down in a small notebook when you encounter them in reading or conversations at work, on the bus, in restaurants, in advertising or on the evening news, even at night in your dreams. Especially notice the ones you, yourself, tend to use without realizing it. When you freewrite, check there for metaphors. Or try teaming up and looking for metaphors while you spend time with a friend or your family over a meal or on an outing. Then, on your own, choose four or five that have real appeal for you—that touch you deeply in some way. Freewrite about your associations with one or two of these metaphors.

13. Drawing and other art forms   For many people, creativity is visual, not verbal. Their best thinking comes when working with colors, shapes, light or spatial relationships in photography or graphic design. Others think best through music, dance or body movement. Any of these non-verbal forms can help you think through a writing project, even something as technical as a report. This is no surprise— metaphors are often visual, and the Tree, the Grid, Clustering, and the Funnel all make use of visual, spatial thinking.

If you're tired of listing, grouping and outlining, put these tools aside and get out your crayons, paints or colored marking pencils, or even your camera. Sit down and draw what you want to say. Get yourself deeply involved in the drawing and see what comes. While writing this book, I often wrote short monthly newsletter columns on herbs. Sometimes the column just flowed together easily from my research, but not always. At times when I just couldn't see how to move forward, I would take a break to make the drawing that usually accompanied the article. Insights for structuring the article came freely as I drew the leaves of mint or dandelion. Dancers, actors and musicians have told me of similar breakthroughs while practicing their art forms.

This tool is especially important if you *don't* think of yourself as an artist. (All of us really *are* artists, but many of us have been scorched by censorship—from outside and from within ourselves.) To get the benefit of this tool, you have to try drawing with colored pens even if it seems ridiculous. The secret is to do it in the spirit of freewriting, not as a performance. No one expects you to be a "great artist." In fact, you don't need to show it to anyone. This is an experiment to get in touch with intuitive ability deep within yourself. Do your drawing or sing your song quickly, without deliberation, without activating those judges inside yourself.

Exercise

A creative fling   Don't skip this one! Make a list of five expressive activities you have enjoyed in the past or might like to try sometime. Anything goes—cooking, roller blading, and arranging flowers are possible, or painting, dancing and playing the guitar. Choose one from your list and take whatever equipment you need for a creative fling. Either try to express your "message" in this alternate form or just spend time expressing whatever is on your mind at the moment. When you return to your writing project, don't judge yourself if a clear-cut solution to your dilemma did not emerge immediately. This technique does not always work in direct ways. Try again and begin to learn how it will work for you.

14. Storytelling   Stories come from a skill we have all admired since childhood. Some people just naturally tell a good story, pouring out the details, drawing us in and somehow pulling things together at the end. Though often written, story is rooted in oral traditions that pre-date written communication. A story may be the answer to a problem or a critical comment on an event. Rarely are stories, as many people in mainstream culture seem to insist, "pure entertainment." Instead they

STORYTELLING HINTS:

Stories differ from explanations, descriptions, analyses and other kinds of communication because they have characters, dialogue, action, a specific place as a setting and a believable voice that tells the story. So try the following:

- Focus on people—characters that really come to life.

- Give pictures of places and scenes with brief details.

- Include blow-by-blow accounts of who said what to whom.

- Find a narrative voice—either you or some-one else—that tells the story and holds the space. The voice has its own rhythm, pace and character. It may use slang. You may find this voice naturally during freewriting.

- Let the details pour out as though you were talking to someone.

- Don't stick to chronological order. Start with something that draws attention to the main theme—whether it happened first, last or in the middle.

convey some idea or message that we engage with in a meaningful way. Their lessons come intrinsically out of the story itself. Every detail in a good story—even those that seem the most random—actually helps get us to this message.

What has helped me tell more fluent stories is a non-judgmental atmosphere, like the one we create in freewriting. I used to share storytelling time with a friend who worked professionally as a storyteller with inner-city children. We would freely compose wild tales about birds' nests, little green doors and whatever came to mind. When you begin to feel uninhibited telling stories, you can lean on this skill in writing. Short bits of stories enliven longer pieces of writing like this book, but there are times when an underlying story shapes an entire report or article. A mass of facts and figures about who lives in your city and their jobs may reduce itself to a simple story, if only you can find that story. Imagine yourself entertaining your seven-year-old nephew or your grandmother with this story, and you may be able to see a clever way to organize the material. After many false starts, a student of mine wrote a very successful statistics paper this way.

Stories fit well into the great logical web we explored through the tree and the grid. A story is like the leaves of a tree branch with the branch as the lesson. Put another way, stories can be the concrete form of abstract ideas. Paulo Freire told the story about the salt to illustrate an idea about the peasants' ability to conceptualize. Stories offer a different way of thinking and can also be more compelling than straight facts or theories. During the housing crisis in my city, I watched hours of public testimony and saw how a personal story of losing one's home not only moved policy makers but also helped them think about a situation they really didn't understand. We need to keep storytelling in our repertoire of tools for social change writing.

Three story exercises	(1) For the first one, you need a group of children or child-like adults. Sit in a circle (unless you are on a long automobile or train ride) and take turns creating a story. The first person starts with "Once upon a time a _____ was doing _____ in the _____." That person continues to tell the story until she feels like passing it to the next person. Then the next person continues adding characters, events, metaphors, strangeness and familiarity to the story. Pass the story to the next person at a high-energy point—a moment of suspense or confusion. Don't try to tell a "good" story—be crazy and wild. Continue as long as you want and make the whole experience as much fun as possible.

(2) Take a writing assignment you are reluctant about and do some freewriting, making the whole message into a funny story and/or imagine you have to explain the subject to a child, a grandparent or a person visiting from another country in story form and do your best to tell it that way.

(3) Stretch your imagination back to your roots and tell the story of your writing project the way your grandmother, great-grandfather, or an even more ancient ancestor would have told it. |

Your Message and the Legacy of Thinking

Don't forget the message

As you work to organize information, remember the high point of thinking: your message. Believe it or not, it's all too easy for your most important ideas to get buried in information. This chapter began with two people from different cultures whose tendency was to tell what happened rather than commit in words to a position on their information. It was hard for Carol to come right out and say *Our office cannot take on this caseload without new funding.* It was hard for Clarence to state a comparative analysis of the five theories. Reluctance to assert is at the heart of silencing. Taking a position puts you out on a limb. Someone could say you're wrong. It could sound impolite. Someone could fire you . . . or worse. It's our habit—and we feel safer—just sticking with the facts, keeping things neutral. But that isn't powerful thinking, and it won't lead to change. To get the funding, Carol can't just tell stories and give information. That's the "what" of her report. The "why" shows that these expenditures are crucial and the best use of limited funds. This is what Paulo Freire meant by "criticity," and the peasant speaking up was an inspiring example. Critical thinking that leads to new positions and action is the goal of the writing we are challenged to do. I've been calling it "critical writing" as opposed to "neutral writing."

In the opening chapters of this book, I mentioned a graduate student from the Middle East who struggled mightily with neutral writing in his thesis research. At that time, political and social silencing were especially strong in his part of the world, but I was astonished that, even then, students from the United States felt genuine fear at expressing ideas they saw as unwelcome in the university. All of them had developed habits of self-censoring, of just giving facts. Doing academic research tempts us to write neutrally, partly because it's easier than formulating new ideas. But more importantly, it's part of a serious misperception that academic work requires neutral thinking. Certain kinds of writing do require neutrality. However, the writing that we most admire—cutting-edge research—always

FROM NEUTRAL SUMMARY TO CRITICAL MESSAGE

	"Neutral" summary	"Critical" message
Letter to the editor	There are three kinds of affordable housing in our city. *(Does not show your position.)*	We are losing all three kinds of affordable housing in our city. *(Clearly states your message.)*
Letter of inquiry for grant support	This program covers food stamps, after-school programs, tutoring, health services and economic resources for families. *(Merely lists services.)*	This program assists children by helping their families survive in hard economic times. *(Shows why the program is unique.)*
Research paper	There are five theories to explain the effects of development on African countries. *(Neutral. Sounds like an encyclopedia.)*	Of the five theories offered to explain development, only one gives a plausible reason for the entrenched poverty in African countries. *(Shows the position you take on the theories.)*

takes a stand. This is not necessarily a risky political stand; it may simply be pulling together why your findings are important. One colleague calls it a "contribution." In every form of writing I've worked with—and in my own writing—I've seen the need to push further from neutral thinking to something closer to "criticity."

Of course there are risks in critical thinking, but we can handle them without suppressing our thoughts. My suggestion is always to write from your boldest thinking. If you can't get in touch with boldness, ask yourself, "Is there anything I am trying not to say here?" Later, if you have to change the writing to feel comfortable making your views public, that is easy. What's hard is to do good thinking when you're afraid or holding back. Once you have put your message fully and honestly into words, the AUDIENCE and FEEDBACK tools in the next chapters will help you figure out how it will be received and how to modify it if necessary.

> *"Is there anything I am trying not to say here?"*

Thinking is our legacy

So what is really going on when we think and create messages? How are the right brain and left brain working together inside your head while you're listing, grouping, outlining, storytelling, or diagramming thoughts into trees? Underlying all the techniques are some natural mental gymnastics. Here is my list of our mental moves as thinkers—and you can probably add others:

- **Making information movable**   The power of ideas comes from applying them in new ways. Move things out of chronological order so you can see new meaning. Move and change chunks of diagrams, categories or grids to get out of familiar ruts in your thinking. Move tree branches to create new relationships and new meaning.

- **Transferring ideas**   Movement also involves transferring a familiar idea to a new situation. Once I realize that oil companies benefit from a war in the Middle East (familiar idea), I can transfer that idea to understand the threat of war in oil-rich Latin America. Grids help us transfer ideas as thinking tools from one column to the next.

- **Analyzing and synthesizing**   Analysis means taking things apart into components. Synthesis means putting the parts back together in new ways for a fuller meaning. Analysis comes from the left brain; synthesis from the right. In Freire's story the intellectuals were "analyzing"; the peasant was "synthesizing." Both processes are powerful, especially when you can use them together.

- **Connecting abstract and concrete**   Finding evidence to support ideas and ideas to explain evidence. Proving your point with facts convinces readers in mainstream culture (in schools, business and public debate). But linking facts with ideas is a universal thinking strength that spans cultures.

- **Comparative thinking**   In listing and grouping, dialogue, contradictions, the grid, the tree, and metaphor we find new connections through comparison and contrast. New connection *is* new meaning, so this activity is at the heart of powerful thinking.

Your most important tool will be your own confidence as a thinker.

These moves will vary in fascinating ways from culture to culture and individual to individual. The more mental gymnastics we learn, the more skill and power we have as thinkers. These mental moves are our legacy as human beings. And it's outrageous that we don't acknowledge them, honor them, teach them to young people and keep them at the forefront as we write. No one should grow up feeling inadequate as a critical thinker. When you grasp the principles behind this chapter, you will come up with your own thinking techniques. And you will know intuitively which ones to use and when to use them. Your most important tool however will be your own confidence as a thinker. Remember your legacy, and don't accept anyone else's approach as more valid than your own.

Dozens of logical tools can help you expand your personal tool kit. Don't look for techniques (or software) that set out to "do it for you." Nothing can take the place of rethinking and reorganizing ideas, to find the easiest and best way to say what you have to say. This will leave you open to the real power of writing—the deepening meaning that comes as you work.

CHAPTER SIX

The AUDIENCE Tool

Who's going to read it?

Put yourself in your readers' shoes. Figure out how they see things and how to get their attention. Stories and exercises help you strategize to get your message heard.

In early 2002 I talked with a woman waiting for a peace walk in her small western town. It was the first time in her fifty years raising children and grandchildren that she'd wanted to do everything in her power to stop government actions she knew were deeply, morally wrong. "I've made calls to Congress, I've signed email petitions," she told me earnestly. "What I haven't done yet is write. I should be writing letters to our local paper, opinion columns, so more people will realize what's wrong with pre-emptive war. But I just can't get myself to be that public. I'm trying to push myself, but it's scary."

Going public is a challenge, yet it's central to making a difference. When we start thinking about who will read our writing, we have to face the deepest issues of our silencing. What will I sound like? How will neighbors, friends and family react? How far will my words travel? Will there be repercussions? Who am I to be saying these things? Even for experienced writers, these unknowns can be intimidating. And often we are writing for several different sets of readers at once—some of them tricky and hard to understand. Getting clear on who is going to read our writing, anticipating their reactions, and figuring out how to get their ear gives us the power to go public with our views and play a role in the events of our time.

The tool in this chapter sharpens our awareness of readers and how to establish a credible relationship with them—the relationship that is at the heart of communication. This tool can reverse silencing by engaging

119

> *Communication is always a balancing process between what we have to say and what readers can hear.*

our positive desires to influence readers and freeing all the energy we tie up worrying about them. Grasping how an audience will see things and empathizing enough to help them change their thinking is what makes social change possible. Here's where writing merges with action and leadership—where writing, itself, becomes empowerment.

When to use this tool

Communication is always a balancing process between what we have to say and what readers can hear, so there is no one perfect time in the writing process to focus on readers. Earlier chapters suggested a "mad draft" before the AUDIENCE tool. Clarifying your own thinking first gives you a solid basis and some momentum. But you can also start with the AUDIENCE tool to analyze your audience and plan your strategy before drafting or even brainstorming. You are the best judge of timing. Try the AUDIENCE tool at any point in the process where it feels useful, including when you are stuck in midstream.

How to use this chapter

A sense of audience doesn't spring up overnight. It grows over time as we learn to be influential in the world. This chapter takes us through the growth in five steps:

- Step one: Realize that you're writing to communicate.
- Step two: Demystify your readers.
- Step three: Analyze your audience to learn where their views differ from yours.
- Step four: Turn your analysis into a communication strategy.
- Step five: Strategize for conflict and confrontation.

Feel free to jump ahead to the section that will help you most at the moment, but don't skip the first steps completely because our schooling leaves everyone with big gaps in understanding how to write for an audience.

Step One: Realize That You're Writing to Communicate

In freewriting we encourage ourselves to write whatever we feel. This is self-expression, and it's hard enough to learn. But to call ourselves communicators we have to do more. How do we say things so people will really hear them? The skill grows with us from childhood. Think of a very young child telling a story. It's usually short and sweet: "Big boom!" That's it from their point of view. Adults have to fill in the what, when and where, so everyone will understand that the child's story is about hearing a plane take off when the family took Grandma to the airport. Children zero in on their own highpoint; they can't yet anticipate what their audience needs to understand the full picture.

Growing up, we learn to focus and fill in the gaps. I learned during my teenage job in a store that sold outdoor equipment. I had to figure out which customers were interested in details about a tent and which just wanted the cheapest way to keep off the rain. I learned to tune in to each person and empathize enough to help that person choose the right tent. My co-workers weren't the greatest models. One just winked and said, "This is a great tent!" Another mentioned every detail about the product while listeners' eyes glazed over. When you start looking at communicators in everyday life, you'll see all kinds—people like my co-workers and people who are really good at getting others to understand. They explain what you need to know (and nothing more), and they can vary what they say to match their audience. They seem to be able to balance what they want to say with what you are ready to hear. This is what communication should be.

In writing, we have to move from a writer-based to a reader-based approach. As writers, we often go into our own little world with the material. Our worlds are so compelling we don't really think about readers, and we assume it's their responsibility to notice what we put on the page. This is writer-based. Alas, just because you include a certain word doesn't mean the idea comes across. It may be buried among other ideas. In reader-based communication, the burden is on the writer to be sure readers can't ignore or misunderstand your points.

A look of awe sometimes comes over people when I ask, "Who are you writing for?" When you haven't thought about it, this simple question opens a door and brings a kind of relief. *Oh! I'm writing for my boss—but also for the community.* Or *I'm writing for friends in the women's movement—but also for my very traditional mother.* Usually in school, the only audience was a teacher, and the only purpose to receive a grade. The first step in audience awareness is to realize that you're writing to communicate with real people, other human beings who may or may not share your sense of reality.

Exercise   **Tracking good communicators**   List five or more people you know who are really good at putting ideas so others will understand. They don't have to be noted experts: look for ordinary people like the woman behind the counter at the Social

Security office or your plumber. They don't say too much and they don't say too little, but the people they communicate with "get it" and feel respected in the process. Choose one of the people you listed and recall several times you listened to or conversed with this person (or watched others do so). What did the person say or do that made the communication work? Now freewrite about this person as a communicator.

Exercise

If you use email   Email can be so writer-based it hardly works as communication. People often write off the top of their heads without thinking how busy readers will experience their message. Sift back through recent memory to a time when response to your email showed that your reader got a different message from what you thought you were communicating. What state of mind are readers usually in when they read email? What, in email, can cause readers to get a different message? What are some of the ways to make email more reader-based? Freewrite about what you discover and next time you email someone, try imagining their reactions before you send the message.

Step Two: Demystify Your Readers

It's hard to be realistic about readers. In person, we can gauge reactions on their faces, but what we can't see can make us uneasy. We want readers' respect. We know their impressions of us through our writing can make or break that respect. The possibility of a judgmental reader, like so many teachers who evaluated our writing in school, can reinforce our worst inner critics. But many fears about readers come from misperceptions.

Elena felt miserable about the writing she was often asked to do in her job, especially letters thanking people who had donated money to her organization. She pictured these readers as distant, powerful figures who were sitting in judgment of her and the organization. This kind of low-level fear makes it very hard to write! When someone organized a social gathering for staff and donors, Elena was surprised. She found herself chatting with people who were enthusiastic about the work they were supporting. Elena's misperceptions melted away and her whole approach to writing the letters changed. Getting to know her readers demystified them.

Jane's view of her audience was a little more complex (as you may remember from Chapter Two). Jane was apprehensive when she began a writing project she had been dreaming about for a long time—a book to help women get more involved in how government spends our money. She had spoken all over the country and written many short articles on this subject. With all this advocacy work, Jane had a real voice for speaking to people who feel fear and resistance around financial matters, and her plan for the book was brilliant. But, for some reason, she couldn't sit down and write.

When I asked about her readers, Jane knew pretty clearly who they would be. Besides her main audience—grassroots women in communities around the country—she was also anticipating some expert readers, an international group of scholars from government and universities. Jane had often shared research and spoken at conferences with them. Many of these people had doctoral degrees and were comfortable with obscure theoretical language. Once she named them, Jane realized that the people with Ph.D.s were making her nervous. Long ago she had chosen to be an activist, not a scholar, and now (with all her expertise) she was secretly worried that university people would look down on her explanations of financial concepts. Once she named these readers for herself, she realized that they held a mystique for her, a power to intimidate that was mostly in her own head! Thinking about the experts aroused her own inner critics and silenced her best thinking. Realizing this brought about a real change for Jane. She saw at once that she was the very best person to write the book she had in mind. If she'd become a university expert, she might have lost contact with the very people she wanted to reach. And she remembered how the scholars always seemed to respect her ability to translate their concepts so ordinary people could understand. Once she was able to put aside her anxiety about the experts, Jane felt all the confidence she needed to move quickly into her mad draft.

In a book about women and blues lyrics, activist-scholar Angela Davis recounts an old African belief that "nommo," or naming—just saying the name of something—gives us power over it. Naming is one way of taking the fear and intimidation out of something, or demystifying it. When things are hazy and confused, we feel anxious and lose our ability to deal with them, but when we identify a problem and name it, we can see it more clearly. This principle works brilliantly in developing audience awareness. When you first sit down to write, there may be many readers' voices swirling in your head. Listing them freely may coax even more of them into the open so you can recognize misperceptions. We may be reacting to a lifetime of obstacles and not seeing that there is a way to deal with this situation.

Not all our fears about readers are misperceptions. There really are judgmental readers out there, and naming them can't always change the power they have over us. Another woman's story taught me a lot about deciding when to speak out and when not to. Alice worked in a world built on layer after layer of silencing. Her job as an advocate for the elderly exposed her to some shocking examples. As she made the rounds of nursing facilities on behalf of the companies that owned them, she began to see cases of abuse. All too often, she observed illegal physical restraints used when staff felt they couldn't handle outspoken elders. One very thin old woman, bound hand-and-foot to keep her quiet, made a huge impression because she looked so much like Alice's own grandmother who had been a Nazi death camp survivor. When this woman leaned toward her and whispered, "Please help me!" Alice knew she had to find a way to speak out. She had already brought up the issue with the company that hired her as a patient-advocate, but her boss had simply ignored her complaints. Alice wanted to go over his head with a story in the local newspaper. But this was a small-town situation. Even if she wrote anonymously, everyone would know who had broken the silence. The industry funded her paycheck, and Alice was sure she'd lose her job and have trouble getting another if she wrote that story.

When a group of us looked realistically at Alice's audience, we could see this was not a problem for an individual writer to solve. Going public would take much more than a good audience strategy. A published story would need to be part of a larger campaign, by a strong and supportive group of people who could stand by the writer and use their collective power to change the elder care industry. We advised Alice to write a draft of the story for herself and close friends but to put her main energy into finding support for a long-term initiative. Alice's solution isn't for everyone. There are many ways to write for intimidating readers, and the rest of this chapter will show you how.

In most cases, naming your readers boosts your morale for writing. For me it's a few special friends and co-workers who always seem to appreciate what I have to say. These are my allies. Picturing their interested faces makes me feel more intelligent and articulate and motivates me to think more deeply and communicate more fully.

Exercise

Naming all your readers, including those that scare you even a little

Make a list—as long as you can—of all the people or groups you imagine will read the writing. Use their names where you can and don't feel you have to be realistic at this point. Include anyone you fantasize, hope, wish or fear may read the writing. Notice your feelings about each. Some names will make you nervous; others may give you a feeling of positive energy. Now look back at your list and highlight any names that make you feel uneasy. Where are the uneasy feelings coming from? Are they realistic or are you just imagining this challenge? If your uneasiness remains, discuss problematic readers with a friend. You can also gain comfort and confidence by systematically analyzing readers who make you uneasy, a process we will explore in Step Three.

Exercise　　**Finding readers who are allies**　Look back at your list and see if any readers might be allies for you—at least in spirit. Does thinking about them make you feel stronger and more competent as a writer? Move your allies to a new list and add any others who come to mind, even if they may not actually read this piece of writing—your sister, a colleague at work, your favorite high school teacher, a mentor. Feel free to add historical figures who would appreciate what you're saying—like Eleanor Roosevelt or Martin Luther King. My lists usually include my own mother who's been dead for many years. Spend some time freewriting about the support you gain from these allies. Later, you may want to ask some of them to comment on your drafts. Your strong desire to reach and influence certain readers can be a positive force in the writing process.

Step three: Analyze Your Audience

Once you've started to think about readers, the next step is to pick the ones you most want to reach and take a systematic look at how they'll see your message. Anticipating their reactions brings you closer to them and gives you more ability to change their thinking. This is the heart of the AUDIENCE tool.

I met Amy in late spring of 2003 when the United States was involved in a full-fledged war, to secure more natural resources, some said, from Iraq and the Middle East. She was passionate about rethinking our country's dependence on oil and gas, not only to restore peace on earth but because—with some training in science—she knew that overuse of fossil fuels was destroying the earth's atmosphere and climate. Amy wanted to use her skills as a writer to help change the root causes of fossil fuel abuse. She decided to begin with a letter to the editors of a magazine that promoted "simple living" but also published a lot of ads from the automobile industry. Amy was particularly upset by ads for a glamorous sports utility vehicle (SUV) that got only 16 miles to the gallon, when there were "greener" alternatives the magazine could advertise.

Amy realized she wasn't trying to change everyone in America with this one letter. She just wanted to influence the magazine editors who could change their editorial policy. If they printed her letter, she might also influence readers of the magazine who sought lifestyles respectful of the environment. After a quick mad draft, Amy was ready to do the analysis—another grid, like those in the last chapter, but focused on readers. After we look at how to do the grid, we'll come back to Amy's letter so you can see her draft and how the analysis helped improve her strategy.

Audience analysis calls for a very large writing surface like a chalkboard, a big sheet of newsprint, or at least the two facing pages of a notebook. You can also do the analysis on a computer if you align the page horizontally and set up tables or spreadsheets with room to write in each "box." First, draw lines dividing your surface into five wide vertical columns across the top of the page and three rows intersecting them down the page. You'll have fifteen empty boxes. Now name the rows and columns. In the columns across the top, write, "**Audience**," "**Your Goals**," "**Their Knowledge**," "**Their Values**" and "**Their Needs**." Down the left side of the page, in the rows under "Audience," identify two audiences you are writing for—in order of importance. In Amy's case, her main audience was *magazine editors* (to be sure her letter would get printed). In the second row she could have put, *readers of X magazine*. (Alternatively, you could add a third row for a third audience or keep it simple with only one audience.)

Exercise   **Setting up your own audience analysis grid**   This tool makes more sense if you are doing your own analysis, so please design a grid for one of your own writing projects. If you don't have a project at the moment, follow Amy's lead and plan to write to a specific magazine to comment on their advertisements. Lay out your grid and get ready for what comes next.

Exercise   **Fine-tuning "Audience"**   Before going further, look at what you wrote under "Audience" for a reality check on who you want to reach with your message. Broad groupings like "the community" need rethinking. Are you writing your peace letter for everyone in your small town, pro and con, or do you want to focus on those who already lean towards peace but don't feel empowered to speak out? Sometimes we're trying to solve too many problems for too many kinds of readers at once. One article probably can't help those at risk for domestic abuse and at the same time set abusers straight. Being very specific about your audience helps set doable goals.

Filling in the boxes

The grid now has eight empty boxes to fill in by writing quickly and spontaneously. Use freewriting or free-listing to get your right-brain energy flowing into the boxes. Work either horizontally or vertically or jump all over the grid, whatever stimulates your thinking, and answer the questions at the top of each column.

The GOALS column   *What are the main messages you want to get across to these readers? What actions do you want them to take?* Thinking about

AUDIENCE ANALYSIS GRID

Audiences	Your goals	Their knowledge	Their attitudes, values, beliefs	Their needs, expectation
Who will read this?	*As a writer, what messages do you want to get across to this group of readers? What actions do you want them to take?*	*What do they know and what do they not know? What do you know that they don't know?*	*Do they have strong attitudes about your message? What do they believe or value? Do they share any common ground with you?*	*What do they need to see in order to be convinced? What will make your writing more accessible to them?*
Your main audience:		**They know:**		**To make it convincing:**
		They don't know:		
Secondary audiences?		**Most important things you know that they don't know:**	**possible common ground:**	**To make writing accessible:**

* adapted from Linda Flower, *Problem Solving Strategies for Writing*

messages and actions helps you move beyond simply giving information, so you won't get stuck in the neutral thinking we discussed in the last chapter. You can start with the goal of *giving information about SUVs and climate change*, but keep writing in the box until you identify a real message, where you take a position on the information: *Our everyday actions are destroying the earth. We shouldn't buy or support advertising for environmentally harmful SUVs.* Or *War hurts our entire society, not just those abroad. This war is not going to make us safer.*

Be sure to include actions you want readers to take as a result of reading your work: *Motivate them to change the ad policy of this magazine.* Focusing on how you want readers to change and what you want them to do gives you more confidence and power as a writer. Putting your goals into words sharpens your awareness of what you want to accomplish with this writing.

The knowledge column *What does this group of readers already know about this subject and what do they not know? What do you know that they don't know?* When you're familiar with a subject, it's hard to gauge accurately what others don't know. This column helps you explore the knowledge gap between yourself and readers. When I wrote the opening paragraph of this chapter, I knew my readers would understand what I meant by "war," but I wasn't sure they would realize that our president had said he was planning a "permanent war" to solve the problems of the country. There was a knowledge gap I would have to bridge if I wanted to use that term, so I changed to the expression "pre-emptive war," which I thought would be more familiar to readers. There were gaps for Amy too, especially because she had a science background that she couldn't expect from her readers: *Will readers know what causes climate change? Are they familiar with gasoline energy efficiency ratings?* When you understand what readers know, you can figure out what to explain or build on. Your skill in doing this will grow as you write for more audiences.

The values column *Do readers have strong attitudes about your message? What do they believe or value? Do they share any common ground with you?* What do they believe to be right or true? What are some of their biases (positive or negative)? This box helps you get outside yourself and think more deeply about readers as complex human beings. What are some of the attitudes that might keep them from hearing your message? *Don't tell me I can't buy whatever car I want!* (It helps to use the language you imagine they would use.) *But this is a business! How can we turn down these advertisers without going broke?* To reach out to readers, you're not just looking for differences

Shared values or common ground will show you how to communicate across the differences.

between yourself and them. Similarities are even more important. A section of the column on shared values or common ground will show you how to communicate across the differences. List here the things you both believe like *I'm reading this magazine because I believe in not wasting environmental resources. Everyone should be able to feel safe and secure.*

If you have no idea what readers believe, try talking to some. My friend who interviewed her haircutter about controversial articles on weapons research (in Chapter Five) was learning about the values of her intended readers. This one might favor defense spending because he believed the nation was at risk and should defend its borders. But he also might feel strongly about government over-spending and be open to hearing that new weapons place unfair burdens on the average tax-payer. This kind of common ground helped her frame her message in a way this reader could relate to. As you list all the values you can think of, there will be common ground somewhere, and you'll begin to feel more empathy for readers.

The needs/expectations column   *What do readers need to see in order to be convinced? What will make this writing more accessible to them?* This column is a "needs analysis" in two parts: (1) what do readers need to be convinced? and (2) what kind of writing will keep these particular readers reading? The first part comes right out of the values column: Given readers' values and attitudes, what will they need in order to accept your message? This question is partly about what information or evidence will persuade them. *They need facts about SUVs and air pollution. They need to see that there can be alternatives without giving up their lifestyles.* It's also about your credibility. *They need to understand that I know how they feel. They need to trust me.*

For the second part, picture your readers sitting down to read. Do you visualize them in an easy chair, on the train, or in an office cubicle with phones ringing on all sides? Now think about their needs as readers. If they're rushed, annoyed or reading because they have to, they need you to get to the point quickly and say why you're taking up their time. If they're browsing to find something that catches their interest for a longer read, they need something to engage their attention deeply, so they'll choose your article instead of another. Most readers are multi-tasking and need help from us to get interested. People in a hurry need headings and bullets to help them skim. In a letter to the editor, they'll be drawn to a classic opening sentence that hooks them to something already covered in the paper. They may delete an entire e-mail if they don't grasp your main point from the subject line. And everyone needs code words explained, ideas in an order they can follow, points made directly (not buried in details), understandable sentences without distracting typos, and a sense of your credibility.

Exercise   **Fill in the boxes**   Work intuitively with the grid you designed and stay open to insights that fall outside the boxes, like how to organize your presentation or what an opening sentence could look like. These may be very valuable later, so be sure to write them down.

Exercise   **Deepening your analysis**   You get the fuller power of the tool by letting your filled-in grid rest briefly (like a mad draft) then revisiting it. If possible do this with a friend, co-worker, or small group—two or more minds can find gaps and strategize better than one person working alone. Questions help you weed out inaccuracies and add insights.

1. Goals: Do they focus on persuading readers? Are they clear? Not too big? Doable?

2. Knowledge: Will readers understand your code words?

3. Values: Have you explored differences? Have you also found some common ground?

4. Needs: Look for both conceptual needs (what they'll need to be convinced) and readability needs (headings, white space and bullets to make reading easier). Use the experience of group members who've read the kind of writing you're doing, and spend some time at the end anticipating the next step. Given readers' knowledge, values and needs, what would make a good introduction to this piece of writing and how will you organize the rest of it?

Connecting with readers even when it's hard

My friend Ann tells a great story about how hard it was to connect with readers when she first began, as a college professor, to write for the public media. During the 1980s, while studying how to save jobs in Chicago's steel industry, she wrote an article in what she considered her best style and sent it to the *Chicago Reader,* a progressive weekly paper available free in drugstores and theaters. When she followed up with a call to the editor, he told her bluntly, "We can't use this piece. We don't need some academic telling us what to do." Ann "felt insulted and wanted to hang up," but made herself stay on the phone another twenty minutes, asking what she could do to make it better. "I tried to really listen," she says, "even though it was hard. The editor wanted something less academic. He wanted more of me in the story, how I had returned to Chicago to study the steel industry, how I felt about the loss of jobs. Trying this in rewriting gave me a voice, and 'The Great Chicago Slump' eventually came out as the lead article in the Thanksgiving weekend issue where it was widely read." Genuinely listening to people with very different values about writing can open our minds to new and effective ways of doing things. Many articles later, Ann says writing for the public has disciplined her thinking and had a feedback effect on her academic work. Now in designing research projects, she uses a form of audience analysis, asking herself: "What are the questions other economists will ask about this? How could I justify it to them?"

Exercise

Listening and audience analysis   Choose an idea you might like to write about in the public media and talk to five people about it, asking them what they think and then listening carefully no matter what they say or how wrong you think they are. Choose people who probably don't share your expertise or your point of view—the person who cuts your hair or waits for the same bus as you do. Even though you may not agree at all, don't express disapproval or argue, but instead try to help the person express what they really think. Notice if there is any common ground between your views and theirs. Afterward, do an audience analysis and see whether you can come up with a way to present your argument that would change these readers' minds.

Multiple audiences

Writers often have to meet needs of very different audiences in the same piece of writing.

Writers often have to meet needs of very different audiences in the same piece of writing. Ann was writing "The Great Chicago Slump" for grass-roots readers of the weekly free paper, but the voice she developed would also reach academics, labor activists and politicians who would probably pick up the article too. In her case, there was no real gap—each group could engage with the same piece of writing, once she moved beyond the academic voice her editor rejected. This was also true for Amy with her letter to both an editor and environmentally aware magazine readers, and for Jane with her book on women and the U.S. budget. But there are many times when it's hard to picture all your intended readers digesting the same set of words.

Picture yourself drafting a controversial report on transportation and energy efficiency in your city. You are writing for engineers, environmentalists, citizens, consultants and the Chamber of Commerce. If you're working for the city, your supervisor and elected officials are also part of your audience. Each group has different knowledge and values on this topic and there are conflicting needs. Engineers are used to reading documents in technical language, politicians and business leaders have their own lingo. And these professionals are comfortable with big words that may turn off community people and the average taxpayer.

If you work out a full-scale analysis for each audience, you'll see that the task is doable. Among all the different agendas, there will be some common ground for organizing your message. Both professional and community-level audiences appreciate a report that is simple and easy to read and includes facts and figures without making the reading process too complicated. When it's time to edit for clarity of language, techniques in the WORD-POWER chapter can help you avoid technical jargon.

Power differences

Power imbalances between writers and readers can throw off your analysis. All of us have experienced this problem writing for teachers, who had the power to give us a grade and who read our writing mainly to evaluate us. Peter Elbow calls teachers "the trickiest audience of all" because the power difference makes it hard to see them as ordinary human readers. Supervisors, editors or influential colleagues hold similar power, with race, class, language, age and gender differences complicating things even more. A young VISTA volunteer told me she felt uneasy writing for "the biggies," the senators, policymakers and CEOs, but especially the owner of a bus company in her city who had the authority to decide whether the youth excursion she had planned would have transportation or not. Even if you are on good terms with such readers, you may need and want their respect so much that you doubt whether your writing sounds credible to them. Some of that fear and mystique we talked about earlier still remains and makes it hard to believe in your own strength as a thinker.

It may not be obvious, but no matter how powerful our readers, we too have some strength in the situation. Our supervisors need the information we have, funders need something to fund, and professors need to feel proud of their students. We have to recognize our power too. Analyzing all sides of the power issue carefully, rather than feeling vaguely anxious, can strengthen our ability to communicate.

> *No matter how powerful our readers, we too have some strength in the situation.*

| Exercise | **Speaking truth to power**   To deepen your analysis of power, try another grid with two columns—one for your audience and one for yourself. In the audience column, list the powers you see in your audience. Consider position (in government, work, family or school), level of education or experience, and gender, class, seniority, ethnicity and language. Is the language, gender, educational level, age of this reader |

(or group) socially privileged above your own (or is it less privileged, or roughly the same)? In some cultures, older people have excessive control and privilege (adultism), but in others ageism causes disrespect of elders. Who holds the reins and how?

In the column on yourself, consider the same kinds of things but look also for non-traditional sources of power—community respect, on-the-job experience and knowledge, dedication to a higher cause, choir membership, peace of mind, knowledge or leadership roles. Look for what your reader really needs from you and what you have to offer in the writing, such as the opportunity to fund a unique project or to be associated with a richly diverse community. If you understand that someone who could give you a job will benefit from your unusual skills, then you have power in the situation. What hidden sources of strength do you have? Are you part of a new movement that has begun to sway public opinion? Often power in writing comes from having a good idea to express and understanding the real needs of your audience. After filling in the columns, freewrite for five to ten minutes on what you learn from this exercise.

Exercise

Using your "power voice" Another way around silencing is to take on the voice of someone with more power in the situation. How do "the biggies" think and talk to each other? This exercise works when you're having trouble stating your arguments to people you believe have more clout than you do. To try it, find a situation like one listed below, but one that is real for you. After doing an audience analysis, role-play a respected peer of your intended reader and have this person make your pitch for you. She or he will have all the credibility you think you don't have. In workshops, we've sometimes invited a person of power to visit, so we can hear how this person would pitch the argument. The pitches are amazingly brief, direct, natural and to the point—demonstrating an effective voice that we can use too.

- You're a young woman with her first job in community development and you have to write a letter requesting a donation from a community member. Since he owns a local bus company, you hope he will donate a bus to take members of your teen leadership program to a conference in a nearby city. Role-play a well-off member of your board of directors, who's a personal friend of the bus company owner, asking him or her for the donation.

- You're a Latin American student who's having trouble explaining to your department chair why you think there should be special arrangements to help international students cope with the pressure of tests and other written assignments in English. Role-play an imaginary Dean of International Students stepping in to present your case to your department head.

- You're a new housing organizer writing to ask a landlord to fix longstanding code violations in a run-down apartment building. Role-play an elected member of your city council contacting the landlord to make the request.

Common ground and cultural themes

Finding common ground is one of the main reasons to analyze your audience. Sharing something with readers, despite differences, helps you find a starting point for getting through to them. Common ground can be shared knowledge, but usually it is shared values. A climate scientist writing for other climate scientists shares a common knowledge of global warming. Most also share a sense of alarm over this situation and a desire for change—their common values. A racial justice advocate, writing for others like himself, shares an awareness of racism and a desire to end it regardless of differences about how to do this. But the same person writing for readers who don't have much awareness of racism will have to dig more deeply for common ground. Maybe these readers care about words like "equality" and "justice." Maybe their relatives were active in the civil rights movement. Maybe the common ground is a belief in democracy.

Sometimes it's hard to imagine what you might share with readers until you explore cultural themes, the beliefs shared by an entire culture. Charlotte Ryan, a consultant to community groups, studies why media coverage so often disempowers mainstream citizens and reinforces silence and the status quo. Ryan points to contradictory themes deeply rooted in our culture—our society respects movie stars and famous people, but we also value the average person. For every hostile, misguided and disempowering theme there is another one with equal power to resonate positively for us under the same circumstances.

> *Sharing something with readers helps you find a starting point for getting through to them.*

SOME CONTRADICTORY CULTURAL THEMES

Disempowering in social change work	Helpful in social change work
keeping up with the Joneses	driving a sensible car
getting the best for yourself	considering future generations
private property	sharing wealth with the needy
respect for wealth and power	equitable sharing of resources
honoring people of privilege	respect for hard work
"winner takes all"	sympathy for the little person
pride in "founding fathers" legacy	"give me your tired, your poor"
honoring mainstream history	cultural diversity
English as the "best" language	richness of multi-culturalism
nuclear family structure	inclusive, loving families

In the debate about SUVs, for example, lobbyists have argued for these huge, heavy vehicles by stressing themes like "family values" (the vehicles are said to hold large families), "safety" (their weight is said to provide protection from accidents) and "freedom of expression" (people should be able to drive whatever kind of vehicles they want). But a long list of opposite cultural values also fit the situation, given the poor gas mileage of these vehicles: "waste not, want not," "don't take more than your share," "sustainability," "an environment for future generations," "common goals above individual interests," and many more. These themes reach just as deep into the American psyche as the value on personal choice. Values we uncover in audience analysis can help us turn the public against risky expenditures, short-term profits, and practices that will destroy the earth for our children.

Exercise	**Using cultural themes** Find a story covered in the public media in a way that seems belittling, harmful or destructive to your community or people you care about. Then make a chart similar to the one above showing: (1) cultural themes the media has attached to the story (victimization of women, welfare cheats, "big government," Latino drug dealers) and (2) cultural themes that could guide a more positive version of the story (resourcefulness of single women heading households, unfairness of super-profits, Latino family values). Go all out on this second list—make it as long as you can and keep in mind that you are opening up new ground and undoing silencing that has been held in place for generations by stereotypes and the media mindset. Freewrite a retelling of the story that evokes the themes you want to emphasize. For a project of your own, brainstorm a list of cultural themes you can build on.

Step four: From Analysis to Strategy

Audience analysis can reveal strategies for turning a mad draft into something that really clicks with readers. The moment I discover a powerful way to make my point, a strategy, I feel a surge of energy that says, "Go for it!" Sometimes I get this feeling accidentally through freewriting, but usually I work hard for it with the tool in this chapter. I know I'm close when I hear myself talking with readers and an opening sentence comes to mind while I'm filling in the boxes of an analysis grid. If this happens to you, write it down quickly because this kind of intuition doesn't last! A strategy can start out as a feeling, a new mental orientation or a new relationship with readers. It quickly becomes a persuasive message, a sequence of points to get the message across, and an opening lead to grab readers' attention. This step includes ways to use your analysis to fine-tune strategy, including how to write introductions.

First, look back at your analysis with a highlighter pen and flag ideas that will help you strategize. These can pop up in any of the columns. What should you emphasize to be convincing? How can you build on what readers already know and value (especially common ground)? How can you lead people step by step through your material? What's the very best starting point for these readers? Now we can come back to Amy's letter to the editor about SUV advertisements. Take a look at her original letter (opposite). When she highlighted her grid (next page), a better strategy emerged.

Strategies for persuasion

The heart of any strategy is what will convince readers to do what you're asking. The "needs" column usually shows how to persuade. Two themes in the needs column jump out for Amy. One is the editors' need for a way to check the facts. Since the magazine is a business venture, Amy knows she can't persuade them to drop all advertising, but access to facts may make environmentally sound choices easier for them. This point is so important, she adds it to the "goals" column. Including a website with reliable information on greener vehicles they might advertise will strengthen her strategy.

The other thing that jumps out is that editors, who have to process hundreds of letters for each issue, need the point made quickly. They appreciate facts, but only the most necessary ones. Amy's mad draft is 250 words long and gives statistics on three different vehicles. It has three medium-length paragraphs. For Amy's busy audience "less is more." She can trim down each paragraph by one third to one half and use only one SUV for illustration.

Amy's early draft anticipated the "knowledge" column on explaining scientific points and built on common ground from the values column: simplicity and consistency. So she didn't have to change those parts of her strategy—only to shorten and tighten her letter. Her final version links her message about choosing greener vehicles to one advertised car, the Chevy Tahoe. Her final letter is brief with everything necessary to make her point, but nothing else. It follows the classic "letter-to-the-editor" form with a hook, a lead, new facts and a new perspective. (You can learn more about this form in Appendix A.)

Strategies for sequencing

A major challenge in longer pieces of writing—like articles or reports—is putting your material in an order or sequence that readers can follow. Audience analysis confirms what we looked at briefly in the PROCESS

AMY'S LETTERS

BEFORE (MAD DRAFT)

Dear Editor:

I was dismayed this month to discover a serious contradiction between your message and product advertising. You advertised ten vehicles, many of which are rated poorly by energy efficiency organizations. I wonder whether inclusion of these ads follows the mantra of *Real Simple*—"a magazine about simplifying your life."

How simple is the Chevy Tahoe (pp. 1 & 2)? The Tahoe gets 14 miles to the gallon (MPG) in the city and 18 MPG on the highway. Annual gas costs are estimated at $1550. The Tahoe emits 18 tons of carbon dioxide and greenhouse gases each year— a weight equivalent to three elephants! In comparison, gas-electric hybrids get three times the mileage, cost 1/3 for gas, and emit 1/3 the gases. With greenhouse gases linked to climate change, including severe weather, the spread of infectious disease, and sea level rise, will the world we leave for our children be simple?

Owning a Dodge Caravan (page 37) could simplify my life by providing extra space for people and things, but greener vehicles *are available within the same size and price class.*

As environmentally conscious crusaders for the simple life, I ask you to educate readers about their effects on the environment and include ads that support this message. Before signing a contract with Chevrolet, check out www.greenercars.com and ensure that the advertised vehicle is not a fossil-burning monster. This extra work may seem complicated, but over time our lives, homes, bodies, and souls will be better for it.

Sincerely,

Amy Schoenfeld   **(249 words)**

AFTER

Dear Editor:

I was dismayed this month to find ads for vehicles that are poorly rated by energy efficiency organizations. I wonder whether including these ads follows your mantra of simplifying life.

How simple is the Chevy Tahoe (pp. 1-2, *RS*, June 2003)? The Tahoe gets roughly 16 MPG, costs $1550/year in gas, and emits 18 tons of greenhouse gases annually! In comparison, gas-electric hybrids get three times the mileage, cost 1/3 for gas, and emit 1/3 the gases. With greenhouse gases linked to climate change, severe weather, infectious disease, and rising sea levels, will driving a Tahoe leave our children a *simple* world?

Greener vehicles *are available within the same size and price class* as the Tahoe. Please ensure that advertised vehicles rate highly within their class (www.greenercars.com). Environmental consciousness may be complicated, but our lives, homes, bodies, and souls will be better for it.

Sincerely,

Amy Schoenfeld   **(146 words)**

AMY'S LETTER TO THE EDITOR

Audiences	Your Goals	Their Knowledge	Their Values, Attitudes, Beliefs	Their Needs, Expectation
Who will read this?	*As a writer, what messages do you want to get across to this group of readers? What actions do you want them to take?*	*What do they know and what do they not know? What do you know that they don't know?*	*Do they have strong attitudes about your message? What do they believe or value? Do they share any common ground with you?*	*What do they need to see in order to be convinced? What will make your writing more accessible to them?*
Your main audience Editors of magazine about simple living	• Point out contradiction between simple living mission and SUV ad policy • Give them info about SUVs, climate change and auto emissions • Show that readers who like the magazine don't like the ads • Convince them to change ad policy • Show how they can find vehicles to advertise that have better environmental impacts.	• They know their advertisers want to advertise big, expensive, trendy cars. • They know their readers haven't stopped driving big cars. • MAY not know the amount of greenhouse gases associated with the Chevy Tahoe & others • May not have checked energy ratings of cars advertised or realize it's easy to do. • May not know the reality, extent, and scope of climate change/global warming. • May not realize many readers are environmentally aware.	• Value a "simple" lifestyle that nevertheless supports consumerism. • Would like to avoid controversy • Maybe believe advertising hype that SUVs are safer & help to maintain a "simple" lifestyle? • Rely on advertising to finance magazine • Value income from automobile industry ads • Don't want to rock the boat. • May believe that global warming is not yet proven? **possible common ground:** • Value "simplicity" • Safety & sustainability • Value children • Want customers to stay happy • Consistency of values & practices.	**to make it convincing:** • Need facts and figures about the vehicles advertised • Need to know source of info. • Need to know there are alternatives—and how to find them. • Is global warming real? • Respect, polite tone • Solutions are appropriate, not overreactions • Need to see this is not coming from the "lunatic fringe." • Writer's expertise **to make writing accessible:** • Get to the point quickly • Follow format for letters to the editor—one main argument • Selective: only the most necessary information • Not too technical
(Secondary audience will be magazine readers)				

138

chapter. The knowledge column helps locate a starting point readers already know a little about, so you can move, step by step, to what they don't know. If you've already written a draft, you can now check whether the steps make sense for readers. Have you explained enough for readers to understand each point, or do you need to prepare them more fully? Have you provided all the information readers need? Have you given them things they don't need?

The needs column will help you think about how many points to make and how much detail to use. Research shows that short-term human memory holds only seven points, plus or minus two. So if you have fifteen or twenty points, even in a long report, you're going to lose people. You'll have to chunk or group your material into fewer sub-points. For letters to the editor, even two or three points are too many. These readers expect only one point. This kind of simplicity has nothing to do with the educational level of your readers; it's just a fact about what the human mind can take in and process.

And what about the "values" column? A sequence of logical arguments against war won't work if the readers you want to reach believe that war is the best way to end terrorism. You'll have to find a way to acknowledge their primary values before they can take in what you have to say. And you may want to reframe your message in a way that's more consistent with cultural themes you can both accept.

Strategies for introductions

Your opening words are the most important part of your strategy, the "itch" that makes your readers want to read on and figure it out. Will they make the commitment to keep reading? Introductions can't be just background. From the start, readers need to feel the connection between what's already important to them and what you're about to tell them. They have to trust you and want to hear what you have to say. Because the best introductions come after you have both a feel for your readers and clarity about your message, most writers write them after the rest is nearly finished.

There's a classic pattern for introductions that experienced writers follow almost intuitively. You can adapt the pattern to writing that is long or short, formal or informal, for news reports or fundraising letters. (High-conflict situations may differ, and they are discussed in the next section.) The pattern for introductions has four parts:

First: Engage the energy
Start with a brief story, fact or set of facts your audience will be curious about because it connects with their values and interests. In news stories

this is called a "lead." In some kinds of writing, the lead will be very brief, maybe only half a sentence. In a long article, it might be several pages. Sometimes a question or a paradoxical statement catches attention, like the one in Amy's letter. The better you know your readers through audience analysis, the more likely you are to find that one point that will be so engaging no one will want to put the writing down.

Second: Reveal your message

Let your readers know your message—and this means your main argument, not just the broad topic you're writing about. The message that's so difficult for many of us to put into words needs to be in an introduction! Directness helps establish trust and prepares readers to think along with you. Glimpsing the forest prepares us to hear about the trees. Some situations call for a different approach, but most reluctance to voice the message directly comes from silencing, not strategy.

> *Directness helps establish trust and prepares readers to think along with you.*

Third: Point out the path

Before continuing your sequence, give an overview of where you're going. Especially in a longer piece, readers need to know not only what they're getting into but how they're going to get there. They need a map. And research shows that readers will mentally construct their own maps—based on misperceptions—if writers don't give this assistance.

Fourth: Establish trust

Readers intuitively expect the first three steps and feel comfortable with a writer who takes care of them. Explaining code words briefly shows you have readers' knowledge needs in mind. We trust writers who seem

AMY'S INTRODUCTION	WHAT MAKES IT WORK
Dear Editor: I was amazed to find ads in your spring issue for vehicles that are poorly rated by energy efficiency organizations. I wonder whether including these ads follows your mantra of simplifying life.	This opening reveals its message quickly. It engages energy by challenging the editors' policy on ads that hype polluting vehicles. It catches attention by pointing out a contradiction between values (simplicity) and realities (gas guzzlers in ads). In a short three-paragraph letter like Amy's, you don't need to point out the path because the reader can see it at a glance.

to understand our needs, respect us and maybe share our values. We feel confidence in writers who speak clearly, don't waste our time, and know what they're talking about.

Exercise

Introductions that get to you   Gather examples of introductions that make an impression on you. Depending on the length of what they introduce, they might be sentences, paragraphs, pages or whole chapters. If you're browsing in a bookstore, which opening pages make you want to read the whole book? If you're rushing through a newspaper, newsletter or material on the internet, which articles do you actually stop and read? Which reports or memos on your desk engage your attention from the very beginning?

Why did these introductions get to you? Look at each one and list the things you responded to. Now look at whether your points match the four elements of introductions. If any element is missing, can you see why the author might have left it out to meet certain reader needs? Are there other elements you would like to add to the four-part pattern?

Strengthening leads in your introductions

People writing for the news media have a special challenge because their audience is free to skip entire articles when they're not interested. So journalists have perfected a way to engage energy with an opening line or paragraph that quickly draws readers into the drama of a story. Usually it's a specific scene, event, quote, personal experience or statistic from the core of the whole story Thus it stands in for all four parts of the classic introduction. It engages energy, reveals the message, points out the path and establishes trust all at once. Phrased in a brief but exciting way, leads are such compelling openings that other writers have borrowed the idea from journalists. Now we find leads—usually longer than in newspapers—introducing proposals, research reports and chapters of books like this one.

A good lead gives a media audience the drama they expect, but it isn't just drama. It also frames the story (and cultural themes) the writer wants to express. Especially if you are writing something for the media world, you need to study other writers' leads and figure out what editors consider newsworthy.

Exercise

Pitching leads to the press   Preparing to speak to the press is a great way to focus ideas. And we need to prep because most of us can't rely on "saying the right thing" spontaneously. Those big black microphones under the super-bright lights of a TV camera scare people into silence. Media consultant Charlotte Ryan encourages practice sessions on giving reporters a clear message and the bits of personal history or vivid facts that provide a good lead. As activists, we want more than an exciting story: we want the reporter to frame things as we see them. (Ryan shows how, when we don't do this, reporters, who don't share our values, can twist our most noble stories into something merely cute, or even harmful to our cause.) Practicing pitching leads like professional PR people will help us write our own.

For this exercise, choose a real situation you'd like the press to cover. It could be a peace walk the media have ignored, a toxic site near your shopping mall, or a concern about unusual storms and global warming. Picture a reporter asking "Why do you think this would make a good story?" Can you come up with a convincing answer, with a lead, in one to three sentences? This is harder than it looks. Write and redraft your answer. If you role-play this exercise with others, you can compare different leads and work together to strengthen an important leadership skill.

Step Five: Strategize for Conflict and Confrontation

At the heart of the AUDIENCE tool is something that reaches much deeper than analysis, the felt relationship you have with your readers. How they will feel about you depends a lot on how you feel about them when you write, and plays a large role in how open they will be to hearing your message. This section looks at one of the most important audience relationships when we face the challenge of speaking out: how to talk to readers when there is disagreement and conflict.

Speaking out in a conflict

> *Confrontation was not the answer, but silence could not be the answer either.*

Many of us wonder how we would react if our voices were suddenly needed in the moments of extreme conflict that come so often in our times. Buddhist teacher Thich Nhat Hanh tells the story of a young nun doing community work in a small village during the Vietnam War. When heavily armed American troops poured into the streets one morning, not long after the massacre of villagers at My Lai, she knew that a small mistake on anyone's part could trigger unspeakable violence. Confrontation was not the answer, but silence could not be the answer either. How could she best use her voice in this highly charged situation? With her Buddhist practice of calming her own mind first, Sr. Chân Không tried to imagine what these military people might be thinking and feeling. Realizing that they, too, were terrified—of enemy troops they feared were hidden in the huts—she stepped gently toward one of them and asked if they were looking for something and if she could help them. Her genuinely calm and respectful presence and her little bit of English created some trust, and the soldier told her they were looking for communists. Knowing the village well, she was able to convince this soldier, and eventually his commanding officer, that there were no communists in the village. Later that morning, the troops withdrew.

In writing, we usually have more time than Sr. Chan Khong did to reflect on our audience and strategize about speaking out. But we often face conflicts that are very intense. We may need to reach and change people who are not only different, but fiercely antagonistic. You may be writing about the death penalty just when a horrible crime has stirred public outcry for revenge. You may need to challenge racism or militarism when feelings are running high. Even among colleagues, you may need to defend an unpopular view. It is in times of struggle, when important values conflict with those of our readers, that we have the potential to wield the most dramatic influence with our writing. How do we rise to these occasions?

The confrontational option

In conflict situations, there are two main strategy options, and either can be powerful. In one you confront the challenge head on; in the other you work hard to empathize with the readers you feel in conflict with (while holding firmly to your own values). I am not going to tell you that one of these options is better because both play important roles. Changing the public mind means using all our voices. Sometimes we

---

MORE RESOURCES ON AUDIENCE STRATEGY

Matching strategy to audience is a time-honored tool. Called "rhetoric," it was a respected art form among the Greeks and Romans. Universities still teach rhetoric, despite the popular misperception that the term refers only to the "cheap tricks" of politicians and PR experts. Linda Flower's book, *Problem Solving Strategies for Writing in College and Community,* pioneered the audience analysis matrix. Her technique for making writing reader-based comes from fascinating research on how readers read and how we anticipate their reactions. For more on non-confrontational ways of communicating, I suggest Peter Elbow's work on "non-adversarial rhetoric" and the FEED-BACK chapter of this book. Non-judging techniques, such as re-evaluation counseling, non-violent communication, and Buddhist listening (including Thich Nhat Hanh's "love letter") are at the core of audience analysis because they help us see how to empathize in order to build truer communication. There is more about writing for media, policy, and other audiences in the resource section at the end of the book.

need confrontational writing that expresses moral outrage, letting the community know, for instance, that we find racist behavior unacceptable. But we also need writing that helps readers find their way out of racism—which, in my experience, rarely happens through confrontation or attack. The second option opens the way to understanding and change, but sometimes it takes the first to awaken readers.

Racism is an excellent ground for learning about both options, as I discovered in the 1980s as I worked with Rosa, then a young mother with roots in the Caribbean. Rosa was planning a letter to the editor showing how the newspaper gave only negative attention to the Latino community in a city with a growing population of Cuban, Puerto Rican, Dominican and Central American residents. Rosa had strong feelings and wanted to start with her strongest point: *It is racist to negatively stereotype Latino-Americans, and the paper is supporting racism in the way it selects stories to cover.* She gave examples and ended with a challenge: *How would editors and readers feel if suddenly placed in a culture where they were a powerless minority represented this way in the press every day?* In the letter she sent, Rosa chose to use this strategy—a very effective use of the confrontational mode.

The Rogerian option and the "love letter"

The other option would have been to go to the "values" column of the audience analysis to see how the editor and the mostly white readers of the paper might view racism. Was there any hint of common ground? Maybe the paper had recently begun to change some of its longstanding negative stereotyping. Were they trying? And could Rosa honestly honor and support those efforts? If so, a letter could begin by affirming some common ground. *I appreciate the steps your paper has taken to avoid the negative stereotyping of African-Americans.* (Here she could mention examples before making her point.) *However, you may not be aware of the need to extend the same respect to other ethnic groups in the city. As a Latina mother, I am very sensitive to the fact that in the past week you have published ten stories of violent crime in the Latino community. What about our abundant professional accomplishments and cultural contributions? What can I tell my teen-age children, who would like to read your paper but see only negative coverage of people like themselves? It is high time to look more carefully into all the cultures that make up this city.*

Strong feelings still come across in the second version, but showing appreciation for the paper's efforts to change may take readers off the defensive and open them to hear the point. This is what Linda Flower calls the "Rogerian mode" of argumentation, after psychologist Carl Rogers, well-known for the psychotherapy technique of letting the answer come from the patient. The Rogerian approach starts with listening to and affirming your readers, on the theory that they are more likely to accept criticism from someone who understands and respects them. If you don't really respect your readers, confrontation will probably serve you better than trying to fake it. They can usually pick up your real feelings.

Some take the Rogerian mode further and say that real change only comes when we truly respect (and even manage to love) our adversary. Thich Nhat Hanh says energy for change comes from the work we put in to feel enough compassion to write a "love letter" rather than an angry letter to those we are challenging. Writing a love letter empowers the writer and creates the possibility for a solution that is outside the box—a transformation in one's adversary (and oneself) that is almost impossible to envision beforehand.

The effects of the "love letter" show up well on the personal level in conflicts between friends, colleagues or family members. My friend Skip, who does a lot of work on racism in his Quaker community, was deeply distressed by two friends, both white men like himself, who jumped to the microphone at a panel discussion ahead of people of color who wanted to speak. Both of them attacked white panelists who, they said, were not doing enough to end racism. Skip was irritated by what he saw as their arrogance in speaking before people of color had a chance. He was also upset that his friends would attack white panelists who had at least taken the risk to speak out. Skip wanted to write an angry letter to his friends, but asked himself what that would accomplish. It was relatively easy for him to attack people like himself; in fact, that's what his two friends had done. Wouldn't he simply be following in their footsteps? The strength of his feeling might be a clue to something he shared with the two other men. His favorite saying, "You spot it, you got it," had always helped him understand situations like this.

After dashing off an angry draft to vent his feelings, Skip decided on the love letter strategy to reach his friends. He wrote several drafts trying to get in touch with their reasons for doing such a thing, recalling a personal story of his own that showed how the panelists might have felt as well as the people of color who had waited to speak. It wasn't easy. Draft after draft, he worked through his anger at his friends until he understood it and them more deeply, until he could honestly say he was in touch with respect for them as people. Then he sent the letters. One of the friends responded with a heart-to-heart conversation that brought the two closer and led to new ideas on ending racism.

Put yourself in a reader's shoes for a moment. Maybe you are a white person who thinks he has found the most effective way of confronting racism or maybe you are a magazine editor annoyed with all the fuss

> *Skip wanted to write an angry letter to his friends, but asked himself what that would accomplish.*

about SUVs. Perhaps you are someone who thinks a war is the best way of ending all wars. You've held your ideas for a long time and others hold them too. What would get you to change your thinking on beliefs that run so deep? Are you more likely to change when someone confronts you in anger or when someone tries to understand your views and respects you even without agreeing?

The Rogerian mode and the love letter both draw on the principle of not-judging that is key to the FEEDBACK tool in the next chapter of this book. Both approaches are undervalued and under-taught in our contentious culture. I'm not ready to give up all confrontation, myself, but I've seen the powerful effects of the love letter on the writer as well as the reader. I think we need both strategies.

Exercise

The angry letter or the love letter?   Generate a list of conflicted situations that call for a choice between angry letter and love letter. You can start with the following:

- A cooperatively-owned community business you admire has started selling expensive sneakers made in sweat-shops overseas.
- Your city manager has just approved the use of a toxic defoliant to kill road-side weeds, but experts say it will also harm wildlife and possibly children.
- Your favorite magazine has just used some language you consider racist.

Add three more situations from your own experience. Then picture the first two columns of audience analysis for each letter. Who would you want to influence? People like yourself or those who "don't get it"? What would be your goals in writing for the audience you choose? Is it more important to have them hear your righteous anger or to open channels for change? Choose one of the situations and do a full audience analysis. Decide on a strategy to achieve your purpose, then draft either a confrontational letter or a love letter. To explore the problem more deeply, draft both kinds of letters and show them to friends to learn which is more effective.

Taking care of yourself

It can be emotionally draining to focus on audience, especially where differences are deep and readers not only don't "get it" but often get angry. My deepest respect goes to people who've made the commitment to keep communicating where there is division and pain. Each generation has its own list of the hardest, most painful issues. Seeking to communicate across differences on race, war, sexual preference and entrenched controversies like the one between Israel and the Palestinians tests our skills to the utmost and can be exhausting. I've often asked myself what it would be like to be an African American working in a mostly white world, every single day making the effort to put myself in the shoes of people who don't see or feel the enormous burden of racism, every day putting myself through the "love-letter" process, over and over, just to get through the day, communicating with people who are unaware that they benefit from racism.

And even when the values gap is not so huge, burn out is easy when your writing is always governed by audience needs. My friend Donna co-directs a center that helps activists ground their work in "spiritual leadership." It's a unique enterprise with multi-racial leadership and multicultural out-reach. Donna told me years ago that she was losing touch with her joy in words because so much of her work was what she called "commodity writing," where utility was more important than expressiveness. During earlier days in the civil rights movement, Donna had kept a small journal with her to jot down poems that would come to her. She saw them as gifts to herself and the close friends she shared them with. Now she was stretched too thin to keep the journal or listen for the poems in herself. Every moment went to strategic, audience-driven writing that would build the center and its wonderful programs. Donna felt she was being sucked into the very system of regulated thought that she was working to change.

Too much audience analysis can throw us out of balance. For those communicating on the front lines of challenging issues and for those using audience-driven writing to build alternative organizations, there are times to leave audience aside and return to private, expressive writing. Even the love letter starts with freewriting that brings out anger, fear or frustration. Balancing between our inner truth and what readers can hear is a deep challenge. We need to take care of ourselves, even if it means taking time out from audience for a while.

When to skip audience analysis

It's healthy to rebel now and then, but some people resist audience analysis for the wrong reasons. This tool can push all the buttons that make writing difficult, our fears and memories of silencing. So people tell themselves they can get away without spending the extra half hour but then get stuck.

If the writing pours out and you feel good about it, then fine. Maybe you don't need an audience analysis. But if ideas are not flowing and if you find yourself confused about which of several paths of organization to follow or even which main point to focus on, then you need to stop and examine who you're writing for, what you want to accomplish with them, and what their needs are.

Summing up

What will help you to go public with your writing, to speak out even when your readers may not share your views? Just thinking about who those readers are will help you see which fears and concerns are realistic. When you know more about how actual readers think and feel, you'll be able to figure out, in most cases, what you can honestly say to change their minds. You'll also be able to get in touch with your own power in the situation. And you may become an extremely persuasive writer when you begin to find enough common ground to have respect for readers who are very different from yourself. This awareness is crucial to reaching out across the boundaries that divide our society. If we can develop a sense of how the other person hears us, we gain the power to be heard. As Zen priest Hilda Ryumon Gutiérrez Baldoquîn put it recently, "We are only useful where we understand how we are understood." That is the essence of this tool. The FEEDBACK tool in the next chapter continues this learning by offering more practice in empathy with readers and showing exactly what leads them to understand you. If you can find some other writers to try it with, you'll learn what goes on in ordinary readers' hearts and minds while they're reading your writing.

> *"We are only useful where we understand how we are understood."*

CHAPTER SEVEN

The FEEDBACK Tool

How do I know it "works" for readers?

Receive real support from a group method that sidesteps traditional critique to help you develop ideas more fully and build grassroots democracy at the same time. Stories and exercises help you give and receive empowering feedback with or without a group.

One year as winter turned to spring, I met with aspiring writers in the deep woods of New Hampshire. One of them, Scott, said he was just there to listen. "I don't write," he insisted. Later he shared a painful story about feedback. As a depression-era schoolboy asked to write a true story, he had written about all the men hanging around town out of work. He wrote about the truth he observed. Other children, he remembers, stuck with flowers and birds. His teacher didn't like his paper and called his parents in to the school, where they scolded him bitterly in front of his friends: "Why couldn't you write something nice like the other kids!" The silencing was powerful. Even though he was good with numbers and became an economist, this man was only now—in his late 70s—beginning to write about the social vision that had motivated his life since childhood.

What passes for feedback in schools like Scott's, and in most homes, workplaces and even friendship circles, is a major tool of silencing. Whether it's called critique, evaluation or constructive criticism, most commentary we receive on our writing is painful. It comes from an authoritarian model, where experts train us in the "right" way to express our thoughts while shaping what those thoughts should be. The expectation of authoritarian criticism runs so deep that most of us are not even aware of it.

It took a visit to South Africa after the fall of apartheid to show me how a new kind of feedback not only strengthens writing but challenges the silencing at its root. To prepare for a workshop there, I interviewed Daphne, a passionate, Zulu-speaking young researcher, who was determined to write policy reports that would help reorganize her country.

During this transitional period, white-led organizations that had opposed apartheid took pride in preparing Black staff like Daphne for leadership in the new society. But there was a huge knowledge gap. Under the old regime, people of African descent had been excluded from subjects like economics and policymaking. An under-funded "Bantu" education system tracked them into manual work and taught English and Afrikaans, a Dutch-related colonial language, by rote memorization. All education—including that of most whites—had been designed on the top-down authoritarian model that had ruled the country politically for so many years. You heard a lecture, you memorized the content, you repeated it back on the test and an expert judged it "right" or "wrong."

Organizations like Daphne's worked to help Black staff overcome the effects of apartheid and generally treated them respectfully—until it came to writing. Then suddenly, it felt like "back to the old regime." Daphne told me it was extremely painful to bring a draft report to her boss, whose feedback was usually, "this won't do," followed by a long list of suggestions and hundreds of corrections in the margins. Anticipating these painful sessions made it doubly hard for Daphne to write. The critique seemed to point to something wrong inside herself. I was more inclined to blame her supervisor until I saw that the problem was much larger. The supervisor was simply offering the same kind of rigorous critique she had received from her own mentors as a privileged white woman under apartheid. The tools that had shaped her were the "master's tools." Though a lifetime activist against injustice, Daphne's boss had not yet learned to question the top-down approach when it came to feedback on writing.

Daphne's story will resonate with many Americans. Except in a few elite settings, our schooling, too, involves rote memorization and a top-down approach. And showing writing always brings risk of negative criticism—whether it's teachers bleeding all over the page with red pens or the legendary tension of supervisors editing employees' writing. As Peter Elbow points out, our parents may have "oohed and ahhed" over our first spoken words, but they probably sent a different message by correcting the spelling on our first written words. And people like Scott remember outright abuse from parents who yelled or punished them for supposed mistakes in writing. Even self-consciously democratic schools perpetuate the judgmental, authoritarian views so deeply embedded in our society: the idea that there are "right" ways to write and that those in power can best tell us what they are.

It's not surprising that most of us internalize the shameful feelings of being corrected. Negative criticism has maximum sting when it hits us where we already feel inadequate. And many of us don't need apartheid to feel, like Daphne, that we are not good enough. If feedback is painful and confrontational, it's partly because that's what's out there. It's also because something inside us expects harsh judgment; people at all levels of achievement have internalized feelings of inadequacy as writers. Maybe we get a little defensive as we swallow our feelings and obediently fix what the "expert" says is wrong. But not thinking for ourselves can't strengthen our writing and actually helps keep the silence in place. It was from Daphne in South Africa that I learned how most of us go along with authoritarianism in receiving feedback and how the tool in this chapter can help us not to do so.

In the new feedback, experts don't tell other writers the right way to do it. We don't judge writing good, or bad, so we don't reinforce the internal judges. Instead, a small group of peers gives writers direct experience with sample readers—what's in their hearts and minds, where they "get it" and where not, how the writing moves them. In short, the new feedback helps writers see for themselves exactly how to solve the problems of persuasiveness that we looked at in the AUDIENCE chapter. Writers learn to empathize with readers and from there can figure out the best ways to get their ideas across.

After Daphne's entire organization had learned to use the feedback tool, it was unclear whether the supervisor's approach had changed. But Daphne impressed me by declaring that even if she did receive judgmental feedback in the future, she would not be cowed by it because she had changed inside. With her new awareness came her striking decision not to play into authoritarian ways. She would have a new attitude about herself, even in the difficult task of writing reports in English. Daphne's transformation is our challenge as we learn this tool.

> *We don't judge writing good, or bad, so we don't reinforce the internal judges.*

How to use this chapter

A tool with so much to offer—especially one that can reverse deep patterns of oppression and collusion—takes a while to learn. This chapter is arranged so you can pick up and use the tool quickly, then explore it more fully later. You'll find:

- An overview of the new feedback tool.
- Suggestions for fine-tuning the process.
- Questions and answers about the method.

- How to start a writing feedback group or adapt the method when you don't have a group.

Even if you are reading this book on your own, with no access to a community of other writers for feedback, this chapter clarifies the social dynamics of silencing and how to extricate yourself.

An Overview of the Feedback Tool

> *The challenge in learning this tool is letting go of the tendency to judge others.*

This version of feedback is really different from what most people expect. It evolved over twenty years as I worked with Daphne and other community activists, friends and students to adapt the techniques of 1960s writing teacher, Peter Elbow. Its essence is listening and awareness, not rules, judgment or analysis. The challenge in learning this tool is letting go of the tendency to judge others. Even though judgment has been so harmful, most of us have plenty of it embedded in us, so don't be surprised if you find it popping up when you try the tool.

The feedback scenario

Picture yourself in a circle with three to five other people. You are going to spend about an hour reading and reacting to two or three pages of writing by one person. You'll be doing a lot of listening and, at the same time, a lot of thinking and reflecting as your understanding of the writing evolves. At several points, you'll have your turn to speak without interruption, but you won't make the usual kind of suggestions until the very last part of the process. Overall, people will be in a good mood and may laugh, joke, or check in about their personal lives before beginning. This is time-out from everyday busyness—a chance to journey together into creativity. The circle has a feeling of anticipation.

The writer of the day hands out copies of her draft, something short, two or three pages or about a thousand words. Maybe it's part of something longer. The writer leads the session, with everyone taking responsibility for helping it stay on course. There are three phases, and a time keeper makes sure each phase gets approximately equal time. Here's how it goes:

The FEEDBACK Tool

Reading phase (20 minutes) The writer reads her work out loud while others follow on their copies and make notes or underlines for phase two. Don't try to be analytical; just listen and stay aware of how the writing is affecting you. The writer asks another person to give the piece a second reading.

Interview phase (20 minutes)   The writer now "interviews" readers with four questions to invite non-judgmental feedback. Avoid traditional give-and-take dialogue. Readers try to give the fullest answer they can at the moment; then resume listening. The writer also listens, without biasing the interview by answering back. There is time later for fuller discussion. One by one, the writer gets an answer from each person and moves on around the circle. Readers always have the option to "pass."

1. **What WORDS AND PHRASES stand out for you?** Simply repeat aloud the words that had special meaning or energy. Just the words. Save explanations for later.

2. **What MESSAGE came through?** Sum up, in one or two sentences, the message that comes through to you in the writing. What was the author trying to say? What meaning do you take away? Give it in your own words, but feel free to build on—or repeat—what someone before you said.

3. **Can you tell us the STORY of your experience as you read?** Talk us through the ups and downs of your reading experience. Moment by moment what were you thinking and feeling? (Elbow calls this "movies of the reader's mind.") Tell your experiences in story form, starting at the beginning of the writing and moving through. Try to use "I statements" *(I heard... I wondered...)*

4. **What is your METAPHOR for the writing?** Give a metaphor or image for what the writing is like—*a tidal wave, a busy intersection, a pin cushion, a half-peeled orange.*

Response & discussion phase (20 minutes)   The group asks the writer: *How are you feeling about this feedback? What is it bringing up for you and are there any dilemmas you want our help with?* The writer gets to say what she's been storing in her mind for the last twenty minutes. Responding to the writer's concerns, the group now offers further feedback and suggestions. At this point, the process opens up to traditional give-and-take discussion.

The session usually ends with wonderful ideas and suggestions that really fit—because after listening to each other, the writing, and the writer for an hour, we understand what the writer wants to say. There is real synergy, so our advice truly helps her. Carefully structuring the discussion pays off in insights that go far beyond what we'd have thought when we sat down. Although the method is time-intensive, it uses time very efficiently since all work is done face to face, without lengthy reading beforehand. (Later you'll learn to apply the method to written feedback.) The group ends by planning the next session, and the writer goes off to figure out how to use the inspiring ideas she's received.

Exercise	**Getting limited feedback** As you make the transition out of the authoritarian feedback mode, it's useful to try just one element of the new feedback. Ask a friend to help, or plan an exchange where you also do the same thing for your friend. You read your writing out loud, then your friend tells you what he thought you were saying (Question 2)—no more. What does this experience feel like for you? Do some free-writing afterwards.

Exercise	**Trying the full feedback process** With a small group, try a session of feed-back with all three phases. Since you are still learning the process, remain aware of any lingering tendencies to offer judgment or analysis as you answer the interview questions. Gently encourage group members to speak up if they notice anyone judg-ing, critiquing or straying from the questions. Spend a few minutes freewriting after-wards to note any concerns about the process.

Fine-Tuning the Process

Each step in the feedback process invites a deeper understanding. This section shows, step by step, how the process works best to help you get the most out of feedback and undo silencing and old habits of judgment.

a. For the best feedback, sit in a real circle.   In daily life, we forget the democratic power of a circle. True circles put everyone on the same level—with no one sitting in the back near the door—to see, hear and speak with equal power. It's much easier to build trust and synergy with people you can see.

In 1990 on the Pine Ridge Reservation, I joined "talking circles" set up around campfires by American Indians 100 years after the Wounded Knee Massacre. In these circles, every person's voice—telling their family's special story of struggle and recovery since that unspeakable event—formed a sacred healing ceremony. A "talking stick" went around, and people spoke without interruption as long as they held the stick. Hearing of this, South African Zulu speakers told me that, for them, "being in the circle" is indigenous democracy. Each voice can comment on what others have said, and a diverse consensus builds without taking sides, squaring off, and winning or losing. Every voice contributes to group insight. No one has the "right" answer—power is shared.

The same can happen in writing feedback circles. The structured questions are our version of a talking stick—to keep us respectful of the circle and the process. To avoid distractions, be sure snacks are available and phones turned off before you start.

b. Reading aloud phase breaks the silence for writers and gives readers new insights   Reading out loud gives us practice putting our voices out there. Even when it's frightening, there's a rush of excitement as our words come rolling out and people react. Reading your own writing aloud (even by yourself), you can hear its "voice." Sometimes ideas make more sense than you thought; other times you trip over rough sentences. Whatever you hear, keep your pledge to listen to yourself without judging. This is a draft and you're looking for information to improve it. The second reading in another person's voice tells you even more—you hear that voice stumble, you realize you left out a connecting thought. You hear repetition. And hearing your words in another person's voice can give them an energy that surprises you.

Hearing writing read aloud helps readers too. For most of us reading is an unconscious process. Listening gives us a chance to notice what goes on in our minds as we struggle to understand the stream of ideas. How do we construct meaning out of the writer's words? (Feel free to make notes while listening.) As you learn more about how your mind interacts with a piece of writing, you'll realize what other readers struggle with, and how to shape your own writing for them.

Avoid discussing the piece before reading it or you won't be able to see if readers "get it" just from what you wrote. Instead you can quickly answer three things:

- Who is your audience?
- How far along in the writing process are you? (Did you write this in a hurry this morning or have you been polishing it for weeks?)
- Are you reading from the beginning, middle, or end of a longer piece?

Keep it brief to save time for what comes later. If the two readings take less than twenty minutes, great! You'll have that much more time for the next two phases.

c. Interview phase: special questions bring out readers' reactions—without debate.   This phase uses structured questions to generate raw information that helps everyone think more deeply. The writer asks one question at a time, moving around the circle to get an answer from each person. (You can vary things by having a different person start each question.) Synergy is key, so feel free to repeat and build on each other. Answer quickly so the process keeps moving, or pass if you wish. As in the talking circle, there is no interruption or rebuttal. Both writer and readers remain in the listening mode until their next turn to speak. This style of discussion may feel unnatural at first, but the need to interrupt and have your say immediately won't be so strong when you know you'll have a turn soon.

There may be tremendous temptation for the writer to "answer back" and correct misunderstandings, but you won't get readers' real reactions if you do. Save all response for the final phase. Readers can help keep the process on course by saying what's in their heart without self-censoring or taking up a lot of time.

While learning this method, we need to coach each other in ways that facilitate without disrupting the process. Timekeeper, readers or writer should intervene if they notice the group has slipped back to evaluating, interrupting, answering back or confusing the questions. (More later on how to do this.) Once everyone understands the reasoning behind the four questions, coaching won't be needed.

d. Question one: WORDS AND PHRASES (What words and phrases stand out for you?) Mention the five, ten or twenty-five words or expressions that have real energy for you as a reader. (It helps to underline them during the reading aloud phase.) Some people love dramatic words or metaphors; others love numbers. Certain words sound special only to you; others resonate with many in the group. If you find yourself repeating what the person before you said, don't worry. Repetition helps the writer see how she's being heard.

Keep the process moving:

- *No explanations at this point.* Explanations mean you're analyzing, not just reacting, and they usually involve judgment. They also slow the process down. Explanation is part of your "story" and fits in later in question three (no matter how natural it feels here).

- *Move it along—no more than a minute and a half per reader.* Pauses for you to think are OK, but don't wait for the writer to copy down each word. You can give her your notes and underlines afterwards and save time for the final phase of discussion. That's what will be most productive.

For the writer, hearing the words that stand out is affirming because they are her words. There may be patterns. Each reader may follow a different train of thought. Or everyone may be on the same track. Already the writer begins to get into readers' mindsets. Even the shyest writers begin to be fascinated with what they hear and eager for more. And this is only the first question.

e. Question two: THE MESSAGE (What message came through?)   This question asks each of us to sum up the meaning of the writing. Try for a one or two sentence version in your own words (in less than a minute). It's not an easy question to answer, especially when the material is complicated or new to readers or when the writer, himself, is struggling with it. The core activity of summarizing draws on both sides of the brain—the left side for memory and detail, the right side for unifying insight. And it comes quickly, almost spontaneously. Researchers who study the reading process have found that, whether we know it or not, we mentally create summaries as we read. The feedback question helps us share this inner process with the writer, cooperatively making meaning as we restate his point in our own ways.

> *The most helpful summaries often come from the reader who's struggling the hardest to understand.*

Everyone in the circle may hear a slightly different message. Some restate points in the order they appeared; others summarize from a new angle. Some build on others' summaries; some diverge. In one group, Ralph, trained as an engineer, seemed to have an uncanny ability to verbalize essential meanings that writers were barely aware of. Writers looked forward to his crisp, factual summaries—no matter how "mad" the draft—because they helped organize information more clearly for the next draft. Other readers go to the emotional heart of an issue. But the most helpful summaries often come from the reader who's struggling the hardest to understand. After all, the writer wants to reach people who don't already get it. So, if you're groping for words or think your answer is too simple, or too fuzzy, just say what you can and you will help the writer tremendously.

These messages are usually very affirming. The writer feels heard, and there is nothing quite so motivating as knowing that four different people have more or less grasped what you've said. You may feel your ideas growing stronger when readers hear more than you actually said or phrase your message more accurately than you did. (Write their words down to help with revisions!)

For this question to move smoothly, readers need to keep messages brief (but meaty) and stick with the writer's ideas rather than straying into their own. The writer needs to remember to listen with full attention, saving comments for the response phase, the finale of the feedback session. And the timekeeper needs to keep an eye on the clock. These first two questions should move quickly because they are only the beginning.

Exercise

Summarizing messages   Brief, interesting summaries are so vital in public life that they can be called a leadership skill. Recall those special people who can help a group make decisions by summarizing a long-winded controversy clearly and fairly—and people you know who write excellent minutes or those amazing two sentences that showcase everything your organization does. Working in feedback groups will sharpen your summarizing skills, but here are two ways to get extra practice: (1) While freewriting, summarize books, articles or speeches. The secret is to write only about the ones that are stimulating to you and to load all the important points into just a few sentences. (2) Find a partner to sit down with you over a cup of coffee with two copies of the newspaper to share oral summaries. Each of you reads the same article quickly. Then take turns sharing the message that comes through. Include what's crucially important, but also keep your message short. Don't feel you have to argue over who got the "right" message. Try several articles in one sitting.

f. Question three: YOUR STORY (Can you tell us the story of your experience as you read?)   Question two brought out the writer's meaning. Question three brings out readers' reactions, not as critique but in story form—stories of what went on moment by moment while they listened to the writing. This includes personal reactions we don't usually discuss (where we stumbled, where we got excited, who it reminded us of). Taking plenty of time, each of us tells a story in the first person, using "I-statements." *I thought about. I wondered. I asked myself. I remembered.* Our story doesn't include the "good" or "bad" judgments we learned to give in school. What we're doing here is really new and different.

If it's hard to tell these stories at first, that's because we have so little consciousness of what goes on in our heads as we read. Which words trigger ideas? Which arouse feelings? What causes confusion? What helps clarify? How do words raise expectations and what satisfies them? Readers' stories eventually demystify the profound mental process of reading—how a living mind encounters words on a page. After a few sessions, you will learn to tell these stories by hearing others tell theirs.

g. Hints for telling stories:

Focus on what intrigued or puzzled you. Think freely out loud and build your story out of reactions from both the head and the heart, or as one reader put it, "the brain and the gut." The more you pin your reactions to specific words or ideas, the more your story will help the writer. (This is a good place to share reactions to words you mentioned in the first question.) Feel free to talk about the parts you didn't quite understand and to use your intuition.

> *The more you pin your reactions to specific words or ideas, the more your story will help the writer.*

Tell your story in the same order as the writing. Start at the beginning and move through—sentence by sentence, thought by thought—telling how you were affected at each point. Don't try to step back and analyze as in a book review or a school critique.

Analyzing (the old way)

Overall this writing is confusing because it goes in two different directions and you don't identify which alternative you recommend. You need to clarify your argument.

The reader steps back from the experience and analyzes, focusing on how to improve. Notice how judgments and advice inevitably creep in when you analyze. How could you say this in story form?

Telling your story (the new way)

I felt outraged when I heard your example of the children who won't get enough to eat under the new program. But then at the same time, I was also feeling a lot of sympathy for the policy makers who don't know how to handle problems with the old system. I felt for them too because I've been in that situation. At the end, I wanted to know whether you were just dumping this unsolvable problem in my lap or whether you, with all your experience, had any idea what to do about it.

Covers the same ground as the analysis, but in story form. Reader shows experience of being pulled in one direction, then another, and also notes what reactions came up at each point.

In the final phase, the group can analyze and solve problems, but this second phase is still the raw-material stage of the feedback process. Think about it. If you were the writer, which would bring out your creative energy—the analysis or the story?

Focus on yourself and your reactions. Stories build on personal feelings and I-statements, not statements about the writer or the writing:

I could picture the kind of neighborhood you were talking about and it made me sad to think of all the lives that were affected.

I was curious to know what you were going to say next.

I felt a sense of hope that so many people are getting involved.

If "I-statements" don't come easily, train yourself to rephrase the old kind of feedback into feelings and reactions. Your group may ask, "Can you rephrase that as an 'I-statement?'"

Analyzing (old way)	Translating to "I statements"
This is unclear	I was lost here.
	I felt confused here.
This needs more detail	I wondered what the place looked like.
	I wanted to be able to picture what you were talking about.

Watch out for phrases like *I feel that this is unclear. I feel you need more evidence.* These only sound like feelings! What made you see the writing as unclear? *I couldn't understand what this second word meant. I couldn't picture this neighborhood.* The more detailed observation in your reaction, the more the writer can come up with specific improvements.

Avoid the word "should" If you hear yourself using this very common word, you know you've slipped back into judging and trying to "fix" the writing (and maybe even the writer). There are important reasons not to let this happen. For one thing, "should" adds your voice to the culture of judgment and silencing. Hearing about what he "should" do or say can put any writer on the defensive and also keep him from finding the best way to solve a problem. If we simply show where we experienced problems, the

SEPARATING OBSERVATION AND EVALUATION

Indian philosopher, J. Krishnamurti once said that "observing without evaluating is the highest form of human intelligence." Krishnamurti's intelligence is key to successful feedback groups, but it's hard for many people to separate observation (noting or giving information) from evaluation (opinions or judgments). For practice, notice which of the following comments are true observations and which use evaluative judgment words such as "repetitive," "dull," or "funny." See if you can rephrase judgments into observations.

The detail is really good here.

The word "implementation" comes up four times in this one sentence.

This part was very dramatic.

There's a choppy quality to this writing.

(Hint: Only the second sentence is an observation.)

When you combine I-statements with detailed observations, writers can see the cause of problems and what to change. So instead of calling the writing *choppy,* you could say

I noticed there were five short sentences in a row and I couldn't follow the flow.

Marshall Rosenberg's book, *Nonviolent Communication*, builds on this distinction between observation and judging or analysis, offering a way to communicate without provoking resistance, an approach that has helped people all over the world.

writer himself can solve them. A reader may think that commas will fix a sentence, when the writer knows the real problem is tangled ideas.

Avoid praise as well as negative judgments. Your instinct may be to praise the writing as brilliant, wonderful, extraordinary, etc., and you may wonder, "How could that hurt? I'm only saying good things." But "good" doesn't tell the writer as much as your story will. It doesn't provoke the deep thinking that strengthens ideas, and many writers don't trust praise of their work. Praise is part of evaluation. It can reinforce the writer's sense that you are smarter than he is and the harmful belief that there is one right way to express something.

Letting go of judgment is especially hard for people with academic training. Evaluation is what universities are all about. But nowhere do we see so clearly how judgment and evaluation are what Audre Lorde called "the master's tools." They are the mechanisms that keep our silencing in place. We cannot use these old tools to free ourselves. The new feedback tool shows us how our writing affects and influences readers, replacing "good" and "bad" with an inner sense of our own strength. (And if you really like the writing, you can say so later on in the last phase of feedback.)

Listen deeply and with curiosity. The writer must put aside any need to defend his writing and listen in a way that encourages readers to tell their stories freely—empathetic listening or deep listening. If you've been burned in the past by comments on your writing, it can be hard to trust enough to listen. What helps is a sense of curiosity, the kind that guides the best qualitative research as well as the best therapy. *What is making these readers tick? What language and images have energy for them?* If you are truly curious about the mental lives of readers, you'll begin to empathize, which is the response that will most help you communicate. A student once gave some writing the highest praise by saying it seemed to anticipate—and then answer—each question that came up as she read. You can develop this skill by listening to how readers' minds work.

It will help if you take notes. If not, try taping the discussions or asking group members to take notes for you. And set aside time immediately afterwards to freewrite about what you remember hearing.

h. Question four: METAPHOR *(What is your metaphor for the writing?)* Here we invite the right brain to react intuitively with a metaphor, an image or thing that is like the writing. *A ladder. A beautiful snake. The view from the top of a mountain.* It's OK to explain the metaphor, but it's also OK not to, just let the possible meanings reverberate in people's minds. The mountain might suggest the writing is awesome, or gives impressive information, or was difficult to climb but rewarding. The beauty of metaphors is they can suggest several things at once. As discussed in the THINKING chapter, metaphors are intrinsic to human communication in dreams, songs and everyday language ("The day *flew* by." "I've got *the blues*.")

If metaphors come more easily for one person in the group, let that person answer first and others will chime in, as in a game. If you're stuck, the writer can ask the question in a different way: *What animal is this writing like? What color is it?* Relax, open your mind and allow yourself to say something strange or silly. The strangest metaphors are often the most helpful. Once your group warms up to metaphors, you'll be amazed at how important they become. Writers often say they help clarify the deepest purposes of the writing.

Exercise

Encouraging metaphor If metaphors are hard for you, reread the section on them in the THINKING chapter and try the exercise there. Like summarizing, skillful use of metaphors is a core communication strength that helps clarify ideas and inspire others.

i. Writer's response (first five minutes of last phase) Now the group changes gears and asks the writer: *How are you feeling about this feedback? What is it bringing up for you and are there any dilemmas you want our help with?* The writer has listened patiently to a lot of input from readers. Now, to kick off the final phase, readers need to hear the voice of the writer responding to their feedback.

This is the writer's chance to say everything she has held back over the past forty-five minutes. Usually writers share feelings about the feedback and new awareness. *I was amazed that so many of you understood what I was getting at, but a lot of my words mean things to you that I didn't expect. I'm going to have to think more about that.* Writers need to identify any changes they are considering or questions they are struggling with after the feedback. *Should I leave this out? Should I restructure this from three points into two points? Do I need to explain who these people are that I'm talking about?* Usually writers are energized by the feedback and have ideas for changes. Often they see their own ideas in a more profound way and want help thinking things through at a deeper level than before. The more significant the problems a writer can raise at this point, the more helpful the last part of the process can be.

Now it's readers' turn to listen deeply, to pick up on themes in the writer's response that may not be obvious even to the writer. She may be voicing a new meaning that didn't appear in the draft or using new and more powerful language. Write down what she says to remind her later. Does she hint at fears or obstacles you can speak to when she finishes talking?

j. Full discussion of writer's concerns (final fifteen minutes of last phase). At this point, the structure falls away and we give advice and suggestions however we want, so long as everyone has a chance to speak. After all the deep listening, everyone is on the same wavelength. Readers are tuned to the writer's concerns and anxieties, so comments can be collaborative and democratic rather than judgmental. Suggestions now come from empathy with the writer's goals, not just from a reader's independent take on the subject. Most groups find the synergy very enjoyable.

Readers have great ideas about where to cut, where to include examples and how to speak to the heart of the issue. They often notice that a writer's response to the feedback makes the piece come to life in a way it didn't on paper. Be sure to allow time for all this to happen—the insights that come up in this last fifteen minutes are the "gold" of the feedback session.

Exercise

Refining the group process   After a few sessions with a group, decide to stay an extra half hour for "feedback on the feedback." Take ten minutes to freewrite on the session you just experienced. What were its high-energy points? How was it from your perspective? Remember that you are learning a process that runs counter to the tradition that's been part of our culture for hundreds of years. Does this explain any problems you're experiencing? Then move around the circle sharing your ideas about the feedback process. After everyone's had a turn, discuss improvements to fine-tune your group's process.

> *There is no "right way" to use the rich jumble of insights and suggestions that come out of one of these sessions.*

k. How to use this feedback to strengthen your writing   There is no "right way" to use the rich jumble of insights and suggestions that come out of one of these sessions. In traditional feedback, a teacher, editor or supervisor, like Daphne's, tells you to clarify your introduction, add examples, or change points of grammar. And many writers have trained themselves to do what they are told no matter how much it distorts their intentions. But with this more democratic tool, there is often no clear mandate. If a writer sets out to fix every point that caused trouble for readers, she may come up with writing that's less coherent and more confusing than the original! Non-judgmental feedback, instead, stimulates the writer's own powers to decide what will improve the writing. Typically writers make fewer superficial changes and more deep ones than with traditional feedback.

Set aside time within the next 24 hours to review all your notes before short-term memory fades.

Even if there's no time to fully rewrite, set aside time within the next 24 hours to review all your notes (including any from group members) to consolidate your insights before short-term memory fades. Piece together the high points of the session, adding, underlining and highlighting. Freewriting can bring back the most powerful moments, which I seem to forget when I'm resisting a transformative insight. While the feedback is fresh, list four or five main changes you want to make later when you do the actual revisions.

In the meantime, insights from that one session can influence the rest of what you're writing or even a different project. People see their groups' faces as they write and internalize each person's feedback. *I know they'll want an example here and they'll need this key idea earlier in the paragraph.*

When you do rewrite, this feedback will help your ideas change and grow in major ways. You'll have a good sense of how to emphasize what was already working in your draft and let go of ideas that are no longer necessary. Writers often return to the group with the same piece a second and even third time, not because they feel stuck but because their ideas are bristling with new energy. After several reviews, the writing becomes something you can feel very proud of. It really is your best work.

Common Questions About the Feedback Tool

An enormous personal change, and one that will contribute to social change, can happen as you learn to use this tool without judgment. At the same time, the quality of your thinking, and your writing too, will improve tremendously. But challenging questions come up as you deepen your experience with this method. Here are just a few:

Wouldn't it be more realistic to read silently? Good question, because studies of silent reading show a different mental process, and we're writing for people who are going to read silently. But reading aloud together connects group members, where silent reading separates them. It also takes longer and makes it harder for readers to look at their own reading process. Reading aloud not only gives writers a chance to try their voices but actually improves feedback.

What if we want to change the questions? These particular four questions keep the process from becoming chaotic and are profound learning tools because they invite information rather than evaluation. If you change them, you lose the protection they offer. Add other questions only if they truly seek information about readers' perceptions. There's one I often add when I've given readers the first few pages of something much longer: *What do you expect me to say next?* And at the end, ask any question you want.

What if people have trouble giving a metaphor?   Keep trying. Metaphors are worth waiting for. Not long ago, I revisited a group that had struggled with metaphors in its first few meetings. A year later, metaphors had become their strong suit. If people have trouble, don't push. You can't force metaphors. Encourage each other to say whatever comes out, no matter how strange. Metaphors may seem complicated, but remember Freire's story about the peasant. Something in you, too, is in touch with metaphoric thinking—a core human strength. Once its power becomes accessible, you'll be glad you didn't give up.

I can't stop being judgmental about others' writing.   Usually judgment masks a feeling, especially when your reaction is strong. Translating judgments into "I statements" gets at the root feeling: *I'm irritated by having to read this word over and over. I'm confused by so many repetitions. I'm annoyed with this long description for wasting my time.* These statements don't blame the writer, but give her important data about a reader's struggles. Quite possibly she will think *Hey. That's useful. I didn't really need those extra words.*

I wonder if I have the patience for all this listening?   Most of us aren't trained as listeners. We value our ability to speak—even to interrupt—and we get impatient. But there's something magical about listening. When you really listen to someone—including thoughts they are barely able to put in words—that person becomes more interesting. And when you are really listened to, you feel more articulate. Deep, committed, empathetic listening is magical and central to this process. When a writer has four or five people really listening to what she says, her ideas and words actually get more powerful. This process is a chance to practice a transformative human skill.

Is a mad draft OK or should it be more polished? And what if most of my writing is longer than two or three pages?   Choose what you think you can learn from. It can be "mad" (if you clear out distracting errors) or it can be polished (if you're still open to changes). It can be an outline or a spoken version or an audience analysis written in bright colors on a flip chart. And for longer projects, feedback on a page or two can guide the rest of the project. Just ask an inspiring group of faculty women who used this feedback process for ten years in the face of their great challenge

> *If feedback could clarify the most confused part, its impact would affect an entire article or book.*

to "publish or perish." In that time all of them got tenure in their jobs, became heads of institutes, or published major books. Afterward they told me that choosing which two or three pages to bring each time was the most important part of the process. One said she always chose her most problematic two pages. If feedback could clarify the most confused part, its impact would affect an entire article or book.

Is it better to have a homogeneous group or one with a lot of diversity? People come down both ways on this. The faculty women's group thrived on similarities. Their fields were close enough to make ideas understandable, and they could help each other with their shared anxiety: "Will my writing be acceptable to the powers that be in the university?" On the diversity side, "outsiders" can often find gaps in thinking that close colleagues miss. More important—especially for those whose writing needs to reach across class and ethnic divisions—diverse groups are a huge source of learning and energy for change. One of the first groups I worked with came from four continents and three language groups. Attitudes and values differed tremendously. The one person from the United States was writing about battered women's shelters. The men in her group from Japan and Saudi Arabia, two relatively male-centered cultures, found women's issues new and challenging. I worried that this group wouldn't provide much insight into how U.S. funders would read her argument, but the writer loved her group. "I'm learning to convince people," she told me. "If I can persuade people in this group, I think I can convince just about anyone!"

Starting a Group and Adapting the Method

How to start a writing feedback group

It always amazes me how many people from all walks of life are drawn to writing groups, but many would-be groups fizzle out because of busy and incongruent schedules. There may also be reluctance to commit to something unfamiliar and bound to change our habits. The following ideas have helped groups get off the ground in friendship circles, schools, workplaces and community centers:

- **Common purpose**   Whether your group is diverse or homogenous, what will hold it together is everyone's urgent wish to become a more effective writer. There are an astounding number of people out there who feel silenced and want to write. Some need writing to succeed in their work, and others feel a commitment to social change through voicing ideas. For many the wish to write is passionate. To start an effective group you need to tap this common passion.

- **Group size** Ideal group size is no fewer than five and no more than seven. For the many times when one person has a sick child or a job interview, it's good to have at least six people in the pool. If one can't make it, there will still be five people (four voices for feedback). Fewer than four people in a group leaves only two voices for feedback, which—though better than nothing—isn't enough for diversity or synergy.

- **Commitment to regular, scheduled meeting time and place** Meetings have to be at predictable, accessible times and places, and each person has to commit to being there regularly and on time. It's not fair to the group to come only when it's your turn or to change your plans at the last minute leaving too few people for good feedback. If members don't attend consistently, the group will quickly lose energy.

- **Reliability** Be ready when it's your turn, and come prepared with copies of your writing. Nothing's worse than four busy people giving up their afternoon for someone who doesn't show up or has to run off to the copy shop on the group's time. None of us is perfect, so it makes sense to have a backup person each time (or a system for contacting replacements).

- **Sticking with the agenda** The first few months of group work are really a training for all members—learning to trust each other, to unlearn habits that silence others and to access deeper instincts for non-judgmental feedback. Because it's such a challenge to replace old habits with ones that are more self-affirming and group-affirming, it's important not to change the agenda until you understand its principles through direct experience.

Adapting to different settings

Without changing the essentials, you can adapt the tool to many situations:

- **At work** If writing is one of your work responsibilities, build an hour for feedback into your weekly schedule. Look at writing by individuals or team-writing. Feedback enhances group strategizing, helps smooth the rough edges of separate voices into one and improves the dynamics of your work-group by shifting competitive, judgmental habits to deep listening and cooperation.

- **With friends**   A writing group among friends can stimulate good work and deepen friendships at the same time. I remember the first group that met at my house to do social justice writing in the mid-1980s. Although most of us lived in the same neighborhood, our schedules were so different we set alarm clocks early and met at seven o'clock every Monday morning. That was real dedication! People took turns bringing muffins, and we always took ten minutes at the beginning to drink coffee or tea and check in with each other. We wrote articles and letters on Central American refugees, violence and children, and women's wages. So as not to "let our friends down," we faithfully completed our writing projects. And we're still friends!

- **On campus**   In the academic world, everyone's expected to produce more and better writing without really being taught how. Some campus writing groups thrive on a mix of faculty, students, staff and international students from a variety of departments. Others narrow their focus to particular fields or peer groups such as support staff or dissertation-writers, like one group at MIT who met for over a decade, with new members cycling in as others graduated. Common challenges strengthen groups who feel vulnerable in the academic world. In a fast-paced university, a firm, regular meeting time is crucial. So are short segments of writing that will reverberate into longer academic projects.

- **With youth**   Because they are often looking for alternatives to the authoritarianism of adults, young people are very receptive to this teacherless method of feedback.

- **In community or labor groups**   A writing group can jump-start written activism to contact newspapers and legislators. A feedback group differs from the media committees of many activist organizations because its main purpose is not so much setting strategy as supporting the important leadership skill of writing. Five or six activists can keep letters to the editor coming at a rapid pace—or start a newsletter—while becoming more confident as spokespeople for the organization. For busy activists, short, regular meetings are important, and because the pieces of writing are brief, you may be able to review several in an hour. (Shorter pieces usually need only one reading aloud.)

- **At dysfunctional meetings**   Community work, and political meetings can be unbearable when a roomful of passionate people tries to agree on a mission statement or other written document. Endless arguments over unimportant phrases bring up all the

This way, disagreements become constructive or interesting rather than painful or divisive.

group's issues, relevant or not. Classic example: the student team that took 46 hours to group-edit their report. Everyone had to have a say about every word in the document. The FEEDBACK tool leads to a more cooperative atmosphere. Ask several people to restate the main point (the MESSAGE question), then call for reactions in "I-statements" rather than "should statements" (the STORY question). The goal is not to revise the document on the spot but to gather responses and suggestions for a small team to incorporate into a second draft. This way, disagreements become constructive or interesting rather than painful or divisive, and it's easier for co-writers to remain open and flexible.

Feedback Without a Group

Even without a group, you can bring some of the new approach into traditional feedback by asking for the kind of information that will strengthen your work. If friends or co-workers are looking at your writing, ask them for two essentials in either written or oral feedback. You'll recognize these as versions of the MESSAGE and STORY questions:

- What do you think I'm saying here?
- Where do you have strong reactions? Where are you especially interested and where do you have questions?

Ask them to spell out their answers fully before they give you any other feedback. If you're working face to face, take some time to share your reactions after you hear their answers. If you're working long distance on paper versions, ask for a one or two sentence message and as much detail as possible in the margins where they have questions. If you're working online, they can type their questions, in brackets or a different font, right into your draft. This way you have a mini-feedback session with just one other person.

Believe it or not this feedback tool can be effective with people in authority. Years of consulting with supervisors and teachers have shown me that many are unsure about how to give productive feedback. Most are not trained as editors with the English language and most have experienced how hard it is to mentor a new writer simply by marking up her pages. Many are searching for a better way. It may take a little more time to summarize, show how you reacted and hear out the writer's response before deciding how something should be revised, but teachers, supervisors and grant officers have told me this tool helps them with their job too. So take heart, if you request the kind of feedback that helps most, you'll be able to produce excellent work.

"Translating" Traditional Feedback When You Can't Change it

There will be times when you can't change the dynamics of traditional feedback, but there's no reason to accept others' judgment passively. As Daphne found in South Africa, your training with the feedback tool helps you interpret authoritarian criticism so it will strengthen, not intimidate, you. The group method gives you so much self-confidence that you won't feel put down by critique. If a teacher, boss or co-worker marks up your manuscript and tells you how to fix it, you'll realize that this is just one person's way of reading your work. I once gave writing to two faculty colleagues and received totally opposite judgments: one said a particular point was great and the other actually crossed it out!

Working with an editor of a magazine or newsletter is a case in point. Most editors mark up your pages in a way that can intimidate new writers. But most assume you'll rethink the changes actively. Editors expect writers to suggest alternate phrasing when a revision doesn't fit the thought they were trying to express.

Once you realize your own power in the situation and know you have choices, you regain your ownership of the writing. Now you can receive criticism—not on the defensive but freely exploring what you can learn. What is going on in this reader's head? If an editor crosses out something important, why doesn't she see its value? Maybe she already understood your message from something you said earlier and doesn't need the extra words. Or maybe she didn't understand at all and needs the idea stated more strongly. Experienced writers stay in control and treat authoritarian feedback simply as more reader information to help them get their point across.

Exercise

Transforming authoritarian feedback situations   Consider the following stories:

A) Steven is newly employed as one of three staff persons in his dream job in an environmental organization. His boss believes in participatory democracy, so Steven is included in most decision-making. As a deadline approaches for their first group-writing project, he struggles with his part of a report that was planned collaboratively. He finishes it a day or so behind schedule but before the final due date. He is shocked at his "democratic" supervisor's response: red marks all over the page and a kind if fury with him for not doing a better job. Suddenly there are absolute rules he is expected to follow and they aren't the same rules he vaguely remembers learning in school. He feels confused and resistant. At the same time his boss is facing a dilemma she hadn't anticipated: it's her responsibility to get the report in on time and make sure it's up to the standards of the profession. Participatory democracy seems to have gone out the window.

B) Christine is part of a group of student women who work with a female professor in a thesis support group. For generations, an "old boy network" has groomed male scholars in their very competitive university department. Somehow it's always the males whose "brilliant" work attracts worldwide attention and the best jobs and privileges afterwards. In graduate seminars, it is the male students who speak up and get attention for their work. With their professor, Christine and the others hope that women-centered feedback in their support group will help to level the playing field. A different person presents her writing each week. But the discussion format resembles that of the official university seminars: each participant looks for flaws in the presenter's argument and what's wrong or needs improvement. Yes, there is praise for strengths, but the goal is to give writers the kind of experience they'll receive when male colleagues and professors attack their work. Their theory is it's important to accept criticism no matter how painful. "No pain, no gain," is a slogan that draws a bitter laugh from Christine. A session is considered successful when it ends with the writer in tears.

On your own or in a group, figure out how the feedback tool could solve Steven's or Christine's problems. How could feedback be more productive for all involved?

Coordinating Feedback with the Rest of the Toolkit

None of the tools stands alone. The FEEDBACK tool can help throughout the writing process—at the beginning, middle, end or even several times during a single writing project. Use this tool with free writing you did half an hour ago or with something you've been revising for weeks. Group synergy can strengthen ideas, language, even overall process or audience analysis.

A Tool for Transformation

At the personal level, people who practice this kind of feedback over weeks, months or years report more confidence as thinkers and writers. Group support heals the pain of past disrespect of one's work and transforms habitual attitudes. Lingering uneasiness about readers begins to dissolve, so we can more accurately sense their reactions. And writing improves as we uncover the layers of thinking hidden in a first draft and learn to support arguments, link thoughts and engage an audience. Research shows this feedback process actually improves critical thinking, and groups often help writers strategize, find publishers and promote their work. At the end of a workshop, people often feel that the people in their group were unusually brilliant or smart. To me this shows that this process brings out each person's full intelligence and helps them appreciate the minds of others.

At the end of a workshop, people often feel that the people in their group were unusually brilliant or smart.

Beyond this, feedback groups do much more than empower writing and writers. For people like me whose heart is in community activism, they are part of what offers hope for peace, justice and a healthy, enduring earth. They join many other new group processes that are working against time to transform our world. Writing feedback groups model a new kind of communication—a consensus-based way of reaching agreement through deep listening, empathy and cooperation. The most improbable people bond firmly in these groups, embodying democracy at a profound level. The groups train us in a new kind of community process, one that respects difference and supports individual strength, yet gives our individual efforts a unity of purpose and voice.

A VISION FOR SOCIAL TRANSFORMATION

One morning in the 1990s as I was beginning this book, I awoke in tears from a stirring dream in which I had joined all those who have been working on communication and social change during my lifetime. Most of them, in reality, know nothing of each other, but in my dream they were all together, among shafts of sunlight, green plants, clear running water and the crumbling remains of ancient stone buildings. Hundreds of them— educators, organizers and peacemakers— were talking with each other about listening, expression, reconciliation, empowerment, and democratic process.

Paulo Freire stood out in my dream, talking with others about critical pedagogy and popular education. Nearby were writing teachers clustered around Peter Elbow and people in the collaborative learning circles from the sixties and seventies. In my dream, too, was Cherie Brown with the co-counseling and Unlearning Racism people, and Herb Walters with the Listening Projects from the rural South, and Marshall Rosenberg with Non-Violent Communication. There were also crowds of oral historians, therapists, mediators and many kinds of Buddhists practicing Right Speech and deep listening to transform suffering.

Over the years that shaped the FEED-BACK tool, the beings of my dream were using similar approaches in thousands of grassroots settings to kindle real democracy, which is now growing stronger. You can read more about these efforts in Frances Moore Lappé's new book, *Democracy's Edge*. In these troubled times, it is hopeful to realize how many American cities have Study Circles or Public Conversation Projects, how many individuals have learned mediation or Non-violent Communication, how many groups use consensus or other methods of genuinely democratic decision-making. These are the best, and perhaps the only, tools we have for addressing the problems of the 21st century.

CHAPTER EIGHT

The WORD-POWER Tool

Review it all and fine-tune your language for readers

Check the action in your sentences, cut out the "lard," and learn to avoid the "grammar gatekeepers" that make so many writers uneasy. Examples and exercises show how to strengthen your power with words and clean up all those little things that frustrate readers.

Luanne came into class one night exasperated. At work, she had two supervisors with drastically different ideas about writing. Last week she'd given a draft to the first supervisor and gotten it back with a lot of red-penciling. This supervisor wanted more formality. He crossed out simple, direct words like *use* and *help* and substituted *utilize* and *facilitate*. He added passive sentences like *it was found* (instead of *they found*) and used stiff phrases like *in consideration of the fact that*. Luanne retyped and gave the draft to her other supervisor for final changes.

Right before class, she'd received her work back from the second supervisor with just as many red marks, maybe more! The second supervisor seemed very disturbed with Luanne's style. He had changed all the big words back to reader-friendly words like *use* and *help*. And he'd removed all the passive verbs because he said they made the writing sound bureaucratic, not appropriate for their workplace. Obviously Luanne liked his version better because it was more like her original, but she felt powerless and upset. How could she possibly write for both these people at once? We sat there talking about how the two bosses needed to work this out with each other and how many people in authority have backward views of good writing style. How do you operate in this kind of situation?

Amazingly, that same night another woman shared a similar story with a different ending. Desiree had given her undergraduate thesis to two professors for feedback. Both of them marked it up heavily and changed her phrasing on every page. The two of them were about as far apart on writing style as Luanne's two supervisors. If Desiree had made every change these two suggested, she would have ended up with a confusing jumble. Instead of taking the corrections at face value, she looked at each red mark as a general sign that something wasn't clear to someone and could be improved. She looked at the red marks and rethought what she was trying to say. Then she made changes, but mostly without using the words her professors had suggested. Instead she restructured whole sentences and paragraphs and made each change in her own way. Her professors both liked the results, and Desiree felt that by thinking each change through on her own, she had taken back the power of her voice.

Desiree had given herself the freedom to make her own choices. Even with all their academic status, she realized, her professors did not know a "right way" to express her thoughts (especially since they couldn't agree between them!). With the WORD-POWER tool, you'll learn there are many different ways to express the same thought. You'll begin to develop the storehouse of options that marks an experienced writer. Like dancers, actors, or hockey players, we instinctively use different moves for different situations. This versatility takes time and effort, but it's the underlying vision of the WORD-POWER tool.

People often feel uneasy looking back over writing, even without teachers or supervisors pushing them to do so. And there are reasons to be uneasy about written language. What's on the page looks strange if it doesn't follow customs for the written word, and there are people who will make judgments about what they see as mistakes. The WORD-POWER tool offers simple principles for looking critically at your own work. You are ready for this tool after (1) You've given your thinking time to evolve and change by writing several versions. (2) You're solid enough to look at your writing without activating the silencing. You managed to avoid the "dangerous method," so now you're ready for the tool that guarantees a "safe method." Now we can make many small changes that strengthen our voices and empower our language on the written page.

> *Now we can make many small changes that strengthen our voices and em-power our language on the written page.*

How to use this chapter

This chapter doesn't try to go into everything a professional editor might need to know. Instead it explores just a few techniques to help ordinary writers make the most significant improvements. The best guide to fine-tuning your language is readers' reaction, not grammar rules. What words and phrases, what sentence forms, will have most power for readers? And what word-habits may distract them and get in the way of communication?

To get at these questions, this chapter covers:

- Looking back over your writing with readers' eyes.
- Cutting words to keep it simple.
- Linking and transitions.
- Grammar is power.
- High-energy language.

Everyone has probably read a guide to writing style without experiencing any real changes in their writing. To change, you have to engage on a deeper level by practicing with your own and others' words—so please don't skip the exercises in this chapter.

Looking at Your Draft with Readers' Eyes

It's deceptively simple. Start by stepping out of your shoes as a writer and rereading your draft as if you were the reader experiencing everything for the first time. Here are techniques to shift your point of view. They will lift you out of the state of mind you were in while writing and help you see through a reader's eyes.

A fresh copy. Make yourself a clean copy. It could be a newly-printed paper copy with no other editing marks (a real luxury to pre-computer old-timers who remember pasted-up pages, arrows and smudged revisions). Especially for shorter letters or things that will be read online, the virtual copy on the computer screen works well too.

New time and space. Let your draft sit and incubate overnight or while you work on something else. One friend tells me this gestation period is magical and opens his eyes to things he couldn't see before. I like to sit down with my draft in a less familiar writing space—my front room, a coffee shop, another person's desk. Now I am someone else, at leisure, reading this writing.

Reading out of order. I sometimes start with final sections of a longer piece and work my way back (or I start in the middle and work both back and forward). This helps break pre-conceived ideas of what I've said and reveals repetitions. It doesn't help me look at whether things flow logically, so if I suspect that's a problem, I don't use this technique.

Reading out loud. Reading aloud automatically shifts you out of the writer's role. You'll see immediately if the words work for readers or not because now you are a reader. Which words flow and which are unpronounceable? Is there breathing space? Where does it sound stilted and where does it sound like a real person? What are the high-energy points? Where is the energy low or stuck?

Read fast, as if it were a magazine or newspaper. Don't stop the flow of ideas to analyze or look for alternatives at this point, just quickly mark places to return to. I use straight lines (underlines or in the margin) for the high-energy parts, the parts that seem to work. I use wavy marks to show where I want to straighten something out. Every writer has things to watch out for. For me it's repeating myself and writing complicated, unreadable sentences. I hear the familiar voices from my feedback group: *I want to see these people. I want to hear them. I'm turning off here. I'm getting tangled up in all this theory.* I hear more irritable voices from way, way back—like my mother's: *How do you expect anyone to know what you mean by vague words like "this"?*

If the old voices make me feel uneasy (and they do sometimes), I try to remember that I can trust the process of writing I am using now. I have written and revised this draft, and I'm about to use the final tool for last minute changes that will make my words and ideas powerful and clear.

> *You'll see immediately if the words work for readers or not because now you are a reader.*

Cutting to Keep It Simple

What do we want this writing to be like for readers? Our job as writers is to save them all the hard work we just did thinking things through. When we get close to a final draft most of us find that we've made it more complicated than readers can deal with. We need tools to reduce the lengthy phrasing that was part of our writing process but will be a stumbling block for readers.

Cutting to make it shorter

Let's start with simple, direct cutting. Say your reader is an editor with a word limit. You've written an op ed column for your newspaper by doing a couple of drafts and letting the message evolve. Bernie, a soccer fan with a lot of international experience, tried this recently with a column about American attitudes toward Germany. Once all his ideas were all in place, Bernie's column was about one third longer than the limit. To get this article published, he would have to cut all the non-

"AS SIMPLE AS POSSIBLE...BUT NOT MORE SO"

While we were working on keeping it simple, a student found Einstein's idea on this subject quoted in his economics book: "Things should be as simple as possible—but not more so." Einstein was talking about the power of ideas that aren't loaded down with related points and qualifications. The fact that he could express a profound breakthrough in the short formula, $e=mc^2$, shows his enormous understanding. With powerful ideas, less is more. Of course, simple thinking isn't necessarily good thinking—like slogans from politicians at election time or shortcuts in logic when someone doesn't take important factors into account. That's the brilliance of "but not more so." Einstein challenges us to figure out just how simple we can make our thinking—and our writing—without making it "simplistic."

essentials without losing his message. Here are before and after versions of Bernie's first paragraph. (To get the most out of the example, cover up the "after" version and try your own.)

BEFORE

World War Two, Hitler, the Holocaust, Cold War confrontation with the Soviet Union, the Iron Curtain and President Reagan demanding that Soviet leader Mikhail Gorbachev "tear down this wall." When most people in the U.S. think of Germany, these are the thoughts and the images that spring into their heads. But the world has changed dramatically since these events were ingrained in the American mind, and Germany has changed with it into a more open and racially and culturally diverse place, a place that no longer fits into American stereotypes and popular images.

92 words

AFTER

Hitler, The Holocaust, The Iron Curtain and President Reagan demanding "tear down this wall." When we think of Germany, these are the images we see. But the world has changed dramatically since these events were ingrained in the American mind, and Germany has changed with it into a more open and culturally diverse place, a place that no longer fits American stereotypes.

62 words

Surprise. When you see the two versions side by side, the shorter one actually looks more appealing. Readers don't get bogged down in details that repeat similar meanings ("cold war" and "iron curtain") or pairs of similar words ("thoughts and images"). And without the extras, ideas are clearer. This kind of cutting is normal process for experienced writers. In early drafts, freewriting and conversation, most of us use 20–30% more words than we need. Bernie's words showed what he knew and pushed his thinking forward. But readers don't need them and even experience them as obstacles.

Most social change writing has to be brief. Op-ed columns are around 700 words. Letters to the editor have a better chance if they're less than 50. Cover letters are no more than one page with plenty of white space. At the same time, all of them need to have deep thoughtful content, sometimes technical, never simplistic. Memos and newsletter or grant-related writing need to be so direct and simple that busy executives can read quickly and yet be touched by the complexities of the situation. Contrary to the common myth, even academic journal readers prefer things no longer than necessary. So cutting words to stay within expected limits without losing content is important.

Exercise

Space limitations.   What can you do to help Michael? His opinion column about SUVs, gas prices and fuel efficiency grew to nearly double the length limit. Michael was having fun with this column. He was trying to regain his playfulness with words, so he put in special touches that he suspected were too much. To have enough room for the factual part of his argument later in the column, he knew he had to cut one third to one half of his opening paragraph. Can you do the cutting for him without losing his key points? Try reading though first to appreciate what he's saying and underline the words and phrases that have power for you. Maybe you can save some of them, but cut as much as you can.

Michael's opening paragraph:

Each morning hordes of Americans begin their day with that wake-up cup of coffee from a nearby coffee house. With prices of coffee ranging from $1.50 to more than $3 for one cup, millions of people reach deep into their pockets and hardly blink their groggy eyes before throwing down their money in exchange for a hot cup of that rousing brew. Meanwhile, across the street at a local gas station, tempers flare as the cost of one gallon of gasoline gets closer and closer to the cost of one cup of Starbucks coffee. For owners of sports utility vehicles (SUVs) and other gas-guzzling vehicles, the reality of rising gas prices hits their wallets that much harder. (116 words)

Hint: When I tried this exercise, I brought the total word count down to 92. Then I tried again and got 74. I think the shortest version would be the most exciting to readers because it's dramatic and moves quickly. It offers one or two clever expressions rather than so many.

My version:

Millions of Americans begin their day with a rousing cup from their local coffee house. With coffee at $1.50 to over $3 a cup, few blink at throwing down their cash. Meanwhile, across the street at the gas station, tempers flare as the price of one gallon of gasoline rises closer and closer to the price of one cup of Starbucks. For owners of SUVs and other gas-guzzlers, rising gas prices hit much harder. (74 words)

Exercise

Sharing the load.   If you're trying to cut your own writing and can't see what words to let go, find someone to do it for you. Ask a friend or coworker to reduce your piece by one third without losing essential meaning. Ask him to use a green or purple rather than a red pen—on the theory that red pens make us feel more defensive—but ask him to be ruthless. When you look at the results, be prepared to see words and meanings lost that you were attached to. When this happened to me without my inviting it, some changes felt wrong but many were liberating! (See The Black Pen exercise in chapter four.)

The paramedic cutting tool

Another cutting technique, the "paramedic method," gets rid of "lard" in sentences that are overloaded or bureaucratic sounding. It's amazing

---

HIDDEN AGENDAS AND BIG WORDS

A surprising tool for cutting is awareness of your own hidden agendas. Years ago in a small business college, I used to team up with a management professor, John Lesko, to teach memo writing. Lesko was the perfect person for this because he had once stood in the students' shoes. He came from a Slovak immigrant family and was the first to go to college. There, he'd struggled to prove his intelligence by using the biggest words he could find. John had also worked for years in the business world. He knew that when you write a memo to your boss or someone else in your organization, people up and down the line will look at your writing style to evaluate you and your worth on the job.

John would tell how, as a young man, he'd been sure that the best way to create a good impression was to make his memos sound like a walking encyclopedia. He might be writing to explain parking rules, but his hidden agenda was always to promote himself. His first memos were lengthy and ornate until his company sent him to a writing class that taught the opposite approach. By trial and error, John learned to write so the messages, not the words, stood out. Much later, John reached his original goal when his teachers in a doctoral program admired the intelligent thinking they could see in his straightforward writing style.

how many of us write sentences like this without realizing it. The tool comes from Richard Lanham, an English professor, who points out that we naturally say, "Jim kicks Bill" or "Jim enjoys kicking Bill," not "Kicking Bill is an ongoing activity hugely enjoyed by Jim." Lanham calls sentences like this last one, "the official style." Usually they don't have an active verb—only an "is" word. Active sentences have a "kicker," a "kicking action," and sometimes a "kickee." Lanham's method locates words and phrases to cut from sentences like this:

This office is in need of a dynamic manager of sales.

First highlight all prepositions and all forms of *is/was/were*. These little words aren't bad in themselves, but a lot of them indicate there's "lard" in your writing.

This office is in need of a dynamic manager of sales.

Then look for the buried action. Ask yourself, "Who's kicking who?" and find a new way to say it, that makes the "kicker" and kicking action clear right away.

This office needs a new sales manager. (7 words, not 11)

The paramedic method alerts us to word habits connected with the lard indicators:

- **Filler expressions** like *in need of, feel like, in respect to.* Most have at least one preposition! Maybe you needed them while writing—but they slow readers down.

- **Buffer words.** You didn't feel confident enough to say, *we were wrong,* so you said, we *tended to make mistakes.*

- **Repeated words, phrases or ideas.** Sometimes repetition helps readers sum up or creates a rhythm that makes a point memor-

---

PARAMEDIC TERMS

Who's kicking who? *(Lanham's way of reminding us about active sentences. In formal grammar, it would be "Who's kicking whom?")*

Prepositions *(small words showing relationships)*

to, from, by, with, of, about, up, down, around, under, at, into, near (and more).

"Is"-words *(Forms of "to be." Verbs that don't show action).*

is, are, was, were, wasn't, weren't, have been, has been, will be, being (and more).

able, as in sermons, speeches or poetry. Do your repetitions help readers or are they a habit you aren't aware of?

- **Pairs of nearly identical words.** *Thoughts and images, promote and facilitate, growth and development,* are so close in meaning they can pile up in a sentence and create a sing-song effect. Each time, ask yourself if you really need two words.

Starting out with too many words doesn't mean you're a bad writer, but don't be surprised if cutting brings up emotion. You birthed these words and you may not want to let them go. Three things help me: (1) Keeping sentences I've cut in a special "parking lot" at the end of my draft (or in a separate computer document). They aren't gone for good, and maybe I'll decide to bring them back. (2) Listening to my writing group to discern whether those words really belong in the draft or not. (3) Getting in touch with the wonderful, light feeling that comes from cleaning out closets and getting rid of what I don't need. Cutting can become a joy when you know that, step by step, it's making your writing stronger.

Exercise

Practicing the paramedic method.   To feel the revolutionary impact of this tool you need to try it often, on others' writing and on your own. Three possibilities:

(1) This sentence from a research paper draft:

The democratic model of health education is an integrative approach, which involves the youth not just as recipients of adult-developed health education learning materials but as the developers of the materials. Developing the materials becomes the educational process from which health-related information (facts and skills) is acquired and incorporated into the daily lives of youth. (55 words)

(2) A paragraph you find in your reading.

(3) A paragraph of your own writing. Choose something that feels dense and awkward but you aren't sure why. Or maybe there's something you intentionally wrote in the "official style:" a request for funding, a letter to your landlord or the city manager. Very often we pick up the "official style" when we're trying to sound more powerful than we feel. Unfortunately it can backfire and have the opposite effect!

A shorter version of (1)
In the democratic model of health education, youth develop their own learning materials rather than simply receiving adult-developed materials. This way they acquire health-related facts and skills, which they incorporate into their daily lives. (34 words)

The noun habit

Using the paramedic or any cutting tool shows how "lard" combines with two related word habits that are hard to break: thinking in nouns and hiding in passive verbs.

Let's start with the nouns. Here's a sentence about a community development corporation that's meant to inspire action for social change. Instead it has so many "lard" indicators it bogs the reader down:

> A primary _aim_ of Urban Edge is the _facilitation_ of tenant _control_ and ultimate _ownership_ of the property. (18 words)

When you look closely, the sentence also has a lot of nouns, and the underlined ones are nouns that could be verbs. There's a lot of hidden potential for kicking here. So what happens when you ask, "Who's kicking who?" and put a kicker in charge of the kicking?

> Urban Edge facilitates tenant _control_ and ultimate _ownership_ of the property. (11 words)

This is better. The community organization is now the kicker and you have freed some action in the nouns. The sentence sounds more natural. But there's a way to make it even shorter and more active. There's an important actor that hasn't become a kicker yet—the tenants!

> Urban Edge helps tenants own and control property. (8 words)

Now the tenants are actors too! They "own" and "control." And the organization's empowering goal is reflected in the new sentence structure. Ideas get energetic when you move beyond the noun habit. This is word-power.

The passive verb habit

Even though we want our writing to undo silence and inspire action, we sometimes use passive verbs just like the bureaucrats. A student named Evelyn helped me understand this back in the 1980s while writing about a California town called Orange Cove. Evelyn's work traced farmworker organizing there in the late 1970s, showing how local people intuitively followed successful strategies. Most of the time she wrote with active verbs, but in one paragraph, she slipped into bureaucratic-sounding verbs:

> By 1978, a more sophisticated strategy was mapped out to elect three Council members. A massive registration campaign was launched to recruit new voters who had never exercised their privilege and youth who had turned voting age. Mass meetings were organized to introduce the candidates and expose the issues. A base had already been established

through the direct action strategies. The results <u>were</u> victories: Mayor Victor Lopez, Councilman Roy Rodriguez, and Councilman Olegario Villarreal <u>were each elected</u> to serve four years. (81 words)

The underlined words are all "is" verbs associated with lard. They don't show kickers kicking. This means they are "passive verbs" with no real actor. They show only passive action, "a strategy was mapped out," instead of direct action, "the community mapped out a strategy."

EXACTLY WHAT IS A PASSIVE VERB?

Active and passive verbs offer two ways to say nearly the same thing. Active verbs put the "kicking" action directly. Passive verbs use is/was/be and state the action as a noun or adjective. Because we don't know who the kicker is unless we add a preposition like "by," passive verbs hide responsibility for an action.

Active verbs	Passive verbs
You decided. The group decided.	It was decided. A decision was made.
Eight out of nine members of our city council decided.	It was decided by the group.
We concluded.	A conclusion was reached.
The group concluded.	A conclusion was reached by the group.
A bomb killed him.	He was killed.
Quick & easy to understand	*Slower, "a lot of big words"*
Upbeat, positive, energetic	*Harder to understand*
Makes the kicker/doer clear	*Dull-sounding*
Responsibility is clear	*Can conceal the kicker/doer*
	Who is responsible?

Evelyn told me she had lived all her life in Orange Cove and her family was part of the mobilization she was describing. She wanted the community and its leaders to stand out as powerful actors. Honoring them was her whole point in writing, so she was shocked at how her language in this one paragraph had disempowered them. Why? She was fluent in Spanish, which uses more passives than English, but there was another possibility. She had worked in City Hall before graduate school. Maybe she had picked up some bureaucratic writing habits? City governments have a different culture from the world of organizing. You don't say things that rock the boat. At City Hall she was used to seeing and writing: *The election was conducted. It was decided.*

Few of us talk in passive verbs. They only come up when we're trying to sound like others or to hide thoughts we don't feel safe expressing openly. And they can become a habit that hides our belief and commitment. Sometimes there's a legitimate use for them, but finding a way to change most passives into active verbs can make writing more readable and our voices more effective.

Exercise

Passive verbs can become a habit that hides our belief and commitment.

Writing with active verbs.

(1) First, change as many of Evelyn's verbs as you can to active ones. (Hint: This will also shorten her paragraph by at least ten words.)

(2) Then do the same thing with the following paragraph from a health researcher in Albuquerque, New Mexico. (Hint: You can easily cut about 15 words.)

In New Mexico, billboards promoting alcohol consumption were eliminated as a result of the work of mid-school students. The billboards were visible by students at the Pojoaque Middle School and three students decided to voice their concerns and take action. A petition was circulated and over 260 signatures were collected. Then the owner of the billboard was contacted. His response was an apology and a replacement of the beer ad with a "Stay in School" ad. (76 words)

(3) Finally, look through your own writing for something with a lot of passive verbs—perhaps it's a paper where you were trying to sound scientific or a letter where you didn't feel comfortable speaking directly. See if you can find and transform passive verbs, and feel free to make any other improvements. In each case, read the before and after versions out loud to see which sounds more natural.

The myth of the short sentence

Whatever your high school English teacher may have said, there is no correct length for a sentence. It's the clear structure of a sentence that makes it work, not the length. Some thoughts take longer to express. Others don't. A balance between short and long seems to work for readers. Artificial cut-offs for sentence length can create a choppy effect and confusion. If you're keeping things as simple as possible, you won't have to worry about over-long sentences because whatever's too much for a reader will get shortened. And choppy, short sentences can be combined for impact and versatility. Experiment with different ways to say something. When you get good at moving things around in sentences, you'll build a storehouse of sentence forms you can pull from.

Exercise   **How many different ways can you say it?**   Just for fun, as you learn the acrobatics of sentence revision, see if you can rephrase this sentence at least three different ways. Try moving words around, putting different ideas first and using simpler words. Use any techniques you've learned so far in this chapter.

> Since the early 1990s, collaboration has become a standard in community development funding circles—either as a mandate or as a strongly encouraged approach. (24 words)

Each version you try will have a different emphasis and might play a different role in the paragraph it comes from. Your versions may not be better than the original, but they are helping you build your sentence options.

Some possibilities:

Since the early 1990s, community development funding circles have encouraged, and sometimes mandated, collaboration. (Active verbs; 14 words)

For the past fifteen years, community development funders have encouraged, or even required, collaboration. (14 words)

Starting in the early 1990s, funders began to mandate, or at least encourage, collaboration in community development projects. (17 words)

Community development funders began, in the early 1990s, to stress the benefits of collaboration. (14 words)

Learning from the cutting tools

Now you have a range of tools for "keeping it simple." You can just plunge in and cut, you can use the paramedic tool, or you can focus on nouns and passive verbs. Any of these approaches will make your ideas more accessible to readers, even mixed audiences--like community people, politicians and engineers—who will all read the same report. Readers at all levels appreciate simplicity. Politicians can easily get lost in technical language, and even the engineers appreciate a clear, quick read.

Linking and Transitions

In every workshop people ask how to link ideas without jumping around. Making connections is one of our most important skills, but the logical groundwork begins when you organize and strategize. No last minute editing, no clever use of transition words, can link ideas that aren't related in the first place. However, good editing can help readers follow your ideas. The principle is to move from the familiar to the unfamiliar, from a thought you've explained to a new, unfamiliar thought.

The classic pattern of linking—"theme" and "rheme"

The pattern shows up in basic sentence "flow." Each sentence starts with a familiar thought then adds a new unfamiliar one. The next sentence echoes the previous new thought and adds a still newer one, linking things one by one down the page. Chapter two highlighted Betty's columns on racial issues. Her writing is a moving illustration of the classic linking pattern:

> Now, I wept, remembering the genocide of the Africans. Everything in our cultural environment fosters forgetfulness of the roots of the African American experience in this country and the unforgiven ravages of slavery and legalized mistreatment. Before a community can heal the deep hurts that divide us, it must forgive. Before people can forgive, they must remember.   —Betty Burkes, *Cape Cod Times*, July 1991

Linguists have some helpful terminology for this pattern. They call the familiar thought the "theme" and the new thought the "rheme." In sentence flow, a thought that was new in one sentence ("rheme") comes up again as the familiar "theme" of the next sentence—weaving a sequence.

> Now I wept, remembering the genocide of the Africans (**new rheme**). Everything in our cultural environment fosters forgetfulness of the roots (**repeated theme**) of the African-American experience in this country and the unforgiven ravages of slavery and legalized mistreatment (**new rheme**). Before a community can heal the deep hurts (**theme**) that divide us, it must forgive (**rheme**). Before people can forgive (**theme**), they must remember (**rheme**).

Probably without even thinking about it, Betty moves readers forward from the familiar to the unfamiliar, from theme to rheme. And this paragraph has a special twist: the final rheme ("remember") is not totally new but also echoes the beginning of the paragraph, giving a circular pattern to the flow.

We don't always need every idea repeated. But if the links aren't obvious, readers get lost, not only from one sentence to the next but also from paragraph to paragraph. The theme-to-rheme flow of ideas helps writers carve a path from point A to point B without confusing readers. The pattern feels comfortable and natural to English-speakers (although some other languages link ideas differently).

Exercise   **Linking ideas with theme and rheme**   Take two paragraphs of your own writing—one that seems to flow naturally and one that was difficult to write and still feels rough. Sentence by sentence, highlight the theme in one color and the rheme in a second color. (The colors will shift from sentence to sentence as the rheme of one sentence becomes the theme of the next.) Does one of the paragraphs more naturally follow the classic pattern? Notice where the pattern breaks down and see if you can move things around to make the links for readers.

Exercise | **Linking paragraphs**   Choose a short article you have read that seemed to flow well, and examine how the paragraphs are linked. Usually you'll find that each one begins with a word or phrase echoing the theme of the previous paragraph. Try highlighting the main theme and main rheme that link paragraph to paragraph, just as you did for sentence linking. Sometimes a paragraph links back to a theme mentioned much earlier, but often you find the same sequence of links we saw from sentence to sentence.

Grammar is Power

A few years ago Martha, who was a poet and a community leader, told me she lived every day of her life with a demon called "grammar fear." Martha speaks eloquently for many people who think they need a rigorous course in grammar in order to trust themselves as writers. Many found grammar a major silencer during childhood schooling—a system of rules, "right" and "wrong" ways of using language, which we could never master. But linguists tell us something very encouraging: by the time we're four years old, all of us have learned the underlying structure of our language (even when caregivers don't speak it perfectly). Even when we can't tell you the rules, we understand a lot intuitively. We should. We created our language over centuries of simply using it with each other. Grammar is far more than the answers we were supposed to give in school. It's the underlying logical system for expressing connections that has evolved as we have. It is already ours, and it offers choices and alternatives for saying just about anything.

Remember Timothy, whose inner-city teachers made fun of his language and ended his youthful dreams of writing poetry? Timothy was so terrified of making mistakes that he deliberately dumbed down his college writing to elementary school level, severely restricting his ability to use his intellect. At one point Timothy asked me for feedback on some freewriting about his grammar fear—completely uncensored, uncorrected writing. I had to tell him that, as far as I could see, this piece of writing had nothing in it that you could call a mistake. Timothy was amazed. Like most people, his natural understanding of the language took over when he wrote freely and spontaneously.

> **Most of us know more than we think.**

Most of us know more than we think. We live in a world where spoken language often differs from written language. So it's not surprising that there's confusion about how writing is supposed to look. And, because we all fear mistakes, many people react by "hyper-correcting," going overboard with imagined corrections that actually make the writing harder to read. Moving beyond anxiety about grammar—and learning that there is flexibility and choice involved—can be a real source of power.

By practicing the cutting tools, you have already revisited the basics of sentence structure—nouns and verbs. This grammar section looks at the three problems that people have raised most often in my workshops—punctuation, pronouns and spelling. If you too have questions on these issues, here's a start on finding answers.

Punctuation, especially commas. *Why do people disagree about commas? Can we put them where we pause in speaking, or is there a better way?*

Some books list 18 or 20 comma rules, but without understanding the underlying principles, no one remembers those rules, and supervisors, editors and even teachers, disagree about them. If you're confused, there's good reason.

There are problems with putting commas wherever you would pause in speaking. The whole point of commas is to establish a consistent, logical signal system for linking ideas—and readers can get really confused if that system isn't there. Unfortunately, speakers time their pauses differently depending on regional, cultural and personal ways of talking. We can't depend on the pause instinct for a consistent signal system. A more reliable guide comes from the most streamlined of all the books on grammar: *The Elements of Style* by William Strunk and E. B. White. This book clarifies three uses for commas: listing, parenthetical expressions and joining full sentences.

Here are some illustrations from writing by Sue, an environmental activist who wants more people to install "green roofs" in order to save on fossil fuel costs by putting soil and plants on their roof.

Lists	*Green roofs can reduce noise pollution, clean the air of dust and toxins, and add to our enjoyment of recreational space.*
Parenthetical expressions	*Chicago's city hall, thanks to a large green roof, will save up to $5,000 a year in heating and cooling costs.*
Joining full sentences with and, but, or, so	*Green roofs alone will not solve all our environmental problems, but they are a realistic investment in the future health of our environment.*

New writers get confused when the first comma rule (for lists) varies slightly from one publication to another. You may see commas before the "and," but you may not. Strunk and White insist that commas should always come before the "and." This way, if a list is complicated and easy to misunderstand, the sentence will always be clear. But, in simple, straight-forward lists, some publications leave that final comma out. Even though confusing, this variation shows perfectly how grammar rules are always subject to change.

What doesn't change is the logic behind the punctuation, and that's what will help you avoid confusion. The three comma uses are really three kinds of logical linking within a sentence. They are easy to remember and can help writers understand other punctuation and grammar as you get to know them. If a sentence feels confusing, and you're tempted to punctuate in some way not covered here, the safest thing is to rewrite so you can use one of these principles. Use your word-power skills to express your idea in a different way. Gradually, you'll become more aware of the logic of our language so you can create sentences that won't trip readers up.

Pronouns. *Using "they," "this," and "it" seems to confuse people, and how do I use "he" and "she" without someone saying I'm sexist?*

Pronouns stand in for longer words, mostly nouns. There are many kinds, but all are short cuts—so we don't have to repeat the cumbersome nouns over and over. But a short cut that works for the writer also has to work for the reader. In speaking we can visually check whether people are following our short cuts; in writing we need to look at our words through readers' eyes.

They and them. Alma was upset about "brownfields"—those deeply polluted vacant lands in urban neighborhoods where toxic industries once stood. She decided to put what she knew about them into a community guide so local residents could play a role in decision-making. She wanted this writing to be very accessible, so she used pronouns like *they* and *them* to keep it simple. But the pronouns in her mad draft turned out to be hard for readers to follow:

Who is at fault, the local residents? No usually <u>they</u> are businesses. However the people who suffer from <u>them</u> are brown and/or poor. <u>They</u> do not have political clout and are ignored by the rest of the world.

The last pronoun was the only one readers could even guess at—*they* must be *the people* from the previous sentence. We intuitively know a pronoun stands for something just mentioned or for a noun at the beginning of the previous sentence. Our intuition doesn't work on the other pronouns, so Alma's short cuts don't work for readers. The "fix" means looking back at a longer segment of the writing, and it won't be simple substitution of nouns for pronouns. It's going to take some of that acrobatic ability to say things a different way.

Exercise

Alma's pronouns.   For practice, try two ways of rephrasing Alma's sentences so they are clear and at the same time engaging for community readers. Read each version aloud to be sure it works.

Two possibilities

Are local residents at fault? No, usually businesses are responsible for brownfields. But the people who suffer from them are brown and poor. They do not have political clout and are ignored by the rest of the world.

Who's at fault, the local residents? No, usually businesses bear responsibility. However the people who suffer from brownfields are brown and poor. They do not have political clout and are ignored by the rest of the world.

Similar techniques work with *this, these,* and *it,* so if you use these pronouns a lot, check to see if readers will be able to follow. Sometimes you'll find that you need to clarify for yourself exactly what *it* or *this* means!

She, he, and they. As in many languages, English privileges the male pronoun. Grammar books once told writers to use *he, him, his* for any person, male or female. But as our awareness of gender and equality evolved, many felt the traditional use of male pronouns reinforced the stereotype of men as movers and shakers ("kickers") and left women out of the action. In my lifetime, consciousness and the language have grown more inclusive. But big changes take time to reach everyone. For these pronouns, think about your audience and your purposes. Is this the time and place to raise consciousness about gender, and how hard can you push? Consider your options and choose a strategy; explain it to your readers if needed and follow it consistently throughout a piece of writing. Here are some strategies you'll see other writers choosing:

(1) **Use plurals and other phrasing.** In English *they, them* and *their* do not call attention to gender. But the matching noun has to be plural too. "*Everyone* has *their* own solution" doesn't work. Try "*People* have *their* own solutions" or "Everyone has a different solution."

(2) **Alternate between male and female pronouns.** Respected authors began to do this in the 1980s, writing one chapter with male and the next with female pronouns. Others shift pronouns with each new example. Caution: if you shift at random or from sentence to sentence, you risk confusing readers.

(3) Provide options each time, like *he/she, his/her, s/he, he or she.* This was an early response when the dilemma first surfaced in the 1970s, but it isn't very reader-friendly. Many gatekeepers criticize the awkward, long-winded expressions, although they may be just right for some audiences.

(4) Use only female pronouns (or only male). Depending on your audience and purpose, using only feminine pronouns may be just the right choice. If your audience is mostly women, you may raise self-esteem, helping readers recover from the long silence. Feminine pronouns can also help mixed audiences rethink their assumptions about gender, if that's consistent with your purpose in writing and not a distraction. I sometimes see current authors using all male pronouns, usually with an explanation or a footnote about their choice. (I have to admit this strategy pushes my buttons and I have to put a lot of energy into trying to ignore the author's writing style.)

(5) While you're at it, look for other gender-neutral expressions like *chairperson, chair* and *head.* How can you avoid a blatant expression like *man-hours* (especially if you're discussing women's work)?

A SOUTH AFRICAN'S VIEW OF *I* AND *ME*

Bobby, one of my first South African friends, raised an important question about the personal pronouns *I* and *me.* As a teacher, I was urging people to take responsibility for their ideas by using first person pronouns: *I discovered* instead of *it was discovered.* Bobby said there would be a problem with my suggestions in post-apartheid South Africa. "In the U.S.," he said, "there's a lot of *I* and *me.* Everything is personalized. At home that's considered arrogant. We don't put ourselves forward as individuals like that. Our whole social movement is about sharing, about the group. It is very hard for me to use *I* instead of a passive verb."

Afterwards I thought a lot about this conversation. My first reaction was why not *we*? The first person plural is also more powerful than the passive: *We discovered.* So there are alternatives for the South Africans. But what about us in the U.S.? Holding up the mirror, yes, maybe North Americans do use our pronouns in a pushy, self-absorbed way: me, me, me, me, me. We've been told over and over to leave ourselves out of it. But we've also been told that the individual is all-important. In reacting to our silencing maybe we sometimes go too far. This is one of those places where a simple thing like pronoun choice carries a deep lesson. How do we express our agency as human beings without crossing over into arrogance? The key is to remember that we have choices. There are always more than one or even two ways to say something.

Spelling. *How do we look up a word if we don't already know how to spell it? Spell-check and the dictionary just get me more confused. And how important is spelling, really?*

Spelling isn't consistently logical in English like it is in Spanish. I know people—from factory shop stewards to college professors—who carry pocket dictionaries at all times, just in case. I've seen graduate students misspelling half the words on a page. And many of us have a mild form of dyslexia, which means we perceive letters in reverse order, like children just learning to write. Many of us were silenced, even shamed, over spelling as children. If spelling is your concern, you're not alone—and there is hope.

There are reasons for the problem. Rules for spelling are fairly new. Before the printing press, hand-copied manuscripts had a rich variety of spellings. And the ones that eventually became correct didn't follow principles. Nevertheless, spelling became a class marker and an excuse for discrimination and exclusion. Today, regional and national spellings vary, across the Canadian border and between Britain and the U.S. And popular media add confusion with deliberate misspellings in ads. Many of us would prefer not to make too big a deal out of spelling, but variations can confuse communication.

My own view is that anything we do to deepen our understanding and connection with words is empowering. Knowing why a word is spelled a certain way strengthens our relationship with that word so we can use it with more precision. This, in itself, is good reason to pay attention to spelling.

No one spells everything wrong: problems fall into limited areas. Learning what those areas are for you, and working on them one at a time, can change your spelling significantly. Are there half a dozen words you always misspell? If so, post a reminder list in your writing space. Seeing the words written correctly begins to reprogram your habit. Are most of your errors the kind spell-check doesn't catch, like *there* instead of *their* or *effect* for *affect*? Again, keep a list and double-check these words while you're editing. To learn what your patterns are, friends can help if you remain proactive and don't let them simply correct mistakes. Instead ask them to identify mistakes, so you can ask questions and learn. Do you have a high quality dictionary that will tell you the history and uses of a word along with the spelling? If so, explore it.

More awareness, a greater degree of collaboration with friends, and more thorough use of dictionaries and spellcheckers will slowly begin to make a difference. Your spelling habits won't change overnight. But as you change them, remember to keep the struggle to spell separate from the struggle to think and write. Spell any way you want when you're

> *Anything we do to deepen our understanding and connection with words is empowering.*

freewriting. Don't let your spelling silence you as a thinker, writer, or social change agent.

Exercise

Customizing your own editing checklist   To pull the work on grammar together, I invite you to become your own teacher. Look over a recent piece of writing with grammar and spelling in mind. If anyone has edited your work recently, keep that person's concerns in mind too. Now create a master checklist of your own problem areas. Include specific types of spelling mistakes, commas, pronouns, and stylistic issues like passive verbs and long-winded sentences. You might want to add things covered in other chapters like unexplained code words or paragraph structure. Include everything you need to consider in reviewing drafts. Once your list is complete, re-organize it, clustering similar issues and arranging in order of importance. If there are items you don't fully understand, spend some time researching them with resources listed at the end of the book. Keep your list handy and check it each time you review a draft. Awareness brings change. Over time, you'll be able to cross some problems off your list.

High-Energy Language

People often worry that their writing sounds boring. They imagine that other people's words have more life and energy while theirs are dull. My first suggestion is to check it out. Writers don't realize the power their words have for others, particularly if strong internal judges are at work. A feedback group or a friend reading your draft may find the writing exciting. And the cutting tool can make a huge difference. Getting rid of unneeded words gives your best ideas room to shine. Of course it helps to read other authors whose words you admire and keep widening the frontiers of your vocabulary. But there are two other important ways to strengthen your language: focusing on detail instead of vague code words and going back to the roots of your power with words.

Use detail—"Show don't tell"

In feedback groups, readers resonate with the most specific words, words that show the reality rather than just telling about it. Phrases like "Salvadorans wearing bright scarves" and "signs in twelve languages" show us the crowd at a rally. Words like "diverse" and "multi-cultural" are "code" words that merely tell us what the writer thought, without helping us imagine the real situation. Numbers are specific detail too. I'm shocked if I read that asthma rates for children went up 74 percent. That's huge.

The power of numbers—and all detail—depends on including just the right amount, not too little, but not too much. In some cultures, people are willing to listen to details just because they respect a writer. But readers in our culture are easily bored: they're looking for the significant details, and they want to find them quickly. Detail gains its power by connecting with the point you're making. In her writing about green roofs, Sue put together just the right facts and figures to support her argument that energy-saving gardens on our rooftops will pay for themselves:

> An investment in green roofs will pay for itself many times over. For starters a roof will last two to three times longer because soil and plants will protect it from intense UV degradation and continued expansion and contraction due to fluctuating temperatures. Conventional roofs have to be replaced every 15 to 20 years. In contrast, green roofs in Germany last 40 years without needing to be replaced, and in this country the Rockefeller Center's green roof, which was created in the mid-1930s, is still intact.

Metaphors that come up in freewriting can also boost the energy of your language. Since metaphors play a role in nearly every tool in the kit, your comfort with them and your ability to find them will grow as you work with all the tools. As with detail, freewriting and first drafts may have much more than you need, but it's much easier to cut in the final stages than to come up with new energy at the end.

Finding the source of powerful language

Undoing silence is about going deeply inside ourselves to find the power with words that is in all of us. Our source of power can be in family or belief systems; it can trace back to passions we felt as children; it can be rooted in dramatic experiences or in dreams. Dictionaries and vocabulary building play only a small role in finding power with words. The real energy comes from connecting with our most authentic voice.

In the mid 1980s I met a remarkable communicator named Linda Stout. Linda's background was very different from what surrounded me at that time. She was southern, low-income and white, and she was an ardent, accomplished peace organizer. I was fascinated with how Linda's stories and analytical expression reached across cultural barriers, so I organized speaking engagements for her in the Boston area, including one at MIT where I was teaching. I didn't think about how hard it might

Dictionaries and vocabulary building play only a small role in finding power with words. The real energy comes from connecting with our most authentic voice.

have been for Linda, coming to our seminar from a community of tenant farmers and factory workers in North Carolina, but as I expected, she was a big hit at MIT.

Later Linda published a book called *Bridging the Class Divide* about building a movement without the barriers of race and class. In a section on the "invisible wall" of language, she shows how her low-income community was excluded by the vocabulary of a college-educated peace movement, where words like "strategy" were more respected than words like "plan." To work across the divide, people like herself had to be bi-lingual, with all the difficulties of speaking in what she called a "language outside their own." As she tells readers, "When I am having trouble translating what I want to say into language that is acceptable to another person, I have a much harder time speaking powerfully and with self-assurance." This is the root feeling of silencing.

Linda tells of plans to develop educational flyers for low-income communities and how a well-known anti-nuclear activist suggested the technical language she could use in a grant proposal to fund this project. But when Linda sat down to write the proposal in the suggested language, she "went crazy."

> I spent a week on the proposal, usually in tears. So finally, I just ripped it up and rewrote the whole proposal in my own language. I wrote a cover note saying that we're always asked to use technical language, but that frankly this is not the way we talk.... If we did talk...using this language, we wouldn't get any response in our community. "I'm sorry," I wrote, "but if using this language is a requirement to get the funding then we can't get it."

Linda mailed the proposal in her own words and got the money, the largest grant her organization had ever received! Her most persuasive language came directly from the words she heard and spoke every day in her community, not from poring over a dictionary or a thesaurus or imitating what she saw in other proposals.

Later, peace groups in wealthy communities across the country used the flyers Linda's group had developed and found them more effective than anything written for college-educated readers. Why do we think we need technical jargon, complex words and long sentences? Linda's advice to all activists is at the heart of this chapter: "'Simplify the message.' This is not about lowering standards, it is about communication." If you're looking for models, look for moving communicators like Linda. Look to the speaking and writing that comes from the labor movement, the women's movement, the environmental justice movement.

Formal and informal grammar

Many ask about how to choose the right level of formality for a writing project. It's often fine to use informal expressions like *OK* or *won't* for *will not*—even in newsletters or communications with funding organizations. If you do it with awareness, you can even break some of Strunk and White's rules. But how to know what's appropriate when? Talking to colleagues or looking into the files at your workplace will show the levels of style people have used in the past and suggest what readers will be expecting. Ask to see other grant applications or articles; read the guidelines that magazines and journals give their writers. But keep in mind the enormous weight of bureaucratic habit in others' writing. You may find a lot of passive verbs and stuffy, hard-to-read sentences. Remember that you can help to shift these norms by writing in a more informal, natural style like Linda's. That, in itself, is social change.

Exercise

Back to the roots to re-energize language   Freewriting with passion can help you find energy, detail and word-power—especially with a prompt to get you going. Choose one or two that appeal (or invent your own) and freewrite to explore whatever comes up. Don't worry if you think you're going off the subject or not passionate enough. Keep seeking that free state where words come spontaneously.

1. When I first got involved with this subject, I saw/heard/felt/wondered

   _____

2. My/Our community would put it this way: _____

3. The reason I know people want to hear about this is _____

4. The person who's most against this whole thing would say _____

5. If I were describing all this to children 20 years from now, I'd tell them

   _____

6. If I had a chance to talk about this to the person who most influenced my thinking on this subject, I'd say _____

Or stimulate word-power by discussing (or arguing) with people who also feel passionate about your subject. Or take time out for music, a film or reading that nourishes your heart and your thinking.

Recognizing your power with words

Your writing gains by looking back at what you wrote with the eyes of readers. We need this final period of reflection—and often of cutting and wrestling with sentences—to bring out the full power of our voices. Linda

Stout summed this up well with her testimony to the effectiveness of the voices we are most comfortable using. Where habits cause writing to sound unnatural—like writing in nouns or using passive verbs—we need to figure out where these habits come from and whom they serve. Most importantly, we need to have confidence that our ideas are important. Revered economist, statesman, Harvard professor and prolific writer John Kenneth Galbraith revised his writing often. At 97, not long before his death, I heard him assure one of his grandchildren: "When you are revising a manuscript, as all writers must do, don't worry about the style or grammar. They will be alright. Be concerned only with the clarity of the ideas that you have propounded. They are what count. They are why you have written."

There is truth in this for all of us. As soon as you start to feel confidence and a sense of power over ideas, you will almost automatically begin to use more powerful language. Then working through revisions and finding new ways to say things will become not a fearful task but a creative activity, a true craft.

CHAPTER NINE

"Lift Every Voice"

Getting active with writing

Lift every voice and sing, let earth and Heaven ring
Ring with the harmonies of liberty.
Let our rejoicing rise, high as the listening skies.
Let it resound loud as the rolling sea
    —"The Black National Anthem, " James Weldon Johnson, 1921

Celebrating the long struggle for justice, respect and true security, this stirring anthem is dear to generations of African Americans. But growing up white, I never heard it. When I first heard "Lift Every Voice" in the 1980s—working with Mel King and the Community Fellows Program at MIT—I saw powerful African American activism as a path for all of us. Since then, I've sung this song in many places, often with tears in my throat, because I know the struggle is mine too. Just as Hurricane Katrina made racism visible to Americans, so have wars, official lies and melting ice caps made clear that great systemic wrongs surround us. More of us understand, and this means there are more opportunities for everyday citizens to play a role. The writing tools can help, but we urgently need louder, more concerted voices. Can we lift our voices together? Can we sing as we claim our communities, our country and our planet?

It is very hard to lift your voice alone. As a yoga teacher for many years, I've struggled with chanting, the voice part of this ancient Asian discipline that the western world has reduced to trendy stretching. I used to groan inwardly when a teacher would say, "We're going to chant the *Om* sound all together three times." The voices around me sounded weak or forced, rising up timidly from scattered parts of the room, and my own voice felt unreal, untrue. I never asked my students to try chanting, even though the ancient *Om* sound is supposed to stir deep healing energies for human and planetary well-being. It always seemed like we westerners were trying too hard, forcing sound to come from a place that was individualistic, too shallow for resonant, powerful voice.

Then one time I was in a yoga class of maybe 50 to 100 people in a huge hall. There was nothing forced about it. We sat quietly with our eyes closed, focusing on the hum of life inside ourselves. Then, with our mouths closed, we began to hum in sync with our inner humming. Quietly, I started to feel just the vibrations of my voice, without audible sound. Still keeping our mouths closed, we allowed our humming to grow louder. Just as I began to hear my own sound, we were invited to open our mouths and let our voices join with each other. Slowly, humming voices of all kinds, at all pitches, started to sound and merge, and the volume began to rise. Confidence seemed to grow as we joined with other voices. Some—maybe even mine—began to soar lower or higher than we had begun. There were roaring sounds and croaking sounds and soft musical sounds and deep throaty rumbles. All of us were humming our separate notes, but we had also become one big, resonant, powerful *Om* sound. And the resonance kept growing. Even when I stopped humming to breathe, the sound covered it. All of us humming together held the space.

This is what I think it means to "lift every voice." Every one of us has our own way to increase, amplify, and reach out, separately and together. No one is alone. Our voices strengthen and cover for each other, whatever the power of silence around us.

Now the silences of injustice, war, big money and unresponsive government surround us. No one of us is alone in our concern for the earth and other humans. How can we lift our voices more powerfully together? We can write with the six tools, but how do we motivate ourselves to sit down and use them? I have four suggestions:

- Find subjects we're passionate about.
- Balance urgency and joy.
- Seek out all the small and larger ways to go public with our writing.
- Find supportive community.

Finding subjects we're passionate about

In 1964, Ken was a young architecture student, barely 20. He was on his way to lunch when he noticed a cluster of other students sitting on the ground around a police car parked on the public plaza of the Berkeley campus. "Oh cool! It's a demonstration," he remembers thinking to himself as he instinctively plopped down onto the pavement with the growing crowd. Ken was unusual. From a conservative background in the Southwest, his prior experience was right-wing political campaigns for law and order, not demonstrations. But something drew him into this historic drama. He soon learned that the police car held a former student arrested for distributing literature on free speech, and that passersby like himself had sat down to immobilize the intruding car. Sitting together over the next 36 hours, discussing the issues with those around him—left, right and center—Ken's views would shift. He would emerge from the Berkeley Free Speech Movement with a new vision of social justice that would shape a lifetime of high-energy work.

We didn't connect around that police car, but I got to know Ken Geiser in the 1980s when we were both teaching at Tufts University near Boston. Ken's passions had led him from architecture into policy. He worked with environmental groups like Greenpeace and Clean Water Action that mobilized citizen efforts. In the growing awareness of massive, industrial poisoning of low-income communities, he and his students broke the story that became the film, *A Civil Action*. Ken's interests spanned occupational health and labor, and we once co-wrote a letter to the editor about a big paper-workers' strike in Maine. Soon he was writing a major book on the toxic materials that ground our entire modern way of life and what we can do to use chemicals less destructively.

Journalists now refer to Ken as a "guru in the field of toxics use reduction." He heads institutes, serves on UN committees and speaks internationally—all of which require writing. Besides his incredible enthusiasm for this work, what impresses me about Ken is his ability to communicate the risk of untested chemicals to all kinds of audiences, from neighbors and Greenpeace activists to diplomats and industrialists. He's been able to convince manufacturers it's in their interests to use less dangerous chemicals in production. And now entire institutes and international programs have taken up his mission. Ken's path is unusual, but his passion is catchy, like the Free Speech atmosphere around the police car. It's something we can cultivate in our own ways once we get started.

Amy Goodman, from the alternative news program, Democracy Now, says writers need to go where the silences are, and some of these missions are very dramatic. Besides covering unreported news stories on her program every day, Amy, herself, went to East Timor where she witnessed a genocidal massacre in the 1990s. Jim Harney, the former priest mentioned in chapter two, traveled often to El Salvador to document repression and creative resistance in the 1980s. Now he writes about the other awakening countries of Latin America. One friend has gone to Haifa and to Gaza where the world ignores brutal violations of

Ken's path is unusual, but his passion is catchy, like the Free Speech atmosphere around the police car.

human rights. Another writes about families he has "adopted" in Iraq. But places of silence also call to us in our own backyards—vacant lots filled with toxins that could be made safe for affordable housing, community gardens responding to early signs of climate change, local youth programs that are being defunded. Mel King is now lifting his voice to write about the vibrancy of city streets. My friends on the Cambridge Peace Commission are writing monthly newspaper columns to share news of small and larger actions for peace by local citizens. Taken together these voices and actions form what another visionary, Joanna Macy, calls "the great turning"—a complete change in our unwise values, policies and way of life. Citizen effort is already making a difference.

Tragically, media silence covers up the most exciting voices for social change. Author and activist Frances Moore Lappé, whose ideas about fear helped explain silencing earlier in this book, has spent decades uncovering grassroots citizens' efforts to retrieve democracy—in all regions of this country. Her book, *Democracy's Edge,* chronicles hundreds of small and larger groups chipping away at needs like clean elections, clean water, economic equality and food security—efforts that cross the borders of red and blue states. As Lappé says, "It's a paradoxical time. Striking examples of the power of organized citizens' influence are emerging even as channels narrow for citizens' voices in shaping public policies." Writing keeps all this effort afloat: writing that shares new ideas and enthusiasms; writing that exposes and links the problems; writing that mobilizes others and helps organizations do their work. Lappé builds a convincing picture that citizen effort makes a difference. Finding where you feel passionately about some part this work is the starting place.

Exercise

What are your passions?　If you had time and no conflicting responsibilities, what are the silences you would be drawn to look into and write about? Start free-listing the possibilities and don't stop until you have at least ten items on your list. Be intuitive, not realistic. Anything that comes to mind goes on this list, grand or humble—biological and nuclear weapons, military recruiting, race and class tensions in your workplace, the vacant lots you played in as a child, the grand sugar maple trees of the Northeast that may not make it through the shortening winters. As your list grows freer from self-censorship, you may find yourself listing twenty or thirty items! Now choose the three that grab you most intensely, even if they're wildly unrealistic, and spend some time freewriting about the appeal of each one. If you are finding and stirring your passions, feel free to add ideas that come up about what form your writing might take, perhaps a letter to Congress, a short story for your neighborhood paper, a proposal for an event to bring people together around an issue of concern.

Balancing urgency and joy

This book puts a lot of emphasis on writing that responds to an urgent need—raising money for your cause, stopping a war, restoring democracy through letters and articles, raising consciousness in a grassroots organization. In the AUDIENCE chapter, you read about Donna Bivens who felt weighed down by "commodity writing," where the effect on the audience is more important than the beauty or joy created. Too much urgent, task-oriented writing can burn you out. Donna's concerns challenge us to balance urgency and joy when we want our writing to make a difference. Self-nurturance is basic, but there's another reason to keep in balance. Writing theorists believe that expressive writing—the poems and personal narratives Donna had put aside for her work—is the root source of all other writing. It's where we find strength and voice for all our more routine work. That's why it's so important to keep FREEWRITING as you move into more task-oriented work.

Donna was able to return to balance and bring her whole organization with her. After making time for personal writing in a feedback group for several years, she and her co-workers at the Women's Theological Center reshaped their newsletter to include personal stories of their experiences discovering spiritual leadership. Writing these stories brought back some of the spontaneity and joy that sustained them. Their organization flourished and is now celebrating its 25th year.

Writing theorists believe that expressive writing— poems and personal narratives— is the root source of all other writing.

Seeking small and larger ways to go public with writing

About the time I was working with Donna, my own struggle with silencing took a leap forward when I left my job teaching in the university. Most of my expressive energy had been swallowed up in "commodity writing" such as memos to colleagues, written feedback to students, proposals to administrators, scholarly articles for the academic community. At the same time, I'd been writing newsletter articles and minutes of meetings in my public role as an activist, informational flyers about South African apartheid, and press releases on environmental justice. Mostly I was not so much following my own deep insights as I was speaking for a group, or, in one case, for a political candidate, when Mel King decided to run for Congress. This work was important and challenging, and I could see its effects. When people and institutions responded, I knew my writing was contributing to social change. But the expressive part of me was not free to create. I rarely had time to follow through on ideas for poems or to explore personal insights in my freewriting. Like Donna, I knew I was choosing to use my most precious creative energy to produce commodities, for my job and for the cause of social justice.

Leaving my job threw me back into balance. Powerful words, metaphors, pieces of poems came up frequently, and I noticed more rhythmic patterns in my freewriting. I also tried the exercises in a wonderful book called *The Artists Way* for "recovering creatives." Before I knew it, I had moved into a regular expressive writing practice that included published articles on subjects I felt passionate about. I wrote a series of monthly columns on herbs for my local supermarket newsletter. (Maybe herbs don't sound like they have social change potential, but I wrote about the politics and cultural history of herbs as well as their role in healing and cuisine.) This excursion into the plant world nourished me.

I also found newsletters in the peace movement where I could place short columns I thought of as "solidarity writing," telling of journeys into silenced cultures—the Lakotas' ceremony to heal the pain of Wounded Knee, the Pittston coal-miners' Camp Solidarity, a tenant ceremony at the landlord's house, a Buddhist walk to stop the flooding of Canadian Native reserves, and many more. I wrote proposals and press releases to launch a "working rainbow coalition" in my city; I wrote outreach material for coalition-building and curriculum for popular education. I wrote hundreds of short invitations to progressive events. I wrote columns for the local paper about tenant rights and nuclear weapons and the city's peace celebrations. I wrote to raise money for Indian country, to bring to life the hidden history of slavery in the Northeast, to stop the planting of water-robbing vineyards in the West. I wrote to advertise and maintain a cooperative housing venture and Buddhist communities that support peace and justice. To my delight, the more freely and joyously I wrote, the more opportunities to write arose for me.

When you want to speak out in writing, and you start to do it, big and small ways to put your writing to use will open up before your eyes.

That's how it works. When you want to speak out in writing, and you start to do it, big and small ways to put your writing to use will open up before your eyes. Many people's passions have echoed through this book—youth programs, marches, even a fair trade business—all of them started with short pieces of writing and grew into major projects. The street newspaper in my community, published by homeless people, always looks for stories that will change awareness and unjust policies, and it reaches a very wide and diverse audience. The internet is another entry point, where new forms like blogs are creating a world-wide citizens' media. The Berkman Center for Internet and Society at Harvard Law School estimates there are 40 to 50 million blogs worldwide. One participatory journalism site, OhmyNews.com in Korea, has over 40,000 citizen writer-reporters around the world, with half a million people a day reading their words on the website. Closer to home you'll find other ideas in an inspiring book called *Fifty Ways to Love Your Country* published by MoveOn.org, a grassroots organization that started over the internet. The fifty ways are described in stories written by ordinary citizens who made a difference by speaking out in the crisis period after September 11, 2001. In most of the stories, writing plays a key role. It did for Greg, a war veteran whose heartfelt letter to the president became a paid peace advertisement that reached 100,000 readers. Others took action with flyers, plans, reports, letters, articles, scripts for phone calls, personal journals or email. The MoveOn book shows dozens of ways to go public with words.

And there is a lot of encouragement for citizen activists and writers. Mary Pipher, a passionate writer and therapist from Nebraska, weaves her own experiences into a book of advice, *Writing to Change the World*. She covers speeches, essays, poems and blogs, and, best of all, she describes the letters she and her friend wrote when plans for a race-track threatened a rare, peaceful stretch of original prairie that had been preserved with all its unique plant and bird life. The letters are touching examples of writing that respects the opposition yet expresses deep feeling about what might be lost to development. Local decision-makers who'd favored the race-track came around when the whole community offered thoughtful, heartfelt testimony, and, as a result, this one bit of prairie remains unaffected. All of us are surrounded with catastrophes in the making, and there are people to write to, publications to address in print and online at all levels—community, local, state, regional, national, global. Everywhere you look you'll find more new ways to get the word out. And they don't have to be big time. Pipher opens her book with a quote from the African American novelist and activist James Baldwin on changing the world through writing, "The world changes according to the way people see it, and if you alter, even by a millimeter, the way…people look at reality, then you can change it." Just getting yourself to write and showing your writing to others is already making change.

Exercise

Finding your own ways to go public   Pick a time to do this exercise when you're revved up—you've just talked to good friends, seen a mind-changing film, taken a profound walk, heard a great speaker or sermon, or done an inspiring freewrite. There's a problem on your mind and you are motivated to speak out. Sit down for a few minutes and explore the possibilities. Write out the following sentence at least seven times, filling in the blanks differently each time: I would like to write a _____ (letter, short article, proposal, press advisory, newsletter article, etc.) to send to _____ (the head of a company, city council, local paper or TV station, Congressperson, a magazine). While you're listing, don't be completely practical. Stay open to intuitions and wild ideas. You can discuss global warming in a letter for a newspaper advice column if it connects with a personal problem. You could write an email to friends and political representatives. New possibilities will come up as you make the lists. Keep adding until you've found several ideas that excite you. Then read over what you've brainstormed and highlight the two or three options on each list that have the most energy for you at this moment. Think for a minute, make a few notes if you want, and freewrite an "instant version" of at least the opening paragraph to one of your choices. Continue if it feels right, and add the other ideas to your list of future projects.

Finding supportive community

This book has looked at so many kinds of support communities for writing—research and work groups where writing is done collaboratively, sharing with friends and family members, courses in adult education centers, and of course the groups described in the FEEDBACK chapter. Mary Pipher's local writing group calls itself "Prairie Trout," and writing groups of many kinds are emerging now. One that could serve as a model for people who want to become activists through letter-writing started years ago at the home of a life-long activist in my community, Yvonne Pappenheim. Yvonne was devoted to racial justice. In the 1950s when speaking up was risky and difficult, she'd organized northern support to overturn Jim Crow in the South. She'd helped start a special library on racism right across the street from the statehouse in Boston. Somewhere Yvonne developed a specialty for writing short, well-informed letters to the editor.

I interviewed Yvonne once about her letter-writing group. With some members in their 80s and 90s, the group had met for decades to practice this form of democracy sitting together in her living room over coffee and cookies. Each time they'd discuss the topic chosen for that day—affirmative action, a weapons program, the U.S. budget—and help each other get up to speed on the issues. Then, everyone retreated to a comfortable corner to handwrite her own letter. They'd read the letters to each other for support and suggestions, then go home to type and mail them. (Today, it would be email.) About once a month someone in the group got published in one of the big city papers, so they knew they were making a difference. Even if one person's letter didn't make it, that letter helped another one catch the editor's eye. Over the years I saw many of Yvonne's own letters in the Boston *Globe*, and you can see one of them in the appendix to this book. Yvonne passed away in her 90s under care of hospice. Two weeks before her death the *Globe* published her final letter—a plea to extend health care to all.

There are so many ways to support and motivate each other. Support communities create a culture of activism and offer resources, even in spread-out national interest groups. A Sierra Club study found that 47 percent of its members had written to a public official, compared to only 6 percent in the general population. The Sierra Club has been building this form of citizen activism for years. Local groups like Yvonne's can help you fine-tune what to write about and how to publish or use it. They'll celebrate your successes because all of you in the group are connected, and that, in itself, is a kind of social change.

Now is the time

Here's what I have to say to people using this book. I want you to find your voices, get really comfortable with them, and more regularly and actively lift those voices. A friend just told me that after activist writing for years (and lots of freewriting), he'd suddenly noticed that writing had become almost effortless. This can happen for all of us once we get in the flow. And the earth needs our voices, the wounded, forgotten people of earth need them, all those misled by the glitter of the consumer world need them. The Department of Peace needs them. Hurricane, NAFTA, and tsunami refugees need them. Perhaps most important, we ourselves need our own voices. Feeling free to use political voice, to respond and play a role in our times, nourishes strength, creativity, wisdom, community and joy. Each of us will find our own way to use our voice, our own pitch and resonance. And as more voices enter into the mix, and more of us do just a little more than before, the collective sound builds.

The people and writing projects I've included in this book continue to fill me with awe and offer new possibilities for my own writing. As soon as I think I have a handle on how we can use writing to make a difference, I meet with another group and hear of still more possibilities. With communication technologies expanding, more and more avenues open up every day. This is the time to reach out, take advantage of every opportunity to express our views, sidestep the oppressor within and write!

He'd suddenly noticed that writing had become almost effortless.

Appendices

Appendix A   Letters to The Editor

Mailing or emailing letters to the editor of a magazine or your local paper is the quickest way to start making a difference with writing. As discussed in Chapter Six, these short, specialized letters reach many readers, if published, and influence media-makers' thinking even if not. Writing these letters regularly is what one of my uncles calls a "civic responsibility." It is also great practice in clarifying thinking, writing and leadership.

Many activist organizations, and some newspapers, offer advice on how to write letters that will click with editors (the gatekeepers for this form of political expression). Editors look for a letter that does the following:

- "Hooks" to a recent event or article and offers perspectives, facts or feelings left out of previous coverage. Personal experience with the subject is a big plus.

- Provides something unique, such as new information or an evocative sound bite.

- Is brief (under 100 words, but can vary with the publication). The shorter, the better chances are of publication.

- Focuses on one subject only and follows classic "letter-to-editor" form.

- Expresses your own feelings or values, in your own voice (from the heart and the head at the same time).

- Uses a tone that editors see as "generous spirited" (can express outrage, but does not bash or vent anger).

Successful letter writers interpret these guidelines differently. Here is classic example from Yvonne Pappenheim, whose dedication to writing these letters and organizing others to write them is discussed in the final chapter of this book. Yvonne's letter came out in the *Boston Globe,* one of two major newspapers in the city, and one that receives 350 to 400 competing letters from readers each week. Note how Yvonne stresses cultural themes (Chapter Six) that reaffirm empowering American values.

Without Yvonne's lifetime of practice, it's hard to write a letter like this without a lot of drafts—and the "dangerous method" can be discouraging. Before I stopped using it, there were a lot of unfinished letters in my file drawer. Most of us need to vent our anger about what we see in the news, and it can take several drafts to come up with one single focused message and a generous but tough tone. The issues we want to write about and our feelings are complex, yet we need a letter that's simple. Mad drafts, incubation, and audience analysis are extremely helpful.

YVONNE'S LETTER

A lesson in humanity

On the same day that the Million Man March expressed a positive attitude toward responsibility and toward the biblical adage "I am my brother's keeper," a Page 1 article in the *Globe* discussed Gov. Weld's cruel welfare proposals as a "campaign play."

The governor has had many advantages that the African-American marchers have not had. Yet, regrettably, his politics are less human than theirs. I hope he, too, will atone and come out with legislation that shows respect for all people— kids born to teen-age mothers, immigrants, all of us.

YVONNE PAPPENHEIM
Cambridge

Hook. Linking "cruel welfare proposals" to the most dramatic news of the day draws readers in.

Lead. Linking to the march is not only a hook but also a lead—a dramatic opening that sets the scene.

Cultural themes: Echoes progressive American values (see Chapter Six).

- Responsibility
- "My brother's keeper"
- Fairness/unfair access to wealth
- All deserve respect

Title is chosen by editor, but you can suggest one that's brief, clever and accurately frames your message.

Classic form First paragraph identifies the article she's responding to and the contradiction she is addressing. The second argues why the governor should match the morality of the marchers.

Length: 90 words.

Sound bite A quotable phrase: "his politics are less human than theirs."

Overall tone is hard-hitting ("cruel") but what editors see as "generous spirited." It doesn't bash, but uses irony to criticize the "humanity" of this governor, who was known as part of a privileged white elite.

Appendix B Two Kinds of Opinion Columns

Citizen-authored opinion columns are another effective way to be heard. I suggest two kinds tailored to national or to local newspapers: the classic "op-ed" column (referring to "opposite the editorial page") for local and national papers and a more personal guest opinion column for smaller, local papers. You can adapt either form for blogs and on-line publications.

Classic op-ed columns offer expertise on a newsworthy subject—to get media coverage for points of view that have been silenced. Expertise includes anything from university or think-tank research to the daily experience of an environmentalist, diversity consultant, or social justice traveler like Jim Harney whose columns on Latin America are mentioned in Chapters Two and Nine. (If you study the issues, you have expertise.) It can take planning and effort to get op-ed columns published, but once you begin and create a bit of a name for yourself, you'll have some momentum. There's a specialized form for op-eds, very much like the one for letters to the editor. Here are economist Ann Markusen's guidelines for writing a successful column, based on her decades of publishing on disarmament and economic issues in major newspapers all over the United States. (Chapters Five and Six tell more about Ann's methods of avoiding the "dangerous method.") Ann says:

> You have to say exactly what you're going to do in the first two sentences and then conclude with a smashing, upbeat ending about how people can respond to the problem. An op-ed is only seven paragraphs long (about 700 words) and you can really put only three basic kinds of evidence into it.

ANN'S FORMULA FOR OP-ED COLUMNS

- **Paragraph 1**   Introduction: Hook it to readers' interests and a current event, and state exactly what you're going to prove.
- **Paragraph 2**   Say what's wrong with everyone else's argument.
- **Paragraph 3**   Give your first argument, with evidence.
- **Paragraph 4**   Give your second argument, with evidence.
- **Paragraph 5**   Give your third argument, with evidence.
- **Paragraph 6 & 7** Sum up and show specifically what people can do about the issue.

Ann's formula can be helpful in training yourself to write good op-eds, but notice that even Ann, herself, doesn't always follow the formula. Once you get good at the classic form, you can decide to vary it.

ST. PAUL PIONEER PRESS, APRIL 7, 2005

Preserving Our Right to Tip

I sat last night at my local diner, so happy to sink into my newspaper and let a smiling, attentive woman bring me water, salad and a hamburger. I stayed for a long time, moving on to a novel, and felt the pleasure of leaving a plump tip on top of the modest check. Looking around the thinly-populated room, I wondered how much my neighbor actually takes home on top of her minimum wage of $5.15 and if it even covers her child care.

If "hospitality" industry lobbyists have their way, the minimum wage hike likely to pass the Legislature this session won't reach this woman at all. They are proposing to freeze the minimum wage for servers at $5.15 an hour and use tips to make up the difference between that and a new minimum wage of between $6.50 and $7.00. They call this a tip credit; servers call it more accurately a tip penalty.

Suppose my neighbor works a 4:00–8:00 dinner shift, the average single meal costs $7.00, she serves thirty people (that would be a good night), and average tips are 15%. Currently, she makes $20.60 in wages and $31.50 in tips, or $13 an hour, barely what a single person needs to meet a basic needs budget working full time. Not counting child-care costs or what she needs for child support. No wonder she also works at the neighborhood quick stop during the day.

If the minimum wage were worth today what it was at its peak in 1969 —$8.69—this server would be making $16.50 an hour with tips. The Senate-assed hike would only partly restore this lost value. Yet if the restaurant and hotel lobby gets its way, this server and tens of thousands of others in Minnesota won't receive any increase at all. The entire hike

ANN MARKUSEN

will go directly into the pockets of owners.

It's our right as customers to tip people who serve us and to know that they receive its full value. Tipping is a direct financial exchange between the server and the customer. It feels good to be able to reward prompt and accommodating service with generosity, and although its not always so pleasant, to skimp on a tip for really poor service. The tipping custom enables restaurants to pay already rock bottom wages for talented servers and be able to rely on their graciousness.

Tips are not considered wages by the government. They are a form of income to the server and thus taxable, but not as part of the wage relationship between the employer and server. The government does not collect any data on tips, so we have no idea what the true range is. Hospitality Minnesota claims that Twin Cities wait staff make around $18 an hour. But the trade association represents only the higher end restaurants and hotels. And it is not clear whether their survey took into account the hours that serving staff work before and after meal hours. Or that many share their tips with cooks, dishwashers, bartenders' assistants and busboys.

Most Minnesota table servers and bartenders work in modestly-priced bars, diners and cafes in middle and working class neighborhoods and rural small towns. They are not offered full time work, health care or retirement benefits or paid sick and vacation time. They are often

working a second job to cobble things together. Business is often slow and disappointing, and their tip income suffers as a result.

The market has already adjusted to tips—they obviously raise the price of a meal, and those of us patronizing places with wait staff are obviously willing to pay for the service. We can choose the fast food alternative if we wish, where minimum wage counter servers make no tips at all. Why should we discriminate against a single class of workers in this long-overdue minimum wage hike? Why should restaurant owners and profitable chains be forgiven their share of this minimum wage hike? One lobbyist argued that the food service industry has already been hard hit by more stringent blood alcohol regs and smoking bans, but it doesn't compute that wait staff should have to contribute their tips to compensate.

Most of us know just how challenging waiting on tables is. If we didn't do it in our youth—I worked at Perkin's—we have parents, children, relatives and friends who have. It's hard work. It can be messy. Customers can be grumpy or worse. You come home with your feet aching and clothes smelling of fat and smoke. I admire the talent of people who wait on tables in my favorite watering holes. They deserve this raise, just as their employers deserve a fair price for the meals and atmosphere they create in their restaurants. Let's help our legislators understand what seems to be an arcane issue. It's straightforward—I want the right to tip my waiter and know that she takes the whole of it home.

Ann Markusen is an economist and Fesler-Lampert Professor of Urban and Regional Affairs at the Humphrey Institute of Public Affairs, University of Minnesota

CAPE COD TIMES, OCTOBER 2, 1992

Building on theme of forgiveness

ROSH Hashana is a significant time of year. It is the Jewish New Year, which began at sunset Sunday and is the celebration of the world's birthday. It is also a festival of forgiveness and renewal.

Since attending my family reunion in Alabama this past summer, I have been struggling with the issues of remembering, forgiving and forgetting.

Every 10 years the family meets on the grounds of the Fegan plantation where Susan and Jake Christain, my great-great-grandparents, were slaves and continued to live, according to the 1870 U.S. Census.

Traveling in the South was uneasy. Memories of my family's past lives felt dangerous. They were filled with stories of lynchings, disappearances, escapes and captures. I found myself looking at white people wondering where their grandparents were in 1860, much the way I feel when I'm in Germany, speculating about every German I meet over 60. I became intensely defensive and aggressive. My level of discomfort accompanied an unmitigated rage about the enslavement of my ancestors and its legacy of racism that impinges on every aspect of my life.

Shortly after I returned home from the reunion, a cousin by marriage came to visit on Cape Cod. Johnny is a successful real estate broker who thinks of himself as liberal, contributing to Jesse Jackson's self-help projects, supporting the NAACP and making money available to inner-city students who want to attend college. He displays no particular self-consciousness about our racial and cultural differences. But during his visit this summer those differences were highlighted and their roots exposed.

One evening after dinner Johnny asked my opinion of the Los Angeles riots. I connected what happened in Los Angeles in 1992 with the many revolts, rebellions and riots that have been going on in this country since Bacon's Rebellion in 1676.

Betty Burkes

Like Los Angeles, Bacon's Rebellion was a multiracial, poor people's response to an economic and political system created to keep them "under." Race and class were used in both cases to rule and divide, but when that failed, the militia was called in to restore law and order. That was business as usual in the new world in the 17th century and in the new world order of the late 20th century.

Johnny wasn't happy with my analysis when I suggested the politics of wealth and poverty linked him to the young black and white youth in Los Angeles and ultimately they shared a common destiny. The centuries of physical and emotional violence disturbed me more than the burning of real estate and the looting of merchandise. He was appalled by my suggestion that his lifestyle, his wealth, his business interests might be contributing factors to the miserable conditions in Los Angeles.

"What do you people want?" he exploded. "We're tired of your complaints and excuses. Come on, now, slavery's no excuse anymore. When are you going to forget about that? You've had civil rights, affirmative action, special programs and you still can't make it. When are you going to start taking some responsibility for the mess you're in and stop blaming white people? We're tired of hearing how bad black people have it here. We don't want to hear it anymore. Everybody has had it hard in this country. They've made it. Why can't black people? We're tired of being blamed. What do you want?"

A response to Johnny's question became clear after spending time with Alan, an old friend, the following weekend.

Alan told me about the project he is part of, organized by two psychotherapists and affiliated with Harvard University. The project includes 12 children of survivors of the Nazi Holocaust and 12 children of Nazis. The object of this project is to provide an environment where survivors of perpetrators can meet survivors of victims to begin the challenging process of listening, remembering and forgiving. The participants are examining the meaning of forgiveness and what changes need to happen for that to take place.

Alan's description of this unique group was an invitation for me to think about my cousin's question, "What do you people want?" I cannot speak for all people of color but I can respond to Johnny's question. An acknowledgement by the descendants of slave owners and those who benefited from slavery that slavery was wrong, and reparations to the descendants of those enslaved for the centuries of injustice, would be a very powerful beginning.

Even though there is no way to repay the devastating loss of human life, Germany has attempted to repay Jewish people who survived, and the world does not forget. Recently, the U.S. Congress attempted to redress the wrong done to Japanese-Americans during WWII.

Isn't it time we addressed the crimes committed against Africa and the millions on whose backs this nation's wealth was built? Where is the wall with those names? Why didn't it occur to Johnny to ask my forgiveness?

Rosh Hashana is a great opportunity to seek out those we may have offended, ask forgiveness and make the appropriate restitution. We can re-create kinships and build new bridges to understanding and justice.

Betty Burkes lives in Wellfleet.

Guest opinion columns   (like Betty Burke's on the previous page) invite a more personal kind of expression and can become a regular weekly or monthly feature in smaller local papers. These columns follow similar guidelines on length and also focus on one main theme, but they often use more personal stories and the first person voice. Inspiring examples are the many columns on People of Color that Betty Burkes wrote over ten years for local papers on Cape Cod (see Chapters Two and Eight).

Appendix C   Letter of Inquiry for Funders

Funders and grant officers are busy decision-makers who want good projects to fund. Writing for this audience challenges us to keep things brief with just the right amount of relevant detail, especially in an initial letter of inquiry. A letter of inquiry is a "first contact" letter that introduces a request and opens the door to follow-up, including a full-fledged grant process. The challenge in letters of inquiry is to choose the few details that will convince readers that we have credentials and that a project is well thought-out, doable and in their organization's interest. In the case of a foundation grant, the project must also fully meet the donor's published guidelines for giving. Most of the problems people face in writing for funders lie in (a) not matching a project to the guidelines or (b) not speaking up directly and clearly about what they are asking for. Writing for funders is excellent practice for the main problem all social change writers face—making a message clear and direct.

Eugenio's letter requesting a computer donation is a great example of this classic struggle. As discussed in Chapter Four, Eugenio wrote to a company on the outskirts of the low-income neighborhood where he worked. He eventually received the computer and opened the doors to collaboration between the company and his youth program—but not without major changes to his letter's strategy and a dramatic clarification of his message. Here are Eugenio's "before" and "after" drafts. The first version focuses on what's important to Eugenio, not to his audience—his status at MIT, his finances and shopping techniques. It tells a very writer-based story, not the story of a donation that would benefit the company. It doesn't reveal his request for a computer until the end and even then is vague about how much it would cost and what he is asking the company to do. This was a good start for Eugenio, but needed a lot of work.

Before the final draft, Eugenio researched the company and found that, although they probably were not familiar with his youth program, the company did encourage community volunteer work and even had a staff person in charge of community relations—a live person he could write to directly. This made audience analysis a lot more real. By using an MIT letterhead and refocusing his message, Eugenio was able to create a strong appeal for a donated computer. Notice how he splices together key details about the funding he has already received (a sign of worthiness to funders) and shows how the donated computer will contribute to youth education and perhaps a future workforce. His opening lead builds an engaging picture of his organization, and he ends with a specific "next step" for follow through. There is very little repetition or lard in this positive, upbeat, confident final draft.

"Before" draft

To: _____ Corporation

My name is Eugenio Munoz-Villafane and I am a social worker based at Centro de Amistad Inc. in Guadalupe, Arizona, a community-based nonprofit organization located about a ten minute drive from your plant. I have recently begun a fellowship at the Department of Urban Studies at the Massachusetts Institute of Technology in Cambridge, Massachusetts.

I hope to develop a Youth Enrichment Program in the areas of the arts and sciences. During the course of my fellowship I will research national youth programs that are effective with youth in both of these areas. It is an intensive program which trains community workers to develop effective programs which we can later implement in our communities.

Each year twelve to fifteen fellows come to MIT sponsored in part by the Kellogg, Ford and Reebok foundations. Since the funding is limited, the fellows must be prepared to manage the limited funding for living expenses (housing, food and incidentals), research and travel. At first the funding seems adequate but for fellows living in the southwest and the west coast, a large portion of this is utilized on travel expenses limiting the remaining monies.

The purpose of this letter is to request partial funding for a computer which I could use for my research over the next eight months at MIT. After pricing the area for a competitive system in today's market (IBM 383 or 486) with a printer and basic software average out around $2,100. Even comparable used computers with letter quality printers start at $1,100, about $700 more than my funding will allow. I am therefore inquiring about the possibility of full or partial funding for a new or used computer system or perhaps acquiring one of your used computers. At this point the need of a computer supercedes the fact that it may be a new or used one.

I would appreciate any support and direction that you may provide with this need. I look forward to your response.

Sincerely,

Eugenio Munoz-Villafane

"After" draft

_____ Corporation
"Jane Smith," Director of Community Services

Dear Jane Smith:

I am a social worker at Centro de Amistad Inc. ("Friendship Center") in Guadalupe, Arizona, a nonprofit organization serving Guadalupe, Chandler and Mesa with counseling, health education and youth development. Through the support of the W. K. Kellogg, Ford, and Reebok foundations, I have been awarded a fellowship in the Department of Urban Studies at MIT to develop effective youth programs.

The purpose of this letter is to request funding for a computer system to support my research, which, upon completion, will become one of several computers used by the students of an enrichment program I am developing here at MIT. The program will target students in junior high and high school, who are at risk of dropping out of school. The program will support their educational experiences and increase the number of college bound students. When provided with the right equipment, youth can achieve and exceed our expectations of them. I believe your company could play a role in the development of the youth of Guadalupe, Chandler, and Mesa by sending a strong message to the community that "_____ cares" about youth.

I have priced the Boston area for a competitive system with a printer and basic software and have concluded that the best value can be found at the tax-free, below-dealer-cost "Computer Connection" at MIT. The Computer Connection sells "bundles" which include monitor, printer, and technical support ranging between $1,650 and $2,150. I have already raised $400 in private funds, lowering the range of need to between $1,250 and $1,750.

I invite you to support this effort. I will contact your office the week of January 10, 1994 to discuss this proposal and to answer any questions you may have.

Sincerely,
Eugenio Munoz-Villafane, MSW
Kellogg Community Fellow

We can learn a lot from Eugenio about how to write for funding. Most important is how to state the main message fully and directly, placing it as close as possible to the opening of the letter. Grant-makers want to know right away why you are writing to them. Notice how Eugenio's message evolved:

EUGENIO'S MAIN MESSAGE

Before	After
Placement: Paragraph 4. Buried.	**Placement:** Paragraph 2. Very visible.
I am therefore <u>inquiring about the possibility of full or partial funding for a new or used computer system or perhaps acquiring one of your used computers.</u>	<u>The purpose of this letter is to request funding for a computer system</u> to support my research, which, upon completion, will become one of several computers used by the students of an enrichment program I am developing here at MIT.
Message is stated indirectly with many buffer words like "possibility of," "full or partial," "perhaps." Looks like he doesn't know what he really wants.	*Straightforward request for funding, tied in closely with how the community will benefit.*

Eugenio's example can help you rework drafts of funding letters by aiming for:

- High-energy "lead" (Eugenio mentions he is a social worker and translates the name of his organization).
- Simply stated message at or near beginning of letter.
- Detail that establishes your reliability as a recipient of funding. (If you've been funded before, include that.)
- Detail about how the funding will be used.
- Only details relevant to the decision to fund you.
- Emphasis on how your audience will benefit from donating.
- Brevity, but include relevant detail. ("As simple as possible but not more so.")
- Upbeat, natural voice. Cut excess words or "lard."

More Resources

Recommended Resources

Here are resources that my students and I have used to understand silencing and create the tools to undo it. Of the many good books on writing, the first section lists just the ones that most helped to shape the tools in *Undoing the Silence*. Other sections cover influential books on freewriting, the thinking tools, writing for specific audiences, and the listening skills that are essential to feedback, as well as resources for editing. Final sections cover resources for understanding silence more deeply, getting inspired to write for change, and references to writing projects mentioned in this book.

For many subjects, such as media reform and the value of listening in communication, new resources are constantly emerging as more voices join the public dialogue. This means that website information may soon be outdated, but these listings will help you connect with a new generation of resources on the World Wide Web.

Essential Authors on Writing

Peter Elbow, *Writing With Power*. Oxford University Press, 1981, 1998. The best extended treatment of freewriting, the "dangerous method," feedback, and much more. Adult readers say this book "feels like it was written for me."

Peter Elbow, *Writing Without Teachers*. Oxford University Press, 1973, 1998. The first book on the feedback method that is adapted in *Undoing the Silence*. Elbow's path-breaking work began a nationwide movement to treat writing as a process not a product.

Other work by Elbow sheds light on themes in this book: "The Shifting Relationships between Speech and Writing," *College Composition and Communication*, Vol. 36, No. 3, October 1985, explores why people good at speaking have trouble with writing and vice versa; *Sharing and Responding*, 1989, 1995, written with Pat Belanoff as a users' guide to *A Community of Writers*, gives excellent suggestions for feedback; Elbow's work also emphasizes non-adversarial communication, writing that "listens" to the value in supposedly opposing views.

Linda Flower, *Problem Solving Strategies for Writing in College and Community*. Harcourt Brace College Publishers, 1997. Develops easy-to-use logical tools and the audience analysis technique adapted for this book. Fascinating research on how readers actually read. In *Writing at Work* Flower and her co-author cover memos, reports and other writing with examples from community organizations.

Pat Schneider, *Writing Alone and With Others.* Oxford Press, 2003. Dramatically expands our awareness of "triggers"—ways freewriting can engage our deepest energy and stimulate creative thinking and voice. With profound understanding of silencing, this book encourages the artist in every person—including writers in low-income communities who provide major inspiration and some exciting sample writing for this book. Good suggestions for working in groups.

Intuition and Freewriting

Gabriele Lusser Rico, *Writing the Natural Way.* Jeremy P. Tarcher/Putnam, 1983, 2000. Explains how right and left brain work in writing and introduces "clustering." Has influenced students, teachers and business people.

Natalie Goldberg, *Writing Down the Bones*. Shambhala, 1986, expanded 20th anniversary edition 2006. Shares powerful insights developed in Zen Buddhist meditation, helping us with "mindfulness," the non-judgmental awareness of what's happening in our consciousness moment by moment, and with "wild mind writing," which is the title of her second book (1990).

Julia Cameron, *The Artist's Way.* Jeremy P. Tarcher/Putnam, 1992. Inspired public imagination in the early '90s, inviting people who have lost touch with their creativity to re-experience—and trust—the flow of insight. As in twelve-step addiction recovery programs (which Cameron's *Way* resembles), creativity is seen as a spiritual phenomenon, a way of striving for something higher in ourselves. Key practices are a weekly "artist's date" (a treat for your "inner artist") and the "morning pages" (three-page freewrites in the morning before the inner judges wake up). People who practice Cameron's techniques report amazing changes in their energy level, their ability to work on new projects, and their self-esteem. Cameron's many newer books are good too.

Freewriting in the classroom:

From math to history, from elementary to graduate school, many courses now require freewriting journals. As part of "writing across the curriculum," freewriting deepens the thinking process and teaches theory by application. Read more in Pat Belanoff, Peter Elbow, and Sheryl I. Fontaine, eds., *Nothing Begins with N: New Investigations of Freewriting*, Southern Illinois University Press, 1991; and Toby Fulwiler, ed., *The Journal Book*, Boynton/Cook Publishers, 1987.

Therapy and personal growth:

Among others using freewriting in therapy, Jungian Dr. Ira Progoff developed the Intensive Journal Process to explore key life changes. His book, *At a Journal Workshop,* and registration for his trainings are both available from Dialogue House (80 East 11th St, New York, NY 10003).

Social change leadership:

Journaling is also popular in many of the trainings developed at the end of the 20th century to help social change workers deal with racism, sexism and other oppressions—and with burnout and conflict resolution. See Katrina Shields, *In the Tiger's Mouth: An Empowerment Guide for Social Action.* New Society Publishers, 1994.

Thinking Tools

Ann E. Berthoff, *Forming, Thinking, Writing.* Boynton/Cook Publishers, 2nd edition, 1988. In sync with Paulo Freire, helps writers find power through dialogic thinking and metaphor.

Louise Dunlap, "Language and Power: Teaching Writing to Third World Graduate Students," *Breaking the Boundaries: A One-World Approach to Planning Education.* Ed. Bishwapriya Sanyal, Plenum Press, 1990. "Advocacy and Neutrality: A Contradiction in the Discourse of Urban Planners," *Writing, Teaching, and Learning in the Disciplines.* Ed. A. Herrington and C. Moran, Modern Language Association, 1992. Both articles, written for teachers, explore cultural roots of the choice to speak out boldly or stick with "neutral writing."

David Siff, "Teaching Freshman Comp to New York Cops," *College English*, Vol. 36, No. 5, January 1975. What blocks powerful thinking and writing. A college teacher in the 1970s found remarkable strides in thinking when police officers with strong prejudices were asked to write "in the voice of someone you consider your social opposite." In doing so, the officers were more articulate and convincing than when expressing the views they had held all their lives.

<www.civicus.org> This "world alliance for citizen participation" offers a toolkit for Writing Effectively and Powerfully that shares early versions of some techniques in this book. Other Civicus toolkits feature funding proposals and other grassroots writing needs. Click on Resources and Services.

<www.austhink.com> Links to good resources on critical thinking, including tutorials for "mind-mapping" logical arguments.

Writing for Specific Audiences

Media audiences:

Charlotte Ryan, *Prime Time Activism: Media Strategies for Grassroots Organizing.* South End Press, 1991. Avoids simplistic conspiracy theories but shows how the media can silence grassroots voices and how we can write for this audience. A sociologist, Ryan works with nonprofit, community and labor organizations on message development and media strategy. With the Media Research and Action Project, she continues to provide materials on the internet at <www.mrap.info>.

Donald M. Murray, *Writing to Deadline: The Journalist at Work.* Heinemann Press, 2000. Shows how skilled and politically sensitive writers inside the press think, write, use leads and shape their articles. Murray is also a revered writing teacher.

Robert Jensen, *Writing Dissent: Taking Radical Ideas from the Margins to the Mainstream.* Peter Lang Publishing, 2002. Shows how to frame dissident ideas for mainstream media. Examples of op-ed articles strategically placed to shape public opinion.

Funders:

Kitta Reeds, *The Zen of Proposal Writing*. Three Rivers Press, 2002.

Andy Robinson, *Grassroots Grants: An Activist's Guide to Proposal Writing*. Chardon Press, 1996.

Mal Warwick, *How to Write Successful Fundraising Letters*. Jossey-Bass, 2001.

Community people and policymakers:

Nancy Brigham with Maria Catalfo and Dick Cluster, *How to Do Leaflets, Newsletters, & Newspapers.* PEP Publishers, 1991. Engaging style and illustrations. Help with writing for grassroots readers.

Michael Jacoby Brown, *Building Powerful Community Organizations: A Personal Guide to Creating Groups that Can Solve Problems and Change the World*. Long Haul Press, 2006. A good book on community organizing with emphasis on "putting it in writing."

Catherine Smith, *Writing Public Policy: A Practical Guide to Communicating in the Policy-Making Process*. Oxford University Press, 2005. Shows how to strategize for audiences in memos, position papers, policy proposals and public testimony. Lots of examples.

Politicized audiences:

George Lakoff, *Don't Think of an Elephant: Know Your Values and Frame the Debate.* Chelsea Green, 2004. Useful material on framing ideas in the conservative v. progressive stand-off.

George Lakoff, and the Rockridge Institute, *Thinking Points: Communicating Our American Values and Vision.* Farrar, Straus and Giroux, 2006. Especially helpful for reaching out to readers with mixed viewpoints.

John K. Wilson, *How the Left Can Win Arguments and Influence People: A Tactical Manual for Progressives*. New York University Press, 2001.

Two websites about communicating across political difference:
      <www. rockridgeinstitute.org>
      <www.metaphorproject.org>

Academic, corporate and public sector audiences:

Howard S. Becker, *Writing for Social Scientists: How to Start and Finish Your Thesis, Book, or Article.* University of Chicago Press, 1986. Classic work exposing overly complex language in academic writing, and heartfelt advice from a plain-talking sociologist.

Dianna Booher, *E-Writing: 21st Century Tools for Effective Communication*. Pocket Books, 2001. Audience-conscious writing.

Sandra E. Lamb, *How to Write It: A Complete Guide to Everything You'll Ever Write*. Ten Speed Press, 1998. Advice and examples on many formats.

Natalie Macris, *Planning in Plain English: Writing Tips for Urban and Environmental Planners.* Planners Press, American Planning Association, 2000. Guide to writing in community and government settings. Brief and simple with excellent layout and examples.

Feedback, Listening and Non-Adversarial Communication

Ann Ruggles Gere, *Writing Groups: History, Theory, and Implications.* Southern Illinois University Press, 1987. Tells the story of writing groups in the United States, including one started by Ben Franklin in 1719. By the 1960s, these groups had evolved from early authoritarian roots into forms similar to the one in this book.

Study Circles, Public Conversations and other discussion models: The Study Circles Resource Center in Connecticut helps cities and communities organize informed dialogue leading to action and change <www.studycircles.org>. The Public Conversations Project offers a model for discussing polarized moral and political issues—one that's worked well in my community <www.publicconversations.org>. The Internet shows new models like "compassionate listening" springing up on websites such as <www.newconversations.net>. Some are reviewed in the Winter 2003 issue of *YES! Magazine* <www.yesmagazine.org>.

Herb Walters and Rural Southern Voice for Peace in North Carolina have developed a method of guided interviews, called Listening Projects, to help change political positions that contradict inherent values. For instance, a project interviewing "pro-war" townspeople concerned about relatives being sent to the (first) Gulf War uncovered strong opposition to that war <**www.listeningproject.info**>.

Cherie Brown and George Mazza, *Healing into Action: A Leadership Guide for Creating Diverse Communities.* National Coalition Building Institute, 1997. A guide for facilitating group listening to move beyond [prejudiced or biased] thinking that keeps us from building alliances. Drawing on the techniques of reevaluation counseling developed in the '70s, one excellent chapter is titled "Listening is Not the Same as Agreeing."

Marshall B. Rosenberg, Ph.D., *Nonviolent Communication: A Language of Life; Create Your Life, Your Relationships, and Your World in Harmony with Your Values.* Puddle Dancer Press, 2nd edition, 2003. Approaches conflict resolution through compassionate communication, showing how to translate strong feelings of judgment and evaluation into statements that can be heard. See also workbook with useful exercises.

Julie Greene, "The Art of Giving and Receiving Difficult Feedback Part I: Barriers," *The Trager Newsletter,* Fall 1996. Applies Rosenberg's techniques to feedback in giving and receiving, but has wider application too.

Thich Nhat Hanh, *The Heart of the Buddha's Teaching; Transforming Suffering into Peace, Joy, and Liberation,* Parallax Press, 1999; *For a Future to Be Possible,* Parallax Press, 1993; *Teachings on Love,* Parallax Press, 1997. The Vietnamese Buddhist monk—whom Martin Luther King nominated for the Nobel Peace Prize during the U.S. war against his country—is especially appealing to socially engaged activists. Of his many books, these give special attention to the Buddhist practices of Right Speech and "deep listening" and describe "the love letter."

Editing

William Strunk and E.B. White, *The Elements of Style*. Macmillan Publishing Co. Brief, clear, widely respected explanations of grammar and writing style. Helpful examples. Many of us reread this book often from cover to cover.

Richard Lanham, *Revising Business Prose*. Charles Scribner's Sons, 1979. Helpful guide to transforming bureaucratic language.

United States Environmental Protection Agency, *Be a Better Writer: A Manual for EPA Employees*. U.S. Government Printing Office, 1980. A very useful guide, but out of print.

Chicago Manual of Style. A huge reference book with answers for just about all questions that come up in research or grad school writing.

<www.plainlanguage.gov> A website on simplifying language, especially in government and legal writing. Excellent materials.

Understanding Voice and Silence

Valerie Batts et al., "Modern Racism: New Melody for the Same Old Tunes," Episcopal Divinity School Occasional Papers, 1998. A quick entry into the ideas behind the VISIONS Inc. training program. This approach is the best I've found to clarify the role of "-isms" in silencing.

Jo Freeman, *At Berkeley in the '60s: The Education of an Activist, 1961-1965*. Indiana University Press, 2004. Recent account of Berkeley Free Speech Movement.

Paulo Freire, *Pedagogy of the Oppressed.* The Seabury Press, 1970. The classic starting point, but Freire continued to explore issues of authoritarian power and dialogue in many other books. I suggest: *Education for Critical Consciousness,* Continuum, 1973; and *Learning to Question: A Pedagogy of Liberation,* Continuum, 1989, co-authored with Antonio Faundez. Freire's insights have sparked an extensive literature on "critical pedagogy" and international networks of grassroots teaching called "popular education."

Carol Gilligan, *In a Different Voice: Psychological Theory and Women's Development.* Harvard University Press, 1983. Psychological research uncovers influences on women's silencing.

Taeku Lee, *Mobilizing Public Opinion: Black Insurgency and Racial Attitudes in the Civil Rights Era.* University of Chicago Press, 2002. Studies the influence of letters written to decision-makers during this era of heightened democracy.

Audre Lorde, *Sister Outsider: Essays and Speeches.* Crossing Press Feminist Series, 1984. A powerful voice on race and silencing, the uses of anger, the "master's tools," and much more.

Tillie Olsen, *Silences: Classic Essays on the Art of Creating*. Delta Press, 1978.

Inspiring Positive Action

Frances Moore Lappé, *Democracy's Edge: Choosing to Save Our Country by Bringing Democracy to Life.* Jossey-Bass, 2006. Lappé interviews hundreds of citizens and action groups successfully changing toxic and unfair corporate practices through organizing and speaking out. She makes a good case that even with looming disaster we have the power to strengthen democracy, and that even though it looks like opportunities to shape public policy are narrowing, in our paradoxical times, citizen voice and influence are on the upsurge.

Frances Moore Lappé and Jeffrey Perkins, *You Have the Power: Choosing Courage in a Culture of Fear.* Jeremy P. Tarcher/Penguin, 2004.

MoveOn.org, *50 Ways to Love Your Country: How to Find Your Political Voice and Become a Catalyst for Change.* Inner Ocean Publishing, 2004. Inspiring stories of ordinary citizens who found ways to make a difference after 9/11.

Mary Pipher, *Writing to Change the World.* Riverhead Books, Penguin Group, 2006. A passionately, and beautifully, written book to encourage all of us to speak out in writing in this time of great injustice, fear, and insecurity. Shows how personal writing in letters, stories, testimonies, and blogs can move others.

Linda Stout, *Bridging the Class Divide and Other Lessons for Grassroots Organizing.* Beacon Press, 1996. Discussed in the WORD-POWER chapter, Linda's work built a remarkable coalition that changed a North Carolina Congressperson's vote from 0% to 80% for peace. Insight on communicating across race and class difference.

Yes! Magazine: Published by the Positive Futures Network, this quarterly publication shows ordinary citizens taking action across a wide range of issues and making a difference <www.yesmagazine.org>.

Projects Mentioned

Donna Bivens, Women's Theological Center, <www.thewtc.org>

Marian David, *Sustaining the Soul That Serves,* <www.sustainingthesoul.org>

Rink Dickinson, co-founder of Equal Exchange, <www.equalexchange.com>

Ken Geiser, *Materials Matter: Toward a Sustainable Materials Policy.* MIT Press, 2001.

The Lowell Center for Sustainable Production, <www.chemicalspolicy.org>

Jim Harney, <www.westernmassafsc.org/colombia/JimHarney.html>

Jane Midgley, *Women and the U.S. Budget: Where the Money Goes and What You Can Do About It.* New Society Publishers, 2005. <www.womenandtheusbudget.com>

About the Author

Louise Dunlap found two vocations during the Berkeley Free Speech Movement in 1964—writing teacher and community activist. Always seeking to combine them, she taught writing at University of Massachusetts, Boston, during its founding years as an urban campus and then in graduate planning and environmental programs at Massachusetts Institute of Technology (MIT), Tufts University, University of California Berkeley, University of California Los Angeles, and many others. She has taught writing to city workers, foundation staff, environmental professionals and adult education students. She offers workshops for citizen activists in the labor, women's, peace, racial justice and environmental movements around the United States and in South Africa. Louise is currently Lecturer in Urban and Environmental Policy and Planning at Tufts University.

Louise Dunlap received her doctorate in English Literature from U.C. Berkeley in 1976 and has since lived in the Boston area without losing touch with her roots in Northern California. She has shared struggles for justice with activists from many movements, serving on the Cambridge Peace Commission and a co-operative housing board, and participating in peace walks and civil action on nuclear weapons, climate change, slavery and racism, the Wounded Knee Massacre, and the Shellmounds of the San Francisco Bay area. She writes and photographs on social and environmental issues and teaches yoga and Buddhist meditation in the tradition of Thich Nhat Hanh.

Index

new village press

The book you are holding was brought to you by New Village Press, the first publisher to serve the emerging field of community building. Communities are the cauldron of cultural development, and the healthiest communities grow from the grassroots. New Village publications focus on creative, citizen-initiated efforts—good news and good tools for social growth.

If you enjoyed *Undoing the Silence* you may like other books we offer:

Art and Upheaval: Artists on the World's Frontlines
    by William Cleveland
Arts for Change: Teaching Outside the Frame
    by Beverly Naidus
Building Commons and Community
    by Karl Linn
New Creative Community: The Art of Cultural Development
    by Arlene Goldbard
Works of Heart: Building Village through the Arts
    edited by Lynne Elizabeth and Suzanne Young
Doing Time in the Garden: Life Lessons through Prison Horticulture
    by James Jiler
Beginner's Guide to Community-Based Arts
    by Mat Schwarzman, Keith Knight, Ellen Forney and others
Performing Communities: Grassroots Ensemble Theaters Deeply Rooted in Eight U.S. Communities
    by Robert H. Leonard and Ann Kilkelly, edited by Linda Frye Burnham

Upcoming titles include:
What We See: Advancing the Observations of Jane Jacobs
    edited by Stephen A. Goldsmith and Lynne Elizabeth
By Heart: Poetry, Prison, and Two Lives
    by Judith Tannenbaum and Spoon Jackson
Asphalt to Ecosystems: Design Ideas for Schoolyard Transformation
    by Sharon Danks

New Village Press is a public-benefit enterprise of Architects/Designers/Planners for Social Responsibility **www.adpsr.org**, an educational nonprofit working for peace, environmental protection, social justice and healthy communities.

See what else we publish: **www.newvillagepress.net**